'The most remarkabl

MANCHESTER
1824
Manchester University Press

'The most remarkable woman in England'

Poison, celebrity and the trials of Beatrice Pace

John Carter Wood

Manchester University Press

Manchester and New York

distributed in the United States exclusively by Palgrave Macmillan

The right of John Carter Wood to be identified as the author of this work has been asserted by him in accordance with the Copyright, Designs and Patents Act 1988.

Published by Manchester University Press
Oxford Road, Manchester M13 9NR, UK
and Room 400, 175 Fifth Avenue, New York, NY 10010, USA
www.manchesteruniversitypress.co.uk

Distributed in the United States exclusively by
Palgrave Macmillan, 175 Fifth Avenue, New York,
NY 10010, USA

Distributed in Canada exclusively by
UBC Press, University of British Columbia, 2029 West Mall,
Vancouver, BC, Canada V6T 1Z2

British Library Cataloguing-in-Publication Data
A catalogue record for this book is available from the British Library

Library of Congress Cataloging-in-Publication Data applied for

ISBN   978 0 7190 86175 hardback
ISBN   978 0 7190 86182 paperback

First published 2012

The publisher has no responsibility for the persistence or accuracy of URLs for any external or third-party internet websites referred to in this book, and does not guarantee that any content on such websites is, or will remain, accurate or appropriate.

Typeset
by Carnegie Book Production, Lancaster
Printed in Great Britain
by Bell & Bain Ltd, Glasgow

For Anja

Contents

List of illustrations

Preface

This book began with a chance encounter in November 2005. Having written about nineteenth-century crime and violence, I was looking to start a new project on similar topics in the early twentieth century. When a colleague asked whether I would take his place at a planning meeting for a new research network that was to take place at the Galleries of Justice, a unique and fascinating crime-history museum in Nottingham, I agreed partly because of the chance that would give me to spend a few days in the Galleries' archives.

While there, the archivist patiently brought me various things in response to my rather vague queries. All the items were interesting but failed to spark any project ideas. 'There is also Mrs Pace', she then remarked. 'Who's Mrs Pace?' I replied. I was intrigued enough by her description of a woman tried in 1928 for the arsenic murder of her husband in the Forest of Dean to take a look at the few boxes of material that had been kept by her solicitor. What I found (her three police statements, a diverse pile of newspaper clippings and a stack of letters from her admirers) made me think there might be enough material for an article examining this largely forgotten case from the perspectives of police, press and public. As it turned out, the Pace case came to preoccupy me for the next five years: the more I looked into it – whether in the files of the Metropolitan Police and Home Office at The National Archives, in the British Library's vast newspaper collection or in Gloucestershire itself – the more I found, and it became clear that this story was about much more than a provincial murder trial.

While the 'Fetter Hill mystery' is itself fascinating, the scale

and style of the press coverage it generated have also allowed
me to examine what we would today call 'celebrity culture' in
Britain between the wars, especially that part of it inhabited not
by actors, politicians and royalty but rather by 'ordinary' people
suddenly turned into household names. Then as now, crimes
(whether proven or merely alleged) were one of the main causes of
such transformations. I also discovered that the case had played
an important (though hitherto unappreciated) role in contemporary debates about the criminal justice system, in particular
those driven by concerns about police powers and perceived
dangers to civil liberties, anxieties that have recurred across the
last century and up to the present day. In addition, the fortunate
survival of the letters Beatrice Pace received from what can only be
called her 'fans' enable a rare glimpse of that mysterious creature
known as 'the reading public'. Understanding the rise of Beatrice
Pace from rural obscurity to national adoration has thus meant
examining this case from various perspectives. I have tried to see
how the matter 'looked' not only from Fleet Street, Scotland Yard,
Whitehall and Westminster but also from the kitchen tables and
writing desks of the people who felt compelled to reach out to a
woman they had only 'met' in the pages of the newspapers. As a
brief technical note: because of the large number of people with
the surname 'Pace' involved in the events considered in this book,
I depart from academic custom and refer to members of Beatrice's
family by their first names. No excessive familiarity or disrespect
is intended.

    While researching and writing about these different perspectives,
I have benefited tremendously from various sources of insight,
encouragement and assistance. Research contributing to this book
was supported by the Arts and Humanities Research Council
(grant AH/F018150/1). Portions of Chapters 4 and 7 appeared
in an earlier form as '"Mrs Pace" and the ambiguous language
of victimisation', in Lisa Dresdner and Laurel Peterson (eds)
(Re)Interpretations: The Shapes of Justice in Women's Experience
(Newcastle: Cambridge Scholars Publishing, 2009), pp. 79–93. In
a somewhat different version, Chapter 9 was published as '"Those
who have had trouble can sympathise with you": press writing,
reader responses and a murder trial in interwar Britain', *Journal
of Social History* 43 (2009), 439–62. I am grateful for feedback
resulting from these earlier pieces.

My present and past colleagues in the Department of History at The Open University, in particular Clive Emsley, Pete King, Paul Lawrence and Chris Williams, have been unfailingly supportive. In different ways, they quite literally made this work possible. I owe a special debt of gratitude to Katherine D. Watson, James Whitfield, Robert M. Morris and James S. Cockburn, who each read complete drafts and offered many helpful suggestions in their areas of expertise. Margaret Gregory kindly helped me in getting hold of relevant birth, death and marriage certificates. Bev Baker at the Galleries of Justice not only led me to this case to begin with but has also been helpful in researching it. Keith Smart has very generously shared insights and materials gained over decades of personal enquiries into the Pace case. Nicholas Rheinberg, HM Coroner for Cheshire, provided helpful information about inquest procedures, and efforts to reform them, since the 1920s. I am also grateful for assistance and encouragement from Howard Brown, Stewart Evans, Andrew Hammel, Andrew Parry and Christina Wipf Perry. I especially thank Barry Martin and his family, as well as Tony Martin, for sharing with me their personal recollections of the woman at the centre of this study and for providing me with useful materials in telling her story. Finally, Anja Müller-Wood has been my most valuable and consistent source of emotional support and intellectual inspiration while writing this book. For that reason, and countless more, it is dedicated to her.

List of key figures
involved in the Pace case

The family

Beatrice and Harry Pace
Dorothy, Doris, Leslie, Selwyn ('Teddy') and Isobel ('Jean') Pace:
    Beatrice and Harry's children
Arnold and Fred Martin: Beatrice's brothers
Elizabeth Porter: Harry's mother
Elton, Leonard, Gertrude and Flossie Pace and Leah Pritchard:
    Harry's siblings and their spouses

Friends, acquaintances and neighbours

Charles Fletcher: fellow hospital patient with Harry who also
    visited him at home
Fred Thorne: acquaintance of Fletcher and amateur masseur who
    met Harry in hospital and also visited him at home
Joseph Martin: a neighbour of Beatrice and Harry
'Mrs Paddock': proprietor of the King's Head Hotel, Coleford
Alice and Leslie Sayes: friends and neighbours of Beatrice and
    Harry
Rosa Kear: midwife and neighbour of Beatrice and Harry
George Mountjoy: executor of Harry's will

The police

Gloucestershire Constabulary
Chief Constable Major Stanley Clarke
Inspector Alan Bent
Sergeant Charlie Hamblin
PC Edith Lodge

Metropolitan Police (London)
Sir William Horwood: Metropolitan Police Commissioner
Sir B. E. Wyndham Childs: head of the Criminal Investigation
    Department (CID)
Norman Kendal: Deputy Assistant Commissioner, CID
Percy Savage: Superintendent, CID
Chief Inspector George Cornish: lead detective in the Pace case
Detective Sergeant Clarence Campion: detective in the Pace case

Lawyers

G. Trevor Wellington: Beatrice's solicitor
William and Florence Earengey: barristers acting on Beatrice's
    behalf from the magistrates' court onward
Norman Birkett, KC: Beatrice's barrister at her trial in Gloucester
G. R. Paling: Department of Public Prosecutions official who
    assisted the coroner at the inquest and argued the case for
    the Crown in the magistrate's court
Sir F. Boyd Merriman, KC: Solicitor-General and prosecuting
    barrister at Beatrice's trial

Medical men

Dr William Henry Du Pré: the Pace family's doctor
Dr Ram Nath Nanda: doctor who also attended to Harry Pace
Dr Norman Mather: doctor who treated Harry Pace in hospital
Charles Carson: local doctor who performed post-mortem on
    Harry Pace
Prof. Isaac Walker Hall: pathology professor at Bristol University
Rowland Ellis: city and county analyst for Gloucester and
    Gloucestershire
Sir William Willcox: pathology expert, Honorary Medical
    Adviser to the Home Office
Dr Robert Bronte: medical expert for the defence at Beatrice's trial

Legal and government officials

Sir William Joynson-Hicks: Home Secretary
Sir Ernley Blackwell: Home Office Legal Adviser
Arthur Locke: head of the Home Office's Criminal Division

Maurice Carter: coroner who supervised the inquest into Harry
    Pace's death
Mr Justice Horridge: the presiding judge at Beatrice's trial
Sir Archibald Bodkin: Director of Public Prosecutions

Politicians

A. A. Purcell: Labour MP for the Forest of Dean and organiser
    of Beatrice's defence fund
Will Thorne: Labour MP who raised concerns about police
    actions in the Pace case
Ellen Wilkinson: Labour MP who raised concerns about police
    actions in the Pace case
Rhys Hopkin Morris: Liberal MP who criticised the actions of
    the coroner in the Pace case
Sir Kingsley Wood: Conservative MP critical of procedure in
    coroners' inquests

Journalists

Bernard O'Donnell: journalist who wrote a series on the Pace
    case for the *World's Pictorial News*
James Douglas: editor of the *Sunday Express*
R. Gittoes-Davies: editor of the Cardiff *Evening Express*
W. K. Bliss: journalist from the *Daily Chronicle*

Introduction

On the afternoon of 6 July 1928 a slim, pale woman in a black dress emerged from the Shire Hall in Gloucester. Her name was Beatrice Annie Pace, and she was met by a cheering throng of well-wishers – numbering anywhere between 3,000 and 10,000 – celebrating her acquittal upon the charge of having murdered her husband with arsenic.[1] Numerous reporters were on hand to record the tumult. One from the *Daily Mirror* described the 'emotional scenes':

> Women clasped one another by the hands and some cried. When the verdict was made known the crowd was smaller than usual owing to the unexpectedly early hour at which it had come, but the news spread around the city of Gloucester like wildfire, and crowds numbering thousands sprang from seemingly nowhere.
> West Gate-street, in front of the Shire Hall, was packed.[2]

According to a correspondent for *The People*,

> the word went forth from mouth to mouth. Men and women yelled it to one another, and the people came running until the street was choked by thousands of howling men and women. Shopkeepers and their assistants rushed out of their stores and raced for the court to join in the demonstration.
> The National Anthem, played by a trumpeter, shrilled above the clamour. In the hush it caused, the judge came out to his carriage, and the crowd rose to him. 'Good old justice!' they bellowed. A woman ducked under the arms of the police and screamed: 'Saved another woman's life! Bless you! God bless you!'[3]

When Beatrice's barrister left the court to return to his hotel, he could pass through the throng only 'with the greatest difficulty', 'being "thumped" on the back by enthusiastic admirers'.[4] 'Through a wavering lane of cheering men and women he walked,' *The People* reported, 'compelled to bow and raise his hat at every step in acknowledgement of the wild greetings of the crowd.'[5]

The waiting thousands were even more eager to see the acquitted defendant. Shortly after Beatrice appeared on the court building's steps accompanied by two of her daughters and someone from her solicitor's office, a car pulled up to the Shire Hall. As a local paper reported: 'As soon as Mrs. Pace appeared in the open light of day, a free woman once again, the waiting crowd got completely out of control. Wildly yelling their delight, they surged forward, slowly but surely forcing the cordon of police inwards toward the waiting cars.'[6] 'In the rush of the crowd as Mrs. Pace appeared', it continued, 'several women were kicked. Some fainted, and one was carried into the Shire Hall by two policemen, who rendered first aid.' It took some time, but a semblance of order was eventually restored.

Then, according to the *Daily Mirror*: 'When at last Mrs. Pace was able to be led to a waiting car the crowd surged round it, men waving their hats and shouting and women waving handker-chiefs and laughing and weeping alternately.'[7] Although 'men and women clung to the car, which for some time could not be moved', the mounted police charged at the crowd where it seemed weakest: 'The crowd gave, screaming women fleeing before the horses.'[8] Through the breach 'the cars hurtled out on the road to Coleford' – the market town near Beatrice's home in the Forest of Dean – and were escorted for three miles by mounted police.[9] The long suspense of the woman sometimes referred to in the press as 'the tragic widow of Coleford' appeared to have ended.[10]

Just as the crowd celebrated their heroes, they condemned those they saw as villains. This was the fate of Beatrice's in-laws, the family of her late husband, Harry Pace. The Pace family – in particular Harry's brother Elton – had been convinced of Beatrice's guilt, and their courtroom testimony had sought to cast her in an unfavourable light. In view of the crowd's vigorous support for Beatrice, it was clear that the Paces would face an uncomfortable departure:

> The relatives of the deceased man were taken away in the police superintendent's car in the hope that they would not be recognised,

but the crowd quickly saw through the ruse and hooted and booed.
They drove away with a mounted guard on either side, and Mr. Elton Pace raised his hat to the hooting crowd, who replied with derisive cheers.[11]

With extensive police protection, however, they escaped otherwise unscathed.

A curious death in the Forest of Dean

The packed streets and the 'wild demonstrations' that greeted Beatrice's acquittal could not have been unexpected.[12] A similar frenzy had accompanied the trial from its opening four days earlier, and long before that Beatrice had become a well-known figure. This was not simply because of her husband's death the preceding January after a long and agonising illness. Without the official inquiries that followed, his passing would have remained as obscure as that of any other working-class person. But investigations by the local police were soon accompanied by dark suggestions of extramarital affairs, hidden wealth and poisoning. The local coroner's decision to postpone the funeral and order an urgent post-mortem suddenly made Harry's demise highly newsworthy, especially when it was later proven that he had died from a large dose of arsenic. Precisely *how* it had gotten into his body was anything but clear, but there were only three obvious possibilities – accident, suicide or murder – and, at first, no way of deciding among them.

It was during the lengthy inquest into Harry's death that Beatrice, widowed and left alone to care for her five children, gradually became both a suspect and a figure of public interest and sympathy. Although on trial for murder, she was seen as a victim: of her husband, of local gossips, of the criminal justice system and of unfair laws and social attitudes. Her story served as a screen onto which newspaper readers (particularly women) could project their own daily struggles. Many saw their lives reflected in Beatrice's 'ordeal'. As a result, 'Mrs Pace' was among the biggest stories of 1928, not only in the scandal-soaked yellow press but also in more serious newspapers. A journalist described the case as

one of the most sensational dramas of life and death ever staged

1 A studio portrait of Beatrice Pace taken soon after her acquittal.

(Courtesy of Tony Martin)

in this country, culminating in the most dramatic murder trial of recent times.

Leading articles have been written in almost every newspaper in the land concerning the death of Harry Pace ... and the ordeal which his widow has been put to since his death in January last.

... Questions have been asked in Parliament and questions there are still to be asked, whilst the Attorney-General, the highest legal representative in the House of Commons, has, with all the dignity of his office, declared his intention of giving the questions raised his earnest consideration.

Beatrice's acquittal, he claimed, 'was enthusiastically acclaimed by Press and public alike in a manner that has never before been known'.[13] This was not strictly true: there had been other high-profile trials before the case (and countless more to follow), and it is in the nature of sensationalist reporting to exaggerate an event's significance. Nevertheless, other papers concurred. *Thomson's Weekly News* referred to it as 'the most dramatic trial' and the *Daily Express* as the 'most astonishing judicial drama' of recent years.[14] The *News of the World* called the case 'one of the most amazing within living memory', while the *Daily Mail* described it as 'one of the most extraordinary murder trials in the annals of English law'.[15] The *Sunday Express* observed that Beatrice's 'martyrdom' – a term widely used to describe her experience – 'aroused universal compassion' and dubbed her 'the most remarkable woman in England'.[16] Photos of her, her children, other figures from the trial and the crowds surrounding Gloucester's Shire Hall appeared on the front pages of several major papers.[17]

We now live in an age when sensational legal dramas are common, and the media frenzy that surrounds investigations into mysterious deaths or disappearances is no longer surprising. In the late 1920s, however, the Pace trial was a *cause célèbre* of a type that was still relatively new, one of a series of dramatic homicide trials that punctuated the inter-war decades. The drawn-out coroner's inquest that preceded Beatrice's trial had made her a celebrity, and her isolated cottage became a magnet for sightseers. Nor did her fame immediately subside with her acquittal: while closing one aspect of the case it allowed others to emerge more strongly. Beatrice sold her story to the press, and, in weekly instalments, readers learned of her childhood and marriage, her experiences during the inquest and trial, and the details of the new life she was seeking to build. If only for a short period in 1928, she became a touchstone for social commentary on marriage, domestic violence and the state of British justice. As the *Sunday Express* put it, hers was a story 'of thrilling interest to the whole nation, which watched her unparalleled ordeal with passionate interest from its tragic beginning to its happy ending'.[18]

Poison, press, police and public

Although neither murder trials nor tales of tragic marriages were uncommon in the inter-war period, the scale of popular fascination with the Pace case stands out. The passions that surrounded it are not difficult to fathom: an agonising death, a postponed funeral, an embittered family, a revealing series of inquest hearings, a bizarrely violent marriage and a climactic courtroom duel between two prominent barristers gave the case an inherent drama which, to this day, remains gripping. To some extent, it may be that the topics of homicide, family intrigue, injustice and individual perseverance against seemingly overwhelming odds have a universal appeal and relevance; nonetheless, Beatrice's case also fit into the particular cultural moment of late 1920s Britain.

What is almost as remarkable as the sudden public fascination with Beatrice Pace, however, is her subsequent disappearance from the historical stage. Fickle then as now, the newspapers quickly moved on to new scandals, new suspicious deaths and new political battles.[19] The shrinking half-life of media sensations involving ordinary people thrust into the limelight is something to which we have become accustomed, and the fact that Beatrice was in the public eye for about a year might even be taken as a suggestion that her story had a distinctive longevity. She has, moreover, not been completely forgotten. In the 1960s, the case merited a prominent place in biographies of Beatrice's barrister and of a renowned forensic expert who participated in the trial.[20] The matter has also received attention as a 'true crime' story, and it has even been the subject of a television dramatisation and BBC radio play.[21] But the Pace case has never received the sort of attention it deserves. Its chroniclers have – whether in the form of short articles or book chapters – mainly focused on the trial evidence and sought to answer some version of the following question: 'Did she *really* do it?' Admittedly, this is a question which preoccupies anyone who delves even briefly into a case such as this, and in what follows the many intriguing facts of the case – forensic and otherwise – will be considered. However, I will also focus on aspects of Beatrice's experiences that have been mostly ignored: her sensational newspaper coverage and peculiar celebrity, the debates that her treatment by the justice system sparked in press and Parliament as well as the intense reactions that she inspired in the British public.

Other than for those directly involved, the case was primarily a newspaper story. Previous studies of it have been based on local coverage and have largely neglected the extent to which Beatrice became a nationally – even internationally – renowned figure.[22] There was a truly enormous amount of reporting and commentary about the case, much of which will be examined here for the first time. The duration of the press interest gave ample opportunity for a variety of voices to emerge, and discussion of Beatrice and her husband was coloured by contemporary attitudes toward marriage, motherhood, poverty and domestic violence.

More than a few politicians and journalists depicted Beatrice as the victim of social injustice and claimed her experiences revealed dangers to civil liberties. The police were a favoured target of such critics, not least since the Pace case occurred amidst a wave of popular concerns about the police. Police sources themselves are valuable in this regard, underscoring the extent to which the police – and Scotland Yard in particular – were apprehensive about their portrayal in the media. The fact that the accused was a woman made police behaviour in this case an especially sensitive and sensational issue. The treatment of women by the criminal justice system is a complex issue to which historians of crime have devoted much attention in recent decades, and the Pace case offers a useful case study for considering the interactions between gender and police procedure.[23]

Analysis of the Pace case also illuminates a poorly understood historical topic: public opinion. Interpreting media sources, such as newspapers, is challenging enough, but they are at least readily identifiable and available. It is far more difficult to catch even a fleeting glimpse of the reactions of their audience: in this case, newspaper *readers*. The press packaged the Pace case for public consumption in a particular way, but the story was not simply dictated to a passive readership. The papers offered what they thought their readers wanted, and one can assume that – as is always the case – people made use of press narratives in individual ways influenced by personal experiences, expectations and prejudices. As a result of her popularity, Beatrice was deluged with thousands of letters from people across Britain who took an interest in her story.[24] A collection of surviving correspondence will offer new perspectives on popular *reactions* to media presentations of crime, gender, celebrity, institutional authority and victimisation.

In what follows, I recount the details of the Pace case while also considering what one woman's story reveals about the history of the police, the development of celebrity culture and the interests of the public in inter-war Britain. Chapter 1 sets the scene: it opens by tracing the puzzling illness that afflicted Harry Pace from the summer of 1927 to his agonising death in January 1928. It then reconstructs a crucial topic of the press's coverage – the courtship of Beatrice and Harry – based upon three different (and sometimes contradictory) post-trial memoirs. Chapters 2 and 3 focus on the police investigation and the lengthy coroner's inquest, the most extensive of the legal tribunals Beatrice would face. Chapter 2 focuses on the evidence given by Harry's kinfolk; Chapter 3 considers the vivid testimony given by the Pace children, the police, family friends and forensic experts. The case's rise into a press sensation is the subject of Chapter 4: during this 'golden age' of the press 'human interest' stories were driving increasing newspaper sales, and crime was central to this world of press sensationalism. Chapter 5 examines Beatrice's trial in Gloucester: involving some of the most prominent lawyers and forensic experts of the age, its abrupt ending added a surprising, dramatic twist.

Her innocence officially confirmed by a decisive acquittal, Beatrice was reunited with her children and began building a new life. However, as Chapter 6 examines, new allegations arose. Vague – but potentially sensational – suggestions about Harry's death reappeared on the front pages, and detectives returned to the Forest of Dean. Had the criminal justice system failed? Or had a cruel conspiracy been hatched against one of Britain's most popular women? The following three chapters deal with the roles of the press, police and public, respectively. Chapter 7 looks into the ways that Beatrice, Harry and their marriage were presented in the press. The Pace issue was more than a personal story, however, and Chapter 8 explores how it became a vehicle for legal, political, institutional and social criticism. Chapter 9 turns to the reaction of the public that seemed to so devotedly stand by this long-suffering woman: more than two hundred letters sent to her following her acquittal offer fascinating insights into the attitudes of Beatrice's admirers and reveal the intense and deeply moving emotions that she inspired. A general conclusion and a postscript evaluate the case's significance and examine what happened to some of its key figures after the name 'Mrs Pace' had, once and for all, faded from the headlines.

1

The 'Fetter Hill mystery': the strange death of Harry Pace

The path to Beatrice's raucous acquittal had its starting point at a lonely farmhouse in Fetter Hill, a hamlet of scattered houses 'on the fringe of the primitive Forest of Dean' a few miles from the market town of Coleford.[1] The Forest of Dean – between the Severn and Wye rivers – was noted for the distinctive culture of its residents, the 'Foresters'. Although much of the Forest belonged to the monarch directly, the inhabitants had claimed freedoms on 'Crown' lands related to mining, quarrying and pastoral farming since the Middle Ages, some of which were only codified in the early nineteenth century.[2] Supervised by Crown administrators, the 'free' miners independently worked – and often owned – small-scale mines (mainly iron and coal) and quarries (predominantly sandstone). Many were bought by large companies in the first decades of the twentieth century, and in the late 1920s the poor market for monumental and building stone was causing economic distress.[3] Haphazard development meant individual cottages and scattered hamlets dotted the landscape.

The Foresters' isolated lifestyle and their long struggle to maintain their independence and privileges contributed to their being seen as 'a people apart'.[4] Known for their insularity, they 'were for many centuries regarded as an unruly people': strangers (known locally as 'foreigners') 'visited the district at their peril'.[5] Winifred Foley, born in 1914 and later a well-known memoirist of life in the Forest, recalled that her youth in the Forest was 'remote', 'self-contained' and 'cut off from the world': 'We were content to be a race apart, made up mostly of families who had lived in the Forest for generations, sharing the same

2 Rose Cottage, with inset images of Dorothy and Leslie Pace.

(©The British Library Board, *Thomson's Weekly News*, 9 June 1928, p. 4)

handful of surnames, and speaking a dialect quite distinct from any other.'[6]

'Rose Cottage', the Pace home, was a 'typical white-washed Forest dwelling a few yards off the main road' from Fetter Hill to the nearby village of Sling.[7] 'Slag heaps scar the surrounding forest', it was noted, 'and a muddy path leads to the lonely hut.'[8] The 'lonely little farm' was on a hill overlooking a 'rugged beauty spot of the forest'; it was 'drab looking' with 'tiny windows' and a 'ramshackle appearance'.[9] 'The Forest of Dean varies between beauty and squalor', one reporter observed, judging that 'Fetter Hill is hardly one of the beauty spots.'[10] 'It is a bleak and isolated spot', another agreed, 'but in the summer the surrounding hills and forest make it beautiful.'[11] Noting that the 'nearest habitation is another solitary house some 200 yards distant', a detective's report described the cottage:

> The house consists of five rooms, a kitchen or living room, into
> which the front door opens, a pantry or larder on the right of it,

and at the back is a wash house. Immediately to the right of the front door in the kitchen there are ten stairs leading up to two bedrooms upstairs ... [T]hese rooms are about eleven feet square, and scantily furnished, and, in fact, the whole house and its surroundings show signs of extreme poverty.[12]

The Paces, both in their late thirties, had lived in Rose Cottage for about four years, the latest of several houses they had rented during their eighteen-year marriage.[13] They had five children: Dorothy (seventeen years old in January 1928), Doris (eleven), Leslie (nine), Selwyn (nicknamed 'Teddy', five) and Jean, a sickly infant girl of about six months.[14] Beatrice had borne five other children who had died in infancy. Harry was a quarryman and had worked at various quarries owned by the United Stone Firms Company, earning a modest £2 per week; a typical Forester, he supplemented his wages by selling sheep he herded on common land.[15] He had, at times, as many as a hundred sheep and lambs.[16] Along with running the household and caring for the children, Beatrice contributed to the family's income by rearing chickens: she sold eggs and young fowls to the hotels and tradespeople in nearby Coleford. Among her customers were, 'on occasion', the Coleford police.[17]

A mysterious illness

Harry had been 'poorly on and off' for about two years prior to 1928.[18] He was diagnosed in the summer of 1926 with gastritis, an inflammation of the stomach lining with many potential causes. In May 1927, Beatrice persuaded him to see their local doctor, William Henry Du Pré, after another bout of illness.[19] Harry suffered from stomach pains, 'wasting' and occasional vomiting of blood. Diagnosing a gastric ulcer or gastritis, Du Pré prescribed bismuth and soda, and Harry soon improved. In late July 1927 – probably the afternoon of Saturday, 23 July – the Paces 'dipped' several lambs. 'Sheep dipping' involves bathing the animals in a chemical insecticide and fungicide to protect them from infestation.[20] Common brands of 'sheep dip', which came in powder form to be mixed with water, contained enormous quantities of arsenic, perhaps some 1,400 fatal doses in a single packet.[21] (A witness at the subsequent coroner's inquest stated sheep were left in the solution for about half a minute: if left in for two or three minutes they would die.[22]) Harry and Beatrice, assisted by two of their children, dipped nearly twenty lambs in a 'dolly tub' near the railway line that ran by their house. 'Leslie and me had to mind the lambs while Mam and Dad dipped them', Doris later recalled: 'Mam got the hind legs and Dad the front legs and pushed them down in the tub and back up again!'[23] The solution was left in the tub until Beatrice emptied it and put it behind the house. The same tub was used for collecting rainwater and, Leslie stated, washing clothes.[24]

That evening, Harry had such bad stomach pains that he rolled about in agony on the ground.[25] He stayed in bed most of Sunday, and although he went to work the next day at the quarry, he returned early and went straight to the bedroom.[26] Du Pré attended him, diagnosing peripheral neuritis and urging hospitalisation. Harry's family – particularly his mother, Elizabeth Porter – insisted on a second opinion, and in mid-August Dr Ram Nath Nanda agreed with his colleague's diagnosis.[27] Suffering acute pain and partial paralysis, Harry was admitted to the Gloucester Royal Infirmary about a week later, on 19 August. When leaving home, he was so ill that he could not be dressed and was carried to the car in a blanket.[28] The numbness had been worsening for 'about a month' following nine or ten days of severe abdominal pain and vomiting. Harry, in one doctor's words, 'was helpless'.[29]

It is difficult to say precisely when and how arsenic was identified as a cause of Harry's illness. Beatrice later told the press that when Harry's health first declined in 1926 Du Pré's predecessor – a Dr Francis – had 'treated him for an illness which was said to be due to arsenic from sheep dip'.[30] Despite that earlier diagnosis and the fact that Harry's symptoms matched those of arsenic poisoning, neither Du Pré nor Nanda seems to have initially considered this possibility.[31] Beatrice said Harry's illness was first blamed on arsenic at the Infirmary: a 'doctor's theory' was that 'while he was engaged in dipping the sheep the poison had got in through the pores of the skin'.[32] Dr Norman Mather, who treated Harry in hospital, thought of arsenic 'as a possible aiding cause' of Harry's symptoms, and he said Harry himself referred to having recently used sheep dip.[33] Du Pré may have talked to Beatrice about arsenical poisoning two or three weeks before Harry was discharged, and a fellow patient also said that Harry had referred to sheep dip as the cause of his condition.[34]

However, at Beatrice's trial, the prosecution would state that hospital doctors 'failed to discover the origin of the neuritis' before Harry came home.[35] While it is uncertain when – or even if – a firm diagnosis of arsenical poisoning was made, the possibility was certainly being discussed.

Although Harry told at least one fellow patient that the doctors thought he had (accidentally) been poisoned with arsenic, he otherwise kept this information to himself. His family said he never mentioned it to them.[36] Harry told his brother Leonard he had 'catched a chill' while washing sheep. (Sheep washing involved standing in running water – without chemicals – up to the waist and cleaning the fleece.[37]) When a neighbour saw Harry at home, he explained his condition was the result of 'getting in the water dipping his sheep, and getting his feet wet'.[38] Fellow patient Charles Fletcher said that when he visited Harry at home, he 'thought he was suffering from rheumatism or neuritis in an acute form, and he thought he ought to have electrical treatment or baths to get it out of him'.[39] Fletcher was 'floored' when Harry mentioned arsenic. He had been seeking to cheer Harry up, pointing out he could now 'see his sheep from the windows', but Harry was inconsolable, saying 'with a half-laugh and a half-cry': 'Not much hopes [sic], the doctors say I have got arsenical poisoning – arsenic in the blood – and I shall not be able to get about for two years. That's the report from Gloucester.' Fletcher asked whether he had been 'slovenly' with the dip or whether water from the dipping tub had been thrown over the garden produce, but Harry said no. Another visitor, Fred Thorne, said arsenic was mentioned only two months after Harry's return.[40] When Harry's mother later asked Dr. Nanda about the cause of her son's death, she claims he said immediately 'arsenical poisoning'.[41]

Harry's condition improved at best only very slightly while in hospital. Fletcher said Harry had been unable to hold a cigarette when first admitted but that later he could. His grip was 'an ebb and flow', alternately improving and worsening.[42] Beatrice doubted that Harry got much better.[43] She visited him twice a week – one witness said she 'never missed a visiting day' – and often brought fruit and cakes which were shared with other patients.[44] Staff and patients said Harry was miserable and doubted he would recover.[45] Dr Mather recalled that Harry was never 'very bright – he was not the kind of patient who was helping the Doctor'.[46]

Harry reportedly said he would rather kill himself than remain a 'cripple', but his family denied he was capable of suicidal intentions.[47] Insistent about going home (he 'pestered' Beatrice about this after only a few weeks in hospital), Harry was released on 24 October 1927, the day after the couple's eighteenth wedding anniversary.[48] Beatrice did not want him to be discharged but he had 'begged' her until she reluctantly signed for his release.[49] At home, he was carried 'in a helpless state' upstairs. His wretched condition was one of the few points on which Beatrice and Harry's family would subsequently agree.[50]

Although a family friend described him as a 'helpless log' with no use of his hands or feet when he returned home, all observers believed his condition improved once there.[51] Fletcher said Harry had made great progress and regained the use of his hands and arms: two days before Christmas, Harry 'was better than [he] had previously known him' and had 'gradually got away from his depression'. Thorne also saw a steady improvement till shortly before Christmas, despite Harry's continuing stiffness in his knees and ankles.[52] He was able to put his boots on and sit by the fire, cut up his food, handle books and move about his room unaided.[53] Except for Harry's kin, all witnesses agreed that Beatrice was a devoted nurse. Du Pré thought Harry had made 'great progress'.[54]

That improvement ended abruptly. Just before Christmas, Harry's stomach pains and occasional vomiting returned. On Christmas morning, Dorothy had, as usual, gone to light the fire in her father's room. He told her not to bother as he would be coming downstairs. Putting the firewood into the grate, she noticed a bottle and placed it on a chest of drawers. Beatrice went upstairs to ask Harry about it, and Dorothy heard him reply, 'I don't know nothing.' With Doris's assistance, Harry came downstairs for the first time since returning home. Rather than a joyful occasion, however, a terrifying scene unfolded. As Dorothy explained, her father, 'in one of his tempers', grabbed the tongs from the kitchen fireplace and attacked Beatrice. Dorothy intervened, and Harry, thwarted, bashed in the fireguard before sitting down. After a pause, he took a straight razor from the cupboard and told his family to 'clear out' or else he would kill them.[55] The two boys fled, and Beatrice sent Doris to fetch Joseph Martin, a neighbour who lived a couple of hundred yards away.[56]

Harry had 'cooled down' by the time Martin arrived, and he then returned to his room.[57] He would never again leave it alive.

Harry cried bitterly that afternoon and begged for his wife's forgiveness. His condition, meanwhile, worsened, and on Boxing Day, Beatrice walked miles through deep snow to Du Pré. She explained Harry's outburst and said he was suffering from stomach pains, 'feverish headache' and shivering. The snow prevented Du Pré from attending until the next day, when he found Harry suffering from severe abdominal pain and vomiting. He diagnosed gastric influenza. According to Du Pré, Harry's condition remained about the same until the morning of 8 January.[58] Other witnesses described a post-Christmas decline. When Thorne came to the house on 29 December, Harry was 'very much altered and very ill'.[59] Fletcher visited on 3 January, finding him vomiting and 'constantly' retching. Harry told him how 'weak and sore' this had made him.[60] Harry's mother said he was 'in agonies of pain' three days before his death.[61] Joseph Martin visited on 8 January and found Harry 'very bad': he was quiet and looked 'thoroughly ill'.[62] Beatrice fetched Du Pré, who found that Harry's stomach pains and his general condition had worsened; he asked for any vomit or urine to be kept.[63] Another neighbour was present at this point: Alice Sayes. She and her husband Leslie were friends of the Paces, and Alice stayed with Beatrice on Harry's last two nights. On the night of 8 January, she saw Beatrice give him brandy mixed with water, his medicine and a cornflour mixture. She testified that he vomited up the latter and had had, on the previous day, severe diarrhoea.[64]

On 9 January, Harry's suspicious mother, Elizabeth Porter, asked him whether 'he was being done right by'. She said he remarked 'there are two packets of sheep dip here' but said nothing more, as Leslie came upstairs. Elton Pace also visited: Harry 'still had his healthy colour', but Elton could see his brother was in 'horrible pain' and could not firmly grip his hand. Asked whether he thought he was dying, Harry responded 'he was sure he was sinking'.[65] Beatrice sought out Du Pré, who came to the house at about 10.30 p.m. He later told the inquest Harry was 'much worse and almost prostrate': he had 'intense pain' in the head and stomach, a 'burning pain' in the throat and had 'ceased' to urinate or vomit. Harry was unable to sit up, and Du Pré thought he was 'helpless'.[66] Alice Sayes helped keep an eye on Harry, giving him water from a glass in the room or from 'an earthenware pan' in the pantry. She also prepared a mixture of egg white and water for Harry in Beatrice's presence. Otherwise, 'whatever was given him Mrs. Pace prepared'.[67]

After two weeks of acute torment, Harry Pace died between 10.30 and 11.00 a.m. on Tuesday, 10 January 1928. Alice Sayes said he 'passed away peacefully with his wife's name upon his lips'.[68] Harry's sister Leah Pritchard, however, claimed he died 'in agonizing pain'.[69] When the coroner later questioned Sayes, she insisted Harry died 'very peacefully' and was unconscious 'at the end', within an hour of his death. She agreed when Beatrice's solicitor suggested that Pritchard's evidence about 'the death scene' was 'pure invention'.[70] Pritchard insisted she was present when Harry died, but Sayes and Beatrice said that only they and Rosa Kear – an 'uncertified midwife' who had assisted with some of Beatrice's pregnancies, including the birth of her daughter Jean the previous summer – had been at Harry's bedside. Kear agreed.[71] The matter remained unresolved. Harry, however, was clearly in agony during his last days. A historian has recently offered a vivid description of acute arsenical poisoning from the victim's perspective:

> Imagine stomach pains so sharp that it seems like rats are gnawing at your insides. The pain is accompanied by a thirst almost impossible to quench, with loss of bowel control and a violent vomiting and retching. Vomit and faeces stain you, your bed, and the floor around you; your family cannot wash the linen quickly enough to keep it clean. The air in the room in which you lie is utterly foul.[72]

At the end, Harry may have slipped into a merciful unconsciousness.[73] In any case, the day after Harry died, Dr Du Pré filled out a death certificate citing influenza, anuria (the cessation of urination), gastroenteritis and peripheral neuritis as causes of death.[74] He certified, that is, a death from 'natural' causes.

'I suppose I was a great fool': when Beattie met Harry

The chain of events that led Beatrice to her husband's deathbed began two decades earlier along a country lane within a few miles of Rose Cottage. The earliest stories about Harry's death noted that Beatrice had married young, but further details of her life were at first scarce.[75] In April, Beatrice explained, 'I was a general servant at Hampstead once and happy. Then I came back to my home near here, but Harry courted me for one day and I married him.'[76] As if to compensate for the lack of detail, the three 'life stories' that appeared after the trial – by Beatrice, her daughter Dorothy and a journalist – focused extensively on the courtship. This aspect of the story not only helps to introduce Beatrice and Harry but also gives initial insight into how the press presented their lives and marriage.

First, it is necessary to point out a curious fact. Both Beatrice and Harry were widely reported to have been thirty-six years old in early 1928. In addition, several stories – including Beatrice's own memoir – claimed she had married at seventeen. Harry's age was less clearly established in the press. Quoting a 'sister of the wife', the *World's Pictorial News* claimed Beatrice had been seventeen 'and her husband a year older'.[77] (This was also what Dorothy said.[78]) A later article in the same paper, however, describes Harry as 'a month *younger* than the girl whom he loved so impetuously'.[79] Beatrice's memoir described Harry as having also been seventeen at marriage.[80] None of these versions was true. Beatrice was born on 24 October 1889: thus, when she married Harry on 23 October 1909, she was nineteen (and would turn twenty the next day).[81] This is correctly stated on their marriage certificate, which also gives Harry's age as twenty. *That*, however, was wrong. Harry was born on 16 November 1890: he was, therefore, about a year *younger* than his bride. When he died on 10 January 1928, he was thirty-seven and Beatrice thirty-eight.[82] The reason for these discrepancies is unclear, and nobody in the press at the time – or in later histories of the case – appears to have noted them.

The various versions of Beatrice's life story are broadly similar in outline, which is hardly surprising since the main source for all three must have been Beatrice herself (though some details may have been provided by relatives and friends). Beatrice seems to have talked to Dorothy about her earlier life on many occasions, and, of course, Dorothy could draw on her own experiences for the couple's more recent history. Journalist Bernard O'Donnell, author of the third memoir, seems to have very effectively gained the family's trust, not least by driving Beatrice to and from the inquest's twenty-two sittings from 29 March to the end of May.

'After the day's hearing', O'Donnell later recalled, 'we would have tea at the home of Mrs. Paddock, a friend of the widow who kept the "King's Head" at Coleford, before driving back to Fetterhill': 'I used generally to spend an hour playing with Doris and her dolls or having a romp with Leslie and Teddy, the latter a regular scamp of a boy.'[83] O'Donnell's handling of the case clearly applied his principle that 'tactful sympathy and practical help will unlock the door to an *inside* story more surely than any amount of uncouth bluster'.[84] He certainly seems to have been the journalist who was most successful in developing a rapport – and even, as he later put it, friendship – with Beatrice and her children.[85] In considering the similarities and differences in the three memoirs, it is important to remember that Beatrice and Dorothy probably did not simply 'write' their stories: if they were not ghost-written (based on interviews), both women would have at least received significant editorial assistance and guidance, which might have pushed their tales in subtly different directions.[86]

All the post-trial life stories used the couple's courtship to shape particular narrative arcs, with Beatrice's depiction as a rural *ingénue* adding to her life's drama, tragedy and pathos. Bernard O'Donnell highlighted the 'extraordinary tragedy which seemed to dog her steps' after meeting Harry.[87] Dorothy, too, saw Beatrice's childhood as the key to understanding her life:

> I am giving you this insight into my mother's childhood days because I think it will help you to understand the type of woman she became. She came from plain, working-class people of the Forest of Dean, and a plain, unspoiled woman she has remained. She lived for three years in London, but she brought away with her none of the ways of the city. She went to London a country girl and it was as a country girl that she returned.[88]

Beatrice also emphasised her origins in conveying the sorrow that she was later to suffer. 'I have never been so happy since my childhood', she wrote, 'and it is with my childhood that I shall begin my story, for unless you understand how pleasant and easy things were for me then you will not be able to realise the terrible change in my life that came with marriage.'[89]

Beatrice was born to Thomas and Mary Martin at a place called 'The Fence' in St Briavels, near Coleford. [90] Her father was a gardener. The family was poor but, as Beatrice put it, 'not too poor to have plenty for everybody'.[91] She had a younger sister and brother as well as four older brothers. O'Donnell depicted 'Beattie' as 'a finely-built, sturdy girl with the frankest smiling blue eyes that one could ever see' and 'rather a tomboy in her young days'.[92] Beatrice said her elder siblings treated her as 'the family favourite', and she 'mothered' the others.[93] The latter role increased when, at the age of twelve, she was taken out of school to care for her cancer-stricken mother. After her mother's death, Beatrice kept the Martin household.[94] There, as Dorothy stated, 'From morning to night she was kept busy in her father's cottage, and many times I have heard her say that few young women of twenty to-day would do, without complaining, what she, as a child of twelve, was compelled to do.'[95] Still, Beatrice claimed to enjoy her childhood: 'I was happy and content and looked for nothing else in life except that quiet, day-to-day existence among people who loved me and whom I loved.'[96] Nonetheless, at about the age of fourteen (though she may have been older), Beatrice, as was common for girls of her class, went 'into service': she had found a position as a domestic servant in London.

There were different versions of how this decision was reached. O'Donnell vaguely notes 'it was decided that she should go into service', depicting it as a contribution to the family's survival: 'She was extremely popular with the other members of the family and they were loth [sic] to lose her but there were many of them, many hungry mouths to feed, and money very scarce.'[97] Describing Beatrice's departure as an act of self-sacrifice fits well with O'Donnell's emphasis on her later willingness to put others' interests (particularly her children's) before her own. Dorothy, however, claimed her mother sought to leave against her family's wishes: 'For a country girl of fourteen it was a big undertaking in those days to leave home ties and friends and go away to far-off London. Mother's dad, a simple man of the forest, at first refused to allow her to go, but in the face of the entreaties of my "Mam" who was desperately keen to go, he eventually gave way.'[98] Beatrice herself provided no explanation at all.

Before leaving, she had a fateful encounter. In early 1928, she told the police simply, 'Just before I went to London I made the acquaintance of Harry Pace, who was living at Ellwood with his parents.'[99] While all three post-acquittal narratives in the press agree that on the eve of her departure Beatrice met Harry along a country lane they describe it differently. Dorothy portrayed it as an amiable meeting. Beatrice was walking to the next village on one of her many 'farewell calls' when she met 'a strange lad': 'as is the custom in the country, they exchanged greetings. And as they walked they talked.' Beatrice told Harry all about her 'great adventure of the morrow' and the pair 'laughingly exchanged names and addresses'. The next day, she had forgotten 'the country boy who had smiled so pleasantly at her when he shook her hand in farewell'.[100] In contrast to Dorothy's idyllic rural scene, O'Donnell emphasised mysterious and romantic – even erotic – elements. When the 'young and beautiful' girl met Harry in the forest, 'it may be surmised that her beauty inflamed the passionate nature of young Pace into a desire to marry her'.

> 'You will write to me every week,' he insisted, 'and I shall write to you and then later on we will get married,' he told the girl.
> There was something masterful about his tone, something dominant in his nature which somehow appealed to the girl, and she agreed to write to him and regard him as her sweetheart. [...]
> With that promise and with his kisses upon her lips Beattie Martin entered her home to make the final preparations for her journey the next day.[101]

The hints of danger (Harry's 'masterful' tone and 'dominant' nature) are, at this point, exciting rather than threatening.

Beatrice described a more disturbing encounter.[102] She had 'passed a boy' on a 'lonely lane' but ignored him: 'I was thinking of something else, and in any case I rarely spoke to strangers.' She heard him whistle, first once then twice, but took no notice: 'I did not know what it meant. No one had ever called me to them on the roads before.' (So much for friendly country 'customs' on wooded lanes!) The boy then spoke to her. 'He did not look at me', she recalled, 'but with his eyes sideways said straight out, speaking low: "How would you like to get married?" That was all he said, and he never looked at me.' Neither amiably nonchalant nor passionately romantic, the situation was confused and anxious: 'I did not know whether to laugh or to be frightened', she wrote.

> I suppose after a while I said something, told him not to be silly or whatever it was. And then I told him, when he asked me again, that I had to leave for London next morning to take up work there. At that he set up a regular argument, saying he wanted me for his wife, and that I must marry him and not go to work in London. He told me he had plenty of money, too.

> But I answered him I had to go – it was all fixed, and my fare paid, and then I ran home. I left next day.

Beatrice thus recounted a discomforting encounter from which she fled. She did, as planned, go into service in Hampstead, where she remained for about three years, returning in August 1909, later telling Dorothy it was the 'happiest period of her life'.[103]

However, she had been unable to leave the Forest of Dean behind her. In Dorothy's version, Harry could not forget 'the little girl with the flushed, excited face who had been his companion for so short a time', and he wrote to Beatrice. 'That was my mother's first love letter,' Dorothy commented, 'written in the crude, uneducated hand of Harry Pace, who, in the excitement of her new life in London, had passed completely out of her mind.'[104] O'Donnell painted quite a different picture, building upon his initial suggestion of a mutual love affair:

> Sometimes [Harry] would sit up far into the night writing crude verses to his sweetheart, and he had an amazing love of forest flowers.
> But never once did he go to London to see his love, nor did she ever visit her home to see her lover or other relatives. It costs a lot of money to travel from London, and that was probably the reason why the twain never met. They were unable to afford it.[105]

For O'Donnell, they were two 'sweethearts' or 'lovers' kept apart by poverty. O'Donnell even suggested that Beatrice felt committed to Harry: 'Her beauty had increased, if anything, and there was more than one young man in London who would have been glad to be the recipient of her smiles. But somehow the passionate, imploring letters of her lover and his declarations of love held her to him.'[106] In Dorothy's view, her mother 'welcomed his letters in a friendly sort of way' but remained 'evasive' about his offers of marriage.[107] According to Beatrice, Harry had 'found out' her address, and his letters simply began arriving. These were 'long letters, sometimes coming along with packets of flowers he had picked'. Harry, she said, was angry when she did not reply and he was constantly 'pestering' her to marry him.[108]

In the summer of 1909, Harry's tone changed. 'At last he threatened that if I did not come back', Beatrice wrote, 'he would come to London and take me back.' Dorothy also described this ultimatum: '"If you do not return to Coleford at once," my father wrote, "I shall come to London and bring you back."'[109] O'Donnell's version was, as ever, the most tempestuous: 'the patience of the young man was strained to its utmost limits. He was but a boy, a month younger than the girl whom he loved so impetuously and utterly that it simply consumed him.'[110] His letters indicated his 'masterful temperament' and he 'could brook no interference with his desires', finally 'commanding' his 'sweetheart' to return.[111] That Beatrice was under a kind of 'spell' became an important theme in O'Donnell's writing on the case.

Discounting the role of sorcery, however, can we reconstruct young Beattie Martin's thoughts? She remembered feeling frightened and ashamed, fearing trouble with her employer if an enraged lover were to show up. Thinking it 'better and safer at home', she returned to her father's house. In O'Donnell's version she had been 'swept off her feet by her headstrong lover'. Dorothy thoughtfully considers the 'terrible position' her mother was in: 'She did not love Harry Pace then. He was little more than a stranger to her.' She had found out, however, that Harry came from a respectable family and was 'well-spoken of' in the area. '"I was really in a fix", was how mother described it to me. "Then I thought, 'Well, perhaps I could do a great deal worse. Here is a young man who professes to worship the ground I walk upon. He seemed quite a nice sort of a lad. Why not go back and marry him?'"' Beatrice depicted her mind as being far from made up upon her return, but Dorothy wrote that the couple was initially very happy. They 'spent every spare moment' together, and Beatrice's doubts were 'dispelled' by his doting attentions. 'His very word and action seemed to breathe the deepest devotion', Dorothy explained: 'In the course of their constant companionship she grew to love the man who had succeeded in bending her will to his own.'[112]

In 1928, Beatrice told the police simply that she and Harry had 'walked out together' before getting married, but her own memoir recalled disturbing events. She had not informed Harry of her return, but he found out within days and began to watch the Martins' house from a 'little lonely wood' nearby.

> In the evenings, as it grew dark, he would whistle from the wood
> – two long notes, up and down, and it got so on my mind that at
> last I went out to him. Even when I had talked with him, he would

not go away but would often spend the night sleeping in a corner
of our pig-sty, so as to be near me.
Every night he whistled from the wood and kept on at me to marry
him. What was so strange, he hardly said anything, but just [kept]
telling me to be his wife.[113]

Thus, Beatrice emphasised Harry's odd behaviour and her
continuing uncertainty. She did marry him, but there is little sign
of either a young woman convinced of her suitor's devotion or a
'forest maiden' swept off her feet: 'He wore me down, I think,
for then I did not love him – I did not know what love was. I was
only seventeen – three years older than when I met him first – and
I had never had a sweetheart or a man friend.' As noted, Beatrice
was actually nearly twenty on her wedding day. In any case,
although her father warned her against seeing Harry she 'came to
feel somehow that Harry was right': 'I felt that he was my fate, as
they say, and at last I said yes.'[114] They married at the Monmouth
register office on 23 October 1909. O'Donnell thought there was
'no doubt' that 'the pretty girl was completely dominated by the
stronger nature of the youth'.[115]

The various narratives are also vague or contradictory regarding
where the couple lived and how well they got along after their
marriage. According to O'Donnell, Beatrice went to her brother's
house for 'over a month' and Harry remained at his parents'
house. 'Surely', he wrote, 'there was never so strange a marriage
as this':

He would come and stand outside the house, and Mrs. Pace, as
she then was, would go out to see her husband. They would go for
walks together, and then – the bride would return to the cottage at
Clearwell whilst her husband returned to his own home.
Over and over again an invitation was sent to him to enter the
house, but he would never do so, and it was Mr. Martin, Mrs.
Pace's own brother … who at length took a house for the pair so
that they might live together.[116]

Beatrice wrote, however, that about a week after their marriage,
they had found a cottage of their own in Clearwell. 'There', she
wrote, 'we settled down and Harry bought a lamb for seven-and-
six.' Within a week or two, Harry began to 'change': his language
turned rougher, he began swearing and he became 'jealous and
distrustful'. 'How bitter was the disillusionment', Dorothy wrote,

'when two months after marriage he changed completely. In the place of the considerate lover she found a cruel, callous husband.' The details of Harry's cruelty became, as later chapters explain, an important part of the case. Nonetheless, Beatrice said that her own feelings had also changed: 'I began to love him – I cannot explain why or how – and once having begun I never left off, not even through all those years when he was terrible to me. He was my man, whatever he did. He had taken me as a girl, and I grew to be a woman with him.' 'I suppose', she wrote, 'I was a great fool.'[117]

A delayed funeral

On the Friday following Harry's death, a brief notice appeared in the local newspapers: 'PACE. – On January 10th at Fetter Hill, Harry, beloved husband of Beatrice Pace, aged 36. Funeral Sunday, leaving house at 3 o'clock.'[118] Beatrice and her children mourned Harry and made preparations for his funeral; however, there were some who viewed his passing not only with sorrow but also with suspicion.[119] Dr Du Pré might have duly certified Harry had died from natural causes, but the deceased's kin – his mother, his siblings and their spouses – were unconvinced. They gathered together on the day Harry died, and it was decided that his elder sister Leah Pritchard and younger sister Flossie should visit Du Pré in Coleford to find out more. Du Pré admitted that a report he had received after Harry's stay in the Infirmary had referred to arsenical poisoning, 'probably due to his dabbling with sheep dip'. Nonetheless, he was convinced Harry had died from influenza. If the family was not, he said, they were free to inform the police.[120] Harry's brother Elton did precisely that, contacting Inspector Alan Bent in Coleford to say the family were 'not at all satisfied' with the official cause of death.[121] Bent, knowledgeable and locally respected, immediately looked into the matter, and it quickly became clear to him that the family spoke with one voice regarding the possibility of foul play. The neighbourhood was awash in rumours. Local gossips suggested Beatrice was having at least one affair and had prematurely taken Harry out of the hospital. They also speculated that Harry had possessed a great, hidden fortune.

Beatrice was well aware of the Pace family's animosities and the local rumours. The first sign that something more serious was brewing reached her doorstep two days after Harry's death. On Thursday, 12 January, Inspector Bent visited Rose Cottage along with another Coleford officer, Sergeant Charlie Hamblin, to tell the widow about his inquiries, suggest she should 'make no further arrangements about the funeral' and ask some questions.[122] Although Bent at this point had no official indication of the cause of Harry's death, he had listened to his family's suspicions: he asked whether there was any sheep dip in the house. Beatrice produced one unopened packet of the lethal powder from a cupboard in the kitchen, remarking 'Harry always kept his stuff for the sheep there.'[123] Asked if there was any sheep dip left from the last dipping, Beatrice told him she was unsure. When pressed, she said, 'I don't know where it is – it is probably burnt.'[124] The next day, Hamblin returned to say plans had been made for a post-mortem and an inquest. The funeral would definitely have to be postponed.[125] Beatrice told him about the bottle Dorothy had found in Harry's room on Christmas Day. She gave it to Hamblin and also – possibly for the first time – mentioned Harry's suicide threats.[126]

On Saturday, the post-mortem was carried out in Rose Cottage by a local doctor, Charles Carson, and his assistant.[127] Meanwhile, Bent had a 'look round the house' and collected a few bottles. He asked Beatrice where the lambs had been dipped the previous summer. She showed him 'an enclosed place near two oak trees towards the railway line'. Asked again about an unused packet of sheep dip, Beatrice repeated her previous answers: either none had been left over or any remainder had probably been burnt. Carson concluded his procedure, handing Bent five glass jars containing some of Harry's organs and a test tube with a blood sample. Bent took the sealed containers and the bottles and powders he had found directly to Bristol University where they were passed along to a locally renowned pathology professor, Dr Isaac Walker Hall.[128] Although Beatrice and her children knew on Friday that the funeral would have to be postponed, it was impossible to get word out to all of those who would attend. Thus some of Harry's friends only found out when they arrived on Sunday, 15 January. This caused, it was noted, 'considerable consternation'.[129]

The actual circumstances surrounding the delaying of Harry's funeral were dramatic enough. However, an even more sensational myth grew around the case, that the funeral was interrupted while already in progress. For instance, the *World's Pictorial News* reported that it was on 13 January that the 'little group of mourners' were preparing to follow Harry's coffin to the grave:

> They were almost on the point of starting out on their sad pilgrimage when suddenly there came a notification from the Coroner that the funeral must be postponed in order that an inquiry into the cause of the man's death might be held. It came as a staggering shock to the family as well it might, for no hint of the necessity for an inquest had arisen until that moment.[130]

Not only are events depicted incorrectly but the date on which Beatrice was informed of the delay (Friday, 13 January) is confused with that of the planned funeral (Sunday, 15 January). The story of the 'suddenly' interrupted funeral has found its way into later summaries of the case.[131]

On Monday, 16 January, the coroner's inquest that was to deal with the 'Fetter Hill mystery' was officially opened. It was the coroner's duty to look into suspicious deaths to determine whether there was good reason to believe a crime had been committed. At the inquest, evidence would be presented before a jury that would be required to deliver a verdict as to what had caused the death and who, if anyone, should be charged with causing it. A nine-member jury had been empanelled, and the coroner, Maurice Carter, met them at Rose Cottage. After being sworn in, they viewed the body and then moved to the nearby George Inn to deal with some formalities.[132] These steps were necessary not only to allow the investigation to officially begin but also to enable Harry to be buried. Beatrice, dressed in black, replied 'calmly' to the few questions she was asked, verifying her address, relationship to the deceased and Harry's occupation. She also confirmed the identity of the body. During her brief interview in an upstairs room the Pace family remained downstairs. Beatrice and her in-laws do not appear to have exchanged a single word during these preliminary proceedings.

The press interest in the case was already noticeable. Bernard O'Donnell later recalled that he had been sitting in his office in London 'when a brief message came over the tapes' about the stopped funeral. Although 'no other details were given', the message 'sent me scurrying off to Coleford to seek out the story behind this incident'.[133] He was not alone: reporters from several

London newspapers were present at the George Inn as the inquest opened, and they did not have to wait long for a dramatic scene. As Harry's relatives were leaving, a sheep marked with his initials appeared at the front door. His sister Leah 'screamed and sobbed hysterically'. '"One of his lambs! He loved them all," she cried: "They never come so far from home as this."'She was not the only one to be overcome by emotion. After Inspector Bent arranged for Beatrice to be driven home, she fainted and remained unconscious for two hours. Two doctors were summoned. 'It was evident', the local paper stated, 'that the great strain had told upon her system.'[134] The coroner, aware that no real progress could be made prior to the completion of the forensic analysis, adjourned the inquiry for a month.

Harry's burial took place the following day, Tuesday, 17 January 1928, at the nearby village of Clearwell.[135] Neither Beatrice – who was reportedly too exhausted – nor any of the Pace children attended. The time of the funeral was not divulged till about an hour beforehand, but Harry's relatives kept an eye on the cottage: 'When news spread that the funeral would take place at 12 o'clock they waited at the Ellwood cross roads until the arrival of the coffin, which was conveyed by motor hearse, and followed in motor cars, the rear being brought up by a motor load of journalists.' The only mourners were Harry's mother and step-father along with his sisters and brothers and their spouses. The funeral, however, was anything but a private ceremony:

> The scene was a strange one, little groups of people from vantage points on the hillside watching the cortege wend its way via Milkwall to the cemetery. While the bearers ... were arranging the coffin on the bier, a representative of one of the London daily newspapers temporarily headed the mourners while engaged in taking down notes whilst a photographer was busily occupied in getting the correct focus.[136]

Inspector Bent and two other officers were also present. One of the three funeral wreaths had a card attached which read: 'In loving memory, from Wife and Children – Now the labourer's task is o'er."'. As hard-working Harry Pace was finally buried, the presence of the police and press symbolised those forces that would dominate Beatrice's life in the coming months. For some of those present at Harry's funeral, their tasks were just beginning.

2

'Where there are so many cruel tongues': investigations and accusations

The opening of the coroner's inquest had been accompanied by the sort of excitement the press craved, featuring a delayed burial, a suspicious family and a fainting widow. The flurry of activity surrounding Harry's funeral and the opening of the inquest was, however, followed by a lull, at least with regard to the law. In the absence of forensic data, the inquiry could hardly get underway. This period of relative official quiescence was extended for an additional month, until 15 March, due to delays in the completion of Prof. Walker Hall's pathology report.[1] In mid-February, the *Daily Express* quoted Beatrice as saying that the stress of waiting and taking care of her sickly baby Jean was taking its toll: 'I have not the faintest idea why it has been necessary for the inquest to be adjourned again', she added, observing, 'Everything is a mystery to me.'[2] In that, she was not alone: the *Daily Mail* thought the case's 'tangle of circumstances' would be 'likely to require skilful unravelling'.[3]

Procedural delays could not stifle, and more likely encouraged, popular conjecture, and the 'Fetter Hill mystery' had 'excited tremendous interest throughout the Forest of Dean'. One of the notions circulating was that Harry may have been accidentally poisoned while dipping sheep.[4] (Some early press reports stated that he had dipped sixteen sheep 'a few days' before his health declined at Christmas, but this inaccurate claim abruptly disappeared.[5]) There had been more than enough information in the press to feed darker rumours, such as references to 'arsenic' and to a bottle marked 'poison' being taken away by the police; thereafter, speculations about poisoning were central in theories about

Harry's death.[6] Beatrice was confronted by gossip even before the inquest commenced: 'There has been talk of him leaving a lot of money and how it will help me if I marry again. I shall not marry again, and if people think there is a lot of money they can make their own inquiries and find out their mistake.'[7] Some locals thought Harry had saved as much as several hundred pounds, and Elton Pace claimed Harry had suggested he had enough to buy a house.[8] There were false rumours that Beatrice had 'taken' Harry out of the hospital and resisted seeking medical advice.[9] Gossips suggested her romantic involvement with other men, most sensationally with Leslie Sayes, Alice's husband. Clearly hurt by the rumours, Beatrice spoke of leaving the Coleford area – 'where there are so many cruel tongues' – as soon as possible.[10]

Suspicions and inquiries

Meanwhile, the day after Harry's funeral, Inspector Bent continued his investigations, asking Frank Blanch, a chemist in Coleford, to produce the book in which he was legally required to record sales of poisonous substances. An entry showed that 'B. Pace' bought two packets of sheep dip on 22 July 1927.[11] Armed with this and other information, Bent went to Fetter Hill on 15 February to confront Beatrice about the rumours. The widow emphatically denied them, and she agreed to make an official statement, remarking 'I have nothing to fear' and 'I will tell you everything.'[12] This produced the first of her three statements to police. In it, she described the circumstances of Harry's illness and admitted – contrary to some of her previous assertions – that her marriage had been 'a most unhappy one' due to Harry's jealousy, infidelity and cruelty.[13] (Hints of this had been published, though Beatrice's earlier claim of a 'happy' marriage continued to be repeated in the press into early March.[14])

On 5 March, while attending a conference at Gloucestershire police headquarters in Cheltenham, Bent learned that Walker Hall's report concluded that Harry had died from a large dose of arsenic.[15] Added to the tangled web of gossip, the police now had an official suggestion of foul play. The county constabulary, however, was not prepared for an investigation of this sort. The next evening, the Chief Constable's office sent a telegram to the Criminal Investigation Department (CID) of London's

Metropolitan Police – better known, then as now, as 'Scotland Yard' – requesting that 'an especially trained detective' be sent. (Given its experience and capabilities, Scotland Yard acted as a reserve investigative force for the nation in especially complex cases.) CID Superintendent Percy Savage offered to send two detectives early the next day. Telegrams were exchanged into the night, as Savage wanted further information as well as some clarification: 'it may be possible', he pointed out, 'that the expenses will have to be paid by the County'. The reply from Cheltenham detailed the 'suspicious circumstances' of Harry's death, noted that 'his wife was suspected to have administered arsenic poisoning to him' and assured 'if necessary, we are willing to pay'. The next morning, 7 March, a final telegram from London announced that the case had been assigned to Chief Inspector George Cornish, who, with Detective Sergeant Clarence Campion, would depart for Cheltenham from Paddington Station at 9.45 a.m.[16]

George Cornish was the son of a Wiltshire farmer. His police career began in 1895 as a constable in Whitechapel, but he had been promoted into the ranks of the detectives by 1905. He was no stranger either to homicide cases or press attention.[17] He had been involved in the investigation into the death of Cora Crippen, for which her husband was hanged in 1910.[18] After the murder of Lady White in 1922, Cornish's work led to the conviction and execution of Henry Jacoby, a pantry boy at the hotel where she was killed.[19] More recently, he had been instrumental in solving the mystery occasioned when the dismembered body of Minnie Bonati was found in a trunk at Charing Cross Station in May 1927. His work on the 'Charing Cross trunk case' resulted in the conviction of estate agent John Robinson, later hanged at Pentonville Prison.[20] A crime reporter's profile contrasted Cornish's appearance with that of the standard 'heavy-footed, stolid police officer': 'Grey hair cropped close at the sides of his square head. Grey, bristly moustache. There is a look about him that is almost studious. His voice is even, gentle, yet wondrously clear.'[21] He also had a reputation for relentless hard work. His colleague Clarence Campion had less experience with homicide cases but was a skilled detective who had dealt with complex counterfeiting and immigration investigations. (A year earlier, he had handled a major blackmail case.[22])

Cornish and Campion began their investigations in the Coleford area on 8 March. Their arrival prompted the coroner to once again postpone the inquest, this time until the end of the month.[23] The detectives' movements were closely followed by the press. On two occasions they 'had to abandon their car and proceed on foot through the broken hillside country, and descend into pits in order to locate men whom they wished to interrogate'.[24] Cornish also spent, as he later put it, 'three long days' with Harry's family.[25] Like Bent, he was struck by their suspicions of Beatrice. At the same time, newspaper articles appeared that quoted Beatrice as saying Harry had asked one of her sons (later identified as Leslie) to 'fetch a box containing what I believe are poisonous lotions for the treatment of sheep from the kitchen to his bedroom'. 'This box', she said, 'which was on the top shelf of a high cupboard, had been regarded in the house as almost sacred, and my husband allowed no one to get near it.'[26]

Early in the morning on 11 March, Cornish sent Bent to Rose Cottage to ask whether it would be 'convenient' for Beatrice, with Doris and Leslie, to come to the police station to answer some questions. She agreed.[27] The specific character of that interview – and of further questioning three days later – were, as we shall see, to become a matter of controversy, but it is undisputed that Beatrice expressed relief when Cornish identified himself: 'I knew Scotland Yard men were down here. I have seen it in the newspapers, and I have heard it from a lot of people. I am very glad you have come, because the rumours about me are all untrue, and I hope you will discover the truth.'[28] While she was questioned in Coleford, Inspector Bent and another officer, accompanied by Beatrice's brother Fred, searched Rose Cottage, collecting various bottles and substances that were passed along to Rowland Ellis, the city and county analyst for Gloucester and Gloucestershire.[29] Beatrice had much to tell the detectives, but any hope they would quickly 'discover the truth' proved illusory. On 16 March, it was reported that, despite working '15 hours daily', Cornish and Campion could not decide whether Harry had absorbed a fatal dose of arsenic while dipping sheep or, as a local newspaper put it delicately, 'more suspicious deductions could be made'. They were at least certain 'that a good deal of what had been regarded as definite evidence amounted to nothing more than gossip and rumour, often emanating from fifth and sixth hand sources'.[30] After ten days, Cornish and Campion returned to London. They could not prove definitively who – if anyone – had killed Harry, but they now had information from Beatrice's in-laws and acquaintances, a detailed forensic analysis and, not least, Beatrice's own statements. And they had a theory.

Cornish's 49-page report to his superiors on 17 March described the background to the case and his findings in the Forest. In trying to 'get a grip on the case', he had begun by interviewing Harry's family.[31] He gave great weight to their claims that Beatrice had had affairs and behaved suspiciously during Harry's illness. Indeed, his investigation was shaped from the start by the family's views. Cornish also spoke to the doctors who treated Harry, finding that their diagnoses had ranged from gastric ulcers to venereal disease.[32] Building on comments from various friends and acquaintances of the family, the report also discussed the Paces' marriage, Harry's mental and physical state and Beatrice's character. Cornish gave particular attention to the rumours he had heard, particularly those regarding infidelity. He had, for example, not only questioned Leslie Sayes but had also had him investigated. In summary, he observed: 'This case is about as complicated, contradictory and mysterious as it is possible for any case to be. The only real outstanding fact, a fact beyond dispute, is that Harry Pace died from arsenical poisoning, and not from natural causes. A fact that has justified the interference of his family and the institution of enquiries.'[33] Cornish devoted the remainder of his report to two alternative possibilities: suicide and murder.

Cornish dismissed suicide on four grounds. First, Harry was too physically feeble to have dosed himself with poison, having been 'helpless in his hands' for several months, 'more-or-less'. (Whether it was 'more' or 'less' would become a crucial issue.) Second, the timing of Harry's symptoms – the waxing and waning of his stomach problems and paralysis – suggested repeated ingestion of small amounts of arsenic, an unlikely pattern for a suicide. A third, related objection was that it was 'out of the question, and contrary to all common sense' that anyone would slowly and agonisingly poison themselves over six months with arsenic when he had other opportunities to do himself in more quickly. Finally, he doubted Harry even wanted to die: 'we have it from the majority of persons from whom statements have been taken, persons who are not connected with the family,' he wrote, 'that this man was anxious to live and to get back to his sheep'.

These factors meant 'the theory of suicide cannot be accepted' and 'some person' must have murdered him.[34]

Since Beatrice had said none of Harry's visitors could have given him something without her knowledge, Cornish saw only one relevant question: 'did Mrs Pace murder her husband?' He was unequivocal: 'My view is that in spite of her emphatic denials and protestations of innocence Mrs Pace is the perpetrator of this crime, and I say this, fully realising the seriousness of such an allegation, and after carefully considering the possibility of it being any other person.' He offered 'a few points' – ten, in fact – in support of this conclusion. First, there was 'no doubt' that Beatrice had had occasional affairs over the preceding years. Second, Cornish believed Leonard Pace's claim that there had been two full packets of sheep dip in Rose Cottage a month after one of them had supposedly been used when dipping lambs the preceding summer. Leslie had said his father had hammered the sheep dip before preparing it on that occasion, suggesting they had used an old packet rather than one of the two new ones Beatrice bought on 22 July 1927. But only one packet of the 'Battle's' brand dip had been found, and Cornish thought Beatrice's claim that the remainder of the other had either been used up or burnt to be unsatisfactory. Third, Beatrice's alleged refusal to allow Harry's family to be alone with him – a claim they all made – was suspicious. Fourth, Harry had complained to visitors that the room sometimes 'went black' or that he had stomach pains or vomited after taking his medicine or eating; if his wife was the only one to have prepared his food (and practically the only person to give him his medicine), this pointed to her guilt. Fifth, Cornish found it curious that Beatrice had waited until after the postponement of Harry's funeral to mention that a bottle was found in his room on Christmas Day. Sixth, Harry's stomach problems had ceased while he was in the hospital, and only recurred at home. Seventh, although Beatrice knew that Harry was suffering from arsenical poisoning while in the Infirmary and the post-Christmas symptoms were 'the same in all respects' as the previous ones, 'she does not seem' to have tried to get 'the arsenical poisoning counteracted, or even to have spoken to the Doctor about it at all'. Eighth, there were witnesses (all of whom, it must be noted, were surnamed 'Pace') who claimed Beatrice had wished Harry dead. Ninth, Cornish stated that Beatrice 'seems to be the only one' who heard Harry express a wish to die or do himself in. Finally, Beatrice had at least two motives: Harry's 'extraordinary conduct and cruelty' and the fact that she was 'infatuated with other men'. His accusation was stark:

> I suggest that Mrs Pace has systematically adulterated her husband's food and medicine over a long period by the addition of arsenic she obtained from sheep dip, and it is possible that she obtained this arsenic by dissolving the sheep dip in water, allowing the sediment to settle and then using the water so adulterated to mix with her husband's food and medicine.

The separation of sulphur from arsenic that Cornish described was a key matter: powdered sheep dip contained far more sulphur than arsenic, yet no significant traces of sulphur had been found in Harry's organs. As we shall see, all of these issues would attract much testimony at the inquest and trial. In the end, many of Cornish's confident assertions would be undermined.[35]

Soon after Cornish's report, other potential sources of arsenic were identified, such as a bottle that Bent had found in the back kitchen at Rose Cottage.[36] It was only half-full with a watery solution of arsenic and a small amount of 'permanganate of potash [potassium permanganate]', and it looked, Bent noted, as if 'it had been on the shelf a considerable time without being disturbed'. It was covered with dust and cobwebs, 'and we had to wipe the bottle with a duster before we could tell the colour of the liquid it contained'.[37] An empty tin of 'Cooper's Tablets' – a 'sheep rot' remedy – had also been found.[38] None of this challenged Cornish's prima facie case. The Director of Public Prosecutions, Sir Archibald Bodkin, was also convinced. Just before the inquest resumed, Cornish reported that Bodkin thought it would be necessary to charge Beatrice even before it ended: 'he proposed to let a certain amount of evidence be taken by the Coroner, and then stop the Inquest when it arrived at the scientific witnesses'.[39] Matters were, however, to take a different course.

A protracted proceeding

The completion of Walker Hall's pathology report and Cornish's initial investigation meant that, having 'dragged on week after week, being postponed time and time again', the coroner's inquest that had formally commenced on 16 January could finally resume on 29 March.[40] The coroner, Maurice Carter, suggested the 'mass' of evidence meant the inquiry was likely to be 'protracted'.[41] From the end of March to late May, the inquest – typically sitting two days a week in Coleford – worked its way through varied and often vivid evidence. Beatrice's Gloucester trial would receive more sensational media coverage, but the Coleford inquest offered more information, being unbound by the rules of evidence that governed trials. Coroners, charged with examining all the circumstances of suspicious deaths, had broad discretion.[42] Although it was undisputed that arsenic caused Harry's death, expert medical testimony could not precisely determine how the poison had entered his system. Thus, much of the inquest considered circumstantial evidence: the state of the Pace marriage, the rumours of Beatrice's affairs, the course of Harry's illness and the care he received. Inquest juries not only declared a cause of death but also, if relevant, named a suspect or suspects. Their charge would lead to a trial at what was then the main court for dealing with serious crime: the centuries-old, semi-annual circuit court known as the 'assizes'.

Most witnesses in the Pace case were questioned by the coroner himself before the nine-member jury. (The jurors could also ask questions.) An exception was made for the medical and expert forensic witnesses. Carter had sought a more knowledgeable official to handle their examination, and the Department of Public Prosecutions had sent G. R. Paling to assist him.[43] Beatrice was represented by G. Trevor Wellington (himself a coroner) from the Gloucester firm of Wellington, Clifford and Matthews.[44] Her brothers, Arnold and Fred Martin, were paying her legal costs.[45] The inquest was open to the public. At one of the earlier sittings, 'there was a large representation of the press', but the courtroom 'was not so well filled by the general public as might have been expected'. Interest, however, increased as the hearings dragged on.[46] A week before the inquest's conclusion, 'there was a good deal of demand, mostly from women folk, for places in the Court Room'.[47] Foreshadowing Beatrice's frenzied acquittal in Gloucester, 'throngs' of people sought to gain entry when she herself testified toward the end.[48] During much of the inquest, Beatrice – always dressed in black – sat behind the solicitors' table, concealed by a screen set up to 'shield her from the public gaze when the proceedings were in progress'.[49]

The evidence presented at the inquest fell roughly into five categories. First, there was testimony from the Pace family (Harry's mother, brothers, sisters and their spouses). Second, three of Beatrice's children testified about their family life and their father's health and behaviour. Third, the local police and Scotland Yard detectives presented evidence from their investigations. A fourth category of testimony came from a diverse group of people – including acquaintances of the Paces and patients and staff of the Gloucester Infirmary – who commented on Harry's physical and mental condition. Finally, there was a significant amount of forensic testimony: Harry's doctors described his symptoms and medical experts discussed what had killed him and how it might have been administered. The evidence was presented roughly in this order, but there were many deviations, with witnesses being re-examined on particular points of their testimony as new questions or contradictions arose. The rest of this chapter deals with the first category – the Pace family – while the next one will consider the other testimony and the inquest verdict.

Accusation by insinuation

It was appropriate that the inquest opened with extensive testimony from Harry's mother, his siblings and their spouses: their suspicions, after all, had postponed the funeral and set the official inquiries in motion. Harry's family were Beatrice's most ardent accusers, and they had a long history of mutual mistrust and animosity. However, despite their obvious dislike of Beatrice and the clear suggestions in their testimony, family members stopped short of making direct accusations. Instead, they wove a net of insinuations regarding Beatrice's morality and her attitude toward, and treatment of, her late husband.

Harry's mother, Elizabeth Porter (she had re-married after her first husband's death[50]), and his brother Leonard were the first witnesses. Leonard was about Harry's age and had been close to him: before Harry's illness, he had seen him nearly every day.[51] Leonard thought Harry had always been healthy until the previous summer. Leonard found him then to be 'very ill', unable to use his legs, arms or hands and suffering from stomach pains and vomiting.[52] Harry suggested he had caught a chill while washing his sheep. Like all family members, Leonard and his mother insisted Harry would not have killed himself, denying he had ever expressed a wish to die. Porter (later described as a 'well-preserved, sharp-featured woman, with clear skin, firm mouth, and keen eyes'[53]) had long been concerned that Harry was 'not being done right by'.[54] She lived only a quarter of an hour's walk away from Rose Cottage, but before her son's illness she rarely visited: despite denying she and Beatrice were 'bad friends', she did not like how Beatrice 'went on' and therefore she 'kept away'.[55] Harry's sister-in-law Gertrude had likewise ceased visiting two years previously. His brother Elton lived nearby and even owned a quarry on property adjoining Rose Cottage but went there only a handful of times during Harry's illness. Even Leonard said that Beatrice's 'bad ways' had kept him away from the house until Harry became sick.[56] Beatrice, they all said, would not leave them alone with Harry, which, in retrospect, was suspicious. (Other witness, however, had been given free access to the sick man.)

Their relative lack of contact, however, did not stop the Paces from claiming to have detailed insight into Harry's illness, Beatrice's character and the couple's marriage. Heading off suggestions that Harry had been anything less than a good husband, they insisted he had treated his wife kindly. Porter recounted a visit to Rose Cottage on the day Harry died. Beatrice had said Harry 'should have a good coffin, as he deserved it'. Porter and other family members also claimed that Beatrice had noted they 'had a rare bit of fun' on Christmas Day, when Harry had tried 'to amuse the children in the character of "Father Christmas"'.[57] (Asked about this later, Dorothy said it had taken place a few days before Christmas.[58])

Specific suspicions were also aired. Porter visited Harry shortly after the onset of his acute symptoms in July 1927. He was bedridden with 'very bad pains in his stomach' and constantly vomiting and retching.[59] Porter started visiting a couple times a week after this. She described a curious event. About a week before Harry went to the Infirmary, Porter had given him some water in the bedroom, but he refused to drink it.[60] She took a sip and found 'it had a very peculiar taste'; she spat it out, throwing the rest, she said, into a 'utensil' in the room. Beatrice, who was present, sent Doris to fetch more water, which Harry drank, describing it as 'lovely'.[61] The 'nasty water' incident would be contested, but Porter stood by her version of events, which naturally suggested something unwholesome in what Beatrice was giving Harry. Beatrice's solicitor asked whether Harry had made 'any complaint about being neglected by his wife'; he had not, Porter admitted, but claimed 'he was afraid to'. She was asked whether she had gone to the police with the family's suspicions, but before she could answer a voice in the court shouted 'I was the man!' The coroner demanded the speaker leave the room until called as a witness.[62]

The man was Harry's brother Elton. Elton's later testimony sharpened the Pace family's accusations.[63] He insisted he had been 'on friendly terms' with Beatrice and Harry even though Beatrice objected to his visits. 'She reckoned I was a bully or something', he said. Disparaging of his sister-in-law, he testified that she often complained about Harry's 'ways' and his stinginess. She 'was always saying she wished my brother dead', he claimed, 'and she wished to be rid of the mingy old bugger'. Elton believed she wanted to be with other men. He claimed that some years previously she had 'confided' things to him: she '"had her eye on Mr. So-and-So." – things like that'. Like the rest of the family, he claimed to have seen Leslie Sayes at Rose Cottage in suspicious circumstances, both before and during Harry's hospitalisation. Alongside suggestions of an affair, Elton also criticised Beatrice's treatment of his brother during his illness. (He had to admit, though, that he had only seen Harry at home about three times while he was sick.) His first visit was about a week after Harry's illness, in late July or early August 1927. He had seen Harry 'doubled up with pain' in bed, and he heard Beatrice shouting 'Harry, Harry, you be dying, we shan't see you much longer.' He thought this very 'pathetic' considering that she had expressed a wish to poison him. Beatrice had also sought to prevent them learning about his medical condition and treatment. Elton claimed, for example, that she had on one occasion deceived him about a doctor's visit: she had sent a note informing him that the doctor would come at 1.30 p.m. when the appointment was actually two hours earlier.

Elton's cross-examination by Beatrice's solicitor developed into a heated duel, with Wellington's 'quiet but relentless questions' contrasting with Elton's 'almost fierce outbursts'. Elton – despite his obvious antipathy – refused to admit being on bad terms with Beatrice. Clearly, the family wished to avoid the impression of a personal vendetta. But under Wellington's insistent questions, he finally acknowledged 'a row' with his sister-in-law, one of several reasons he kept away from Rose Cottage. Wellington named a different source of conflict. Elton and Beatrice were on bad terms, he proposed, because Elton had made 'indecent overtures' to her and even attempted an 'indecent assault' when rebuffed. Elton vehemently denied this, insisting that the problem was Beatrice's behaviour and Sayes's visits: 'Because I had my own opinion', he stated, 'on the morals of a married woman being visited by a married man when her husband was at work.' Elton had become 'suspicious' after finding out 'two or three days' before Harry's death that he had been suffering from arsenical poisoning. Wellington tried to draw out a clear statement of whom Elton suspected:

> Do you suggest that [Sayes] administered poison to your brother? – I don't know who administered poison.
> Do you suspect anyone? – That is for the jury to find out.
> At the last hearing you took credit in dramatic fashion for having given information to the police which resulted in stopping the funeral? – It was not dramatic ...
> Mr. Wellington pressed his question again as to who was suspected and witness reiterated 'I suspected no one.'
> Why did you give information to the police? – Because I knew he had been poisoned.

This was as close, in court, as any of the Paces would come to a direct accusation.

Similarly, Elton's sister Leah Pritchard claimed that she and her family were not 'unfriendly' with Beatrice while leaving a clear impression of intense dislike.[64] She claimed outright that Beatrice had been 'associating with other men', had spoken badly of her husband and had – due to the expense involved – resisted having him hospitalised and seeking a second opinion. (Other witnesses, such as Dr Nanda, thought Beatrice 'quite willing' to see Harry hospitalised.[65]) Like Elton, Pritchard was convinced that Harry was kind and indulgent to his wife; indeed, she cast Beatrice as the troublemaker in the marriage. Pritchard described a conversation she had had with Dr Du Pré about Harry and

Beatrice. 'They don't get on very well together, do they?' Du Pré had asked. Pritchard told the court she responded, 'I can't say doctor, but if she had many men to deal with they would make mincemeat of her.'[66] She denied that such comments were not 'friendly' to Beatrice. Furthermore, she, like the rest of her family, suspected an affair involving Leslie Sayes. She claimed that he had been 'walking my sister[-in-law] about in my brother's absence as much as three years ago'; when asked what she had against him, she said, 'I don't think he is a man' and pointed to an incident in late December in which her mother had seen Sayes 'reading a newspaper by the fireside in the kitchen downstairs'. (At this point, Beatrice 'became faint' and, accompanied by a policewoman, left the court.)[67] Finally, Pritchard defiantly refused to believe other witnesses' claims that Harry had spoken of suicide. Highlighting Pritchard's stubbornness, Wellington observed: 'And if the Archangel Gabriel told you so you would not believe it?' 'No, I would not', she responded.[68] Another of the dead man's sisters, seventeen-year-old Flossie, also claimed that Beatrice had prevented her from seeing Harry alone. She also recalled him complaining of being hungry while Beatrice cared for him.

The next week, Leonard's wife Gertrude took the stand. Unlike other family members, she did not even make a token effort to conceal a hostility caused by Beatrice's 'ways'. Gertrude alleged Beatrice said 'on several occasions' that she could poison Harry and that 'she wished he would come home stiff from work'. Cross-examined, she could give no dates for when she had heard these things, but it had been about two years previously and it had stopped her from visiting. Nonetheless, she claimed to know that the couple was 'always on friendly terms', and Harry was 'good' to his wife. They were, she said, 'very happy together'. Questioned by the coroner, Gertrude said she had seen a man named Harold Cole at Rose Cottage when Harry was in the hospital. Wellington sought to prevent such speculations, but Carter insisted he would continue to allow questions in this direction: there would, the coroner said, be no screening of names, 'no reference to "Mr. A", or "Mr. B"'.[69] (Cole later denied any improprieties, claiming he had come to the Pace household for 'the performance of a neighbourly act': he had occasionally helped Beatrice to tend the family's sheep.[70])

Murder for love or money?

As a sign of how seriously the court took the Pace family's accusations (infidelity, of course, would establish a homicide motive), both Leslie and Alice Sayes were questioned at length. Beatrice was close to both of them, and they, particularly Alice, were depicted in the press as her staunchest and most loyal supporters. (Beatrice typically arrived at the inquest 'accompanied by Mr. and Mrs. Sayes'.[71]) Testifying in early May, Alice and Leslie both firmly denied any improprieties.[72] Alice (described by the *Dean Forest Guardian* as 'the best dressed woman witness so far') stated that she knew her husband went to Rose Cottage – which was only a few minutes' walk from her own house – both before and after Harry became ill to bring the Paces eggs and poultry. Alice had also looked after the Pace children when Beatrice visited Harry in hospital, and she had accompanied her to bring him home. Afterwards, she was there 'almost every day and did all she could to help'. Rumours about a possible affair had led her to question her husband 'and also Mrs. Pace separately, and when they were both together'. She had concluded that the gossip was groundless. (A year earlier, similar talk had already driven her to confront Leslie.) Two jurors asked whether she suspected her husband, but she insisted she did not. Cross-examined by Wellington, she said that the rumours originated with Harry's family. Wellington sought to end the speculations about an affair:

> The suggestion is that you knew your husband and Mrs. Pace were carrying on an illicit relationship, and as the Pace family have been kind enough to suggest that one obstacle has been removed, has it occurred to you that you are apparently the next obstacle and that some method will be found of getting you out of the way. And is that all perfect nonsense?

'I should say so', she responded.

Leslie Sayes said he had visited Harry regularly upon his return from hospital, but he denied having been in his home while Harry was away. He had even gone to see Porter and Pritchard the previous spring after Alice had drawn his attention to rumours he 'was paying attention to Mrs. Pace'. Porter said Pritchard was the source of the gossip, but, when confronted, Pritchard had called her mother 'a damned liar'.[73] Leslie also denied another rumour:

that he had borrowed money from Harry to buy his house. Obviously, a substantial debt would also have provided a motive for murder. Leslie had been extensively questioned by detectives on that issue, but he emphatically denied receiving 'a shadow of a farthing' from Harry. 'The whole thing is moonshine, is it not?' asked Wellington, and Sayes agreed. Wellington decried the Pace family's 'campaign of slander'. Among other things, he alleged that Elton followed Sayes in Coleford, accusing him of poisoning Harry and loudly declaring him an 'Armstrong'.[74] Although 'Armstrong' would today be an innocuous, even bewildering, epithet, in 1928 its intended meaning would have been perfectly clear. It was a reference to Major Herbert Armstrong, who had achieved widespread notoriety after his trial for murder in 1922. The Armstrong case would be mentioned more than a few times during the Pace inquest, and, as it would have been one of the most well-known poisoning cases at the time, it merits a brief digression.[75]

Armstrong was a solicitor and magistrates' clerk in Hay-on-Wye, on the border between Wales and Herefordshire. In late 1921, a series of illnesses afflicted the household of Oswald Martin, a neighbour and fellow solicitor. Suspicion fell upon Armstrong not only because he was then involved in a contentious property transaction with Martin, but also because one of Martin's illnesses immediately followed his having taken tea at Armstrong's house. Questions were also raised by the fact that Armstrong's wife had died the preceding February. Her death had been certified as from 'natural causes'; however, her doctor was also attending to Martin, and when tests found small amounts of arsenic in his system, the doctor communicated his concerns to the Home Office. Discreet investigations began, followed by Mrs Armstrong's exhumation. When forensic analysis revealed she had died from arsenic, Armstrong was charged both with her murder and attempting to murder Martin. Like the 'Fetter Hill mystery', the Armstrong case quickly became a local – and then a national – sensation. The schoolroom where the inquest was held proved far too small for the crowds who 'arrived in motor-cars, on cycles, and on foot'.[76]

Although their specific circumstances were very different, there were some parallels between the Pace and Armstrong cases. Both deceased were at first certified to have died naturally until forensic examination revealed the true cause of death. Evidence was largely circumstantial: even when arsenic was established as the cause of Mrs Armstrong's death, there was no direct proof of who administered it. In both cases finding the likely source of arsenic was paramount. Armstrong was an avid gardener, and his near-obsessive eradication of weeds led to frequent purchases of arsenic in order to mix his own herbicides. Armstrong's 'weed killer' became a focus of attention in much the same way as Pace's 'sheep dip'. One surprise during Armstrong's ten-day trial was the production of a small packet of arsenic found 'wedged at the back of the bureau in the prisoner's study, six weeks after both the Scotland Yard officers and the local police had failed to find anything in that very drawer'.[77] Similar attention was given to a variety of bottles and packets found in the Pace household. Both cases involved suggestions that pecuniary and emotional motives had been mixed. Armstrong had changed his wife's will to his own benefit, and it was claimed he was having a relationship with a woman he intended to marry after his wife's demise. Each alleged perpetrator was depicted as having wished to rid themselves of a domineering spouse: Mrs Armstrong reportedly dominated her husband, in public as well as in private, and despite Beatrice's initial claims of a 'happy' marriage the extent of her husband's domestic tyranny would slowly emerge during the inquest. Finally, each defendant claimed that their presumed victims had poisoned themselves, forcing both inquests to consider the deceased's mental state.

Armstrong was convicted and hanged, and though he protested his innocence to the end, press and public opinion appears to have strongly backed the court's verdict. *The Times* praised the wisdom of the judges who rejected his appeal. They 'had as little doubt as the public generally' about his guilt: 'He has been convicted of one of the worst forms of murder, if one can say that there are degrees of moral culpability in the commission of such a crime. A poisoner is not a man who, with foul intent, has been able to "screw his courage to the sticking point" and strike a sudden blow.'[78] In calling Leslie Sayes an 'Armstrong', then, Elton Pace not only accused him of murder but also mocked his manhood. But it would be wrong to conclude from the editorial's obvious contempt that poisoning was quintessentially an unmanly 'women's crime', a long-standing but false assumption.[79] While it has been argued that female poisoners were especially disdained, press reactions to Armstrong give reason to doubt this generalisation.[80] The gender of the personal pronouns in *The Times*'s depiction of a typical poisoner could be reversed without fundamentally changing its significance:

> He is the insidious, calculating villain, who can watch his victim dying day by day and week by week. He administers his potions in the guise of nourishment, and he pretends to fondle the life that it is his purpose to destroy. Under a mockery of devotion he lifts his poisoned chalice to another's lips. It is therefore not surprising that society feels gratified when a poisoner has been brought to justice.[81]

Accusations in the Coleford streets of being an 'Armstrong' amidst a police investigation and a flurry of local rumour-mongering could hardly be ignored. The Sayeses complained to the police and contacted a solicitor – none other than Wellington – who sent Elton a letter threatening slander proceedings. At the inquest, Elton was defiant about the letter: he 'did not reply to it, declining to waste a penny stamp on such a thing'. His public harassment of Sayes, however, seems to have ceased.

Deliberate poisoning has long been seen as 'the ultimate secret crime', and since its symptoms could easily be confused by non-experts (or inattentive doctors) with those of natural death, investigations often began with suspicions on the part of people closely related to the deceased.[82] Harry's kinfolk also appear to have been behind at least some of the local gossip. In their testimony, the Paces claimed Beatrice cared little for her husband, treated him poorly, hindered his medical care, openly wished him dead and cheated on him. They even insinuated she was an uncaring mother: Pritchard thought she planned to find others to take her children once Harry was out of the way, and she suggested Beatrice was not above using them, as lookouts, to facilitate trysts at Rose Cottage.[83] They clearly thought that Beatrice (perhaps with Leslie Sayes) had poisoned Harry, whether for love or money. These alleged circumstances matched the profile of a 'typical' poisoning: nearly half of the seventy-five women accused of poisoning their husbands between 1750 and 1914 were known to have had a lover, and there had been high-profile recent cases (committed either by women or men) with similar motives.[84] Poisoning for passion had become a criminal cliché, yet the Pace family refrained from making any outright charges at the inquest, relying instead on insinuation. Still, they succeeded in casting a spotlight on Beatrice's behaviour and morality, issues which would occupy much of the inquest's time. It would be too easy to write off their suspicions simply as spite. Their doubts that Harry had died from 'natural causes' turned out, after all, to be correct. But determining just how, and at whose hand, he had died required other clues.

3

'I cannot tell you, sir – I cannot tell you': mysteries and circumstances

The 'seemingly interminable' inquest stretched through April and May, attracting ever more attention.[1] By mid-May, the *World's Pictorial News* observed: 'Throughout all these months of inquiries, throughout all the ten hearings before the Coroner, the widow has been called upon to face the gaze of curious eyes. Crowds flocked into Coleford from villages for miles around to see the woman who had become such a figure of public interest.'[2] Having heard the suspicions of Harry's family, the inquest turned to four other categories of evidence: testimony from three of the Pace children (Dorothy, Doris and Leslie), the police, family friends and acquaintances, and medical experts. Finally, the court would hear from the woman at the centre of the matter: the 'tragic widow' herself. The inquest jury would have much to consider, and when it finally reached its decision, the result would be both dramatic and controversial.

'Dad threatened to kill us all': the children

Seventeen-year-old Dorothy was the first of the Pace children to testify.[3] She was seen as a hesitant and frustrating witness, speaking haltingly and claiming to have a poor memory. She had returned home from domestic service in November 1927 at her mother's request to help care for her father and sickly infant sister. She got on well with her relatives, she said, except for her aunt Flossie (who was the same age). She admitted that she often quarrelled with her mother but said that the family was 'happy together' after her return. Curiously, she claimed to have heard no 'miswords' between her parents while also saying her father had a 'violent temper' and would sometimes lock them out of the house or beat her mother. The coroner found her testimony contradictory, but she insisted her parents were on 'good terms' except for when Harry 'got his fits of temper'. One of these had occurred on Christmas Day, when Harry threatened his family and bashed in the kitchen's fireguard. Somewhat mockingly, Carter suggested, 'Because he could not have his revenge on your mother, did he have it on the guard?' The coroner does not seem to have regarded the episode with the 'unfortunate guard' as especially grave: Harry had 'cooled down' after hearing the neighbour had been sent for, and since he knew how long that would take, the quarter of an hour that followed was, in Carter's words, 'not a very serious one after all'.

He noted that Dorothy seemed disinterested in her father's illness; reluctantly, she admitted that she 'had no affection for him at all'. 'Well, sir,' she said in response to a surprised query, 'he was never kind to me.' Dorothy was later recalled, and, it was noted, 'as before, great difficulty was experienced in getting information from the witness'.[4] Jurors asked about inconsistencies in her testimony, the lack of 'miswords', for example, seeming to contradict the 'threatenings and beatings'. Dorothy insisted that the threats and assaults had happened. She also said her father was 'often depressed': she had 'heard him cry several times' and threaten suicide. Rose Cottage was 'a difficult house to hide anything away in', she pointed out, and whatever 'was done to the food was done in the sight and presence of them all'. Alice and Leslie Sayes were frequently at the house. Alice 'helped her mother' and was a great friend 'to both her father and mother'. Leslie visited with her father and 'came in and [did] little jobs such as a man would do about the house'.

There was also confusion about 'salts of lemon' she had sent home while in service, a popular name for binoxalate of potash: though highly poisonous, it was a common commercial bleaching product.[5] After diluting it in a saucer, Dorothy used it to 'get some stains out of her apron' and discarded what remained. However, when re-questioned by detectives during the inquest, she said she mixed it in a *bottle*: since several bottles had been found, this was of interest. Wellington suggested that detectives had put pressure on her during four hours of questioning: 'Did you tell them over

3 Dorothy Pace holding her infant sister, Isobel Jean
(known as 'Jean'), and Selwyn ('Teddy') Pace, holding a few
of the many dolls sent by the public to his sister Doris.

(©The British Library Board, *Daily Sketch*, 7 July 1928, p. 1)

and over again you mixed it up in a saucer and not in a bottle, and
did they refuse to believe you and called you a little liar, and if you
are to be believed, you say they told you they would keep you there
all the day and get the truth out of you somehow?' 'Yes, sir', she
answered, saying she had agreed to the detectives' assertions about
the bottle simply 'to shut their mouths up'. Wellington was clearly
irritated: both with the detectives, for questioning her while he
was otherwise occupied, and with Dorothy, for not having the
'common sense' to have sent for him before she was questioned.
(This would not be the only reference to questionable police
methods in this case, as we shall see.) The 'salts of lemon' played
no role in the subsequent trial (they did not contain arsenic),
but Dorothy's testimony reveals not only the determined tactics

4 Leslie and Doris Pace.
Images of the Pace children were prominent in press coverage
of the case and helped to generate sympathy for the family.

(©The British Library Board, *Daily Sketch*, 7 July 1928, p. 1)

employed by detectives in their investigation but also what may
have been a sometimes rocky relationship between Beatrice and
her eldest daughter. The whole issue of the 'salts of lemon', in fact,
had arisen due to a statement to police by a young man named
Jesse Clack. Dorothy had stayed with the Clack family while in
service and had, she said, 'kept company' with Jesse. Beatrice
disapproved of the relationship, which Clack resented. (Wellington
referred to him as a 'disgruntled suitor'.) When he came to Fetter
Hill to see Dorothy, Beatrice refused to let her see him.[6]

Rather different insights were given by Dorothy's younger siblings, Doris and Leslie. Eleven-year-old Doris was described as a 'model child witness': 'bright', 'quick' and with a detailed memory. She reportedly 'won everybody's heart'. She inspired a few of the inquest's rare light-hearted moments, such as describing the label on her father's medicine as reading 'You've got to take it'. But her matter-of-fact statements on life at Rose Cottage were also chilling: 'Were you all happy at home? – No sir. Why not? – Because Dad threatened to kill us all. When was that? – Before Christmas, and on Christmas Day.' Her father, she said, always had 'bad tempers'. Wellington had argued that it was 'undesirable that a child of that age should have come there at all'; however, given the chance, he did ask a few key questions. One was about the 'nasty water' incident described by Harry's mother. Doris said that after her grandmother had complained about the water being 'nasty' Beatrice took the glass and drank what remained.[7] Porter stuck adamantly by her claim the remaining water had been discarded. As the local press stated laconically, 'a conflict of evidence remained', but, as Wellington pointed out, 'If Mrs. Pace drank the water there is another of your suspicions "gone west" you know!'[8] Leslie, about to turn ten, testified about the previous summer's dipping.[9] The remaining sheep dip was put in a small packet which was placed into what the family called the 'sheep box' kept on the top shelf in the kitchen. After Harry's return from Gloucester Royal Infirmary, Leslie said, he had briefly been left alone with his father, his brother Teddy and the baby. His father asked him to fetch the 'sheep box', looked at something in a packet and placed it back into the box; rather than asking Leslie to return it to the kitchen, he told him to put it in a bottom drawer in the upstairs bedroom. What that meant would be the subject of some speculation.

'Be very careful with them': Beatrice and the police

The police evidence was mainly presented by two witnesses: Inspector Bent and Chief Inspector Cornish.[10] Bent explained his investigations, including interviewing the Paces, collecting various materials and powders at the house and taking Beatrice's first statement on 15 February. About a month later, on 11 March, he had brought her to Coleford to give her second statement. On 14 March, Bent went to Beatrice's again with the detectives. She handed Cornish a letter (from a man named Slinger who had been a patient in the Infirmary), and Bent heard her tell him, 'I was coming to see you about this this evening, and there is something else I want to see you about.' Later that day, she made her third and final police statement. These three statements were central to police evidence.

The 15 February statement was entered into the official record and read aloud in court.[11] It revealed the marriage to have been 'most unhappy' due to Harry's 'jealous nature' and 'cruelty'. One passage reprinted in the *Dean Forest Guardian* went:

> Even on the day of the wedding he beat her in his temper and he had done the same off and on until he was taken ill. Just before the last baby came he beat her with a stick and once before with a wire rope. Once she ran to her father's home, and he said if she put her head out of the window he would shoot her, and he had a gun in his hand.[12]

She had reported the matter to Sgt Hamblin 'several years ago'; later she had summoned Harry at Coleford magistrates' court on a charge of cruelty, when he had been bound over 'to be of good behaviour for 12 months'.[13] She had insisted to police that there was 'no truth' to the rumours about men seeing her 'for immoral purposes'. Leslie Sayes was 'occasionally' at her house to 'look after the sheep when my husband was ill, [and] he used to sit with my husband and tell him what he had done'. A man named Joe Hale did 'odd jobs' for Harry; however, 'this man never came inside my door, and certainly no intimacy took place between either of us'.[14] She emphasised her care for her husband, whom she thought careless with sheep dip, and she noted his despondency, threats to take his own life and refusal to take his medicine.[15] Other than the children's comments on the 'Christmas Day incident', her statement gave the first detailed description of marital abuse. One paragraph was not read aloud: judging by the original, it referred to Harry's alleged sexual predations.[16] Beatrice claimed one of his victims was her sister Florence when she was twelve or thirteen years old. Beatrice asserted that Harry had 'connection' with other women. On at least one occasion she had caught him *in flagrante*, and in another case she had paid the young woman's father 7s 6d to prevent Harry being charged with sexual assault.[17]

Cross-examined, Bent confirmed that the police had been contacted via Elton Pace and that the Paces' statements to him were not exactly the same as those given in court. He agreed that Beatrice had 'rendered him every assistance': she had not appeared to have concealed anything and had spoken to Scotland Yard willingly. All of the substances found were typical of those kept by sheep farmers. A 'red powder', for example, turned out to be 'used for marking sheep'. Some 'lysol' had been bought for the post-mortem. He confirmed that Beatrice had complained to the police about Harry's cruelty and Hamblin had warned Harry.[18] He had also seen a damaged fireguard and tongs that fit the description of Harry's alleged Christmas outburst.

Chief Inspector Cornish was called to testify on 10 May.[19] He told the inquest that Beatrice was quite willing to be interviewed (a point Wellington emphasised). When she came to the station on 11 March she began 'talking very rapidly' about her married life. Cornish had told her the 'fairest way' to proceed would be via a statement that could be written out and which she could then sign. 'She said', Cornish told the court, 'she would be very glad to do so.' This 'all took several hours to accomplish'. Indeed, as later chapters discuss, debates about what happened during those 'several hours' attracted intense press – and political – attention. Despite the statement's significance, however, it was not read aloud at the inquest; after the coroner had ordered particular paragraphs ('as to the advisability of which he had been concerned') to be covered up, it was given to the jury, 'who, in groups, read it through as the pages were passed on' for somewhat more than half an hour. (The statement consisted of twenty-six sides of folio paper and 'two experienced journalists' estimated that it was 8,000 to 10,000 words long.)

Cornish also confirmed that he and Bent had gone to Rose Cottage on 14 March.[20] Beatrice had handed them a letter from a former Infirmary patient and told Cornish she planned on coming to Coleford to meet with the detectives a second time. She gave him a small tin labelled 'Cooper's Tablets' she had found in a cupboard. Similar to sheep dip, they contained a mixture of arsenic and sulphur and were given to sheep to destroy internal parasites. She remembered Harry saying, 'If you are tired of

life, take one of them [and] you will soon bloody well die.'[21]
The subject that Beatrice wanted to discuss with Cornish was
apparently a difficult one.

> Mrs. Pace came to the station a little later and told them something,
> and in consequence he said 'We had better take another short
> statement from you.' She agreed and it was written down and signed.
> After this voluntary statement was completed she complained of
> illness and fainted. A doctor was called in and when she recovered
> said she was fit to go home, and he sent her there in a car.[22]

The jury was told that the 14 March statement 'contained a name
or names which the jury were told to keep entirely to themselves'
and then it was given to them to read. Cornish did not comment in
court about it. Bent said simply it 'referred to the matter excluded
from her statement, which it had been agreed had no relation
to the subject matter of the inquiry'.[23] This was not, strictly
speaking, true. It dealt not with Harry's infidelity but rather with
the rumours involving Beatrice's; however, as its contents never
became public, it will be discussed later, in Chapter 8.

Wellington failed to get Cornish to express doubt, as Bent had
done, about some of the Pace family's statements. Cornish quipped
that he had only been able to follow their comments through the
press, the reliability of which, he suggested (to the appreciative
laughter of the court), was imperfect. His cross-examination
ended 'with some amusement' when Wellington referred to his
own advice to Beatrice on dealing with the police:

> 'I told her to tell the truth,' said Mr. Wellington, 'and do you know
> what else?'
> The Inspector (hesitating): To be very careful with them!
> Mr. Wellington: Sound advice was it not?
> Witness: Very, I thought.[24]

In his testimony, Cornish presented a neutral case far removed
from the decided opinions of his report. Police testimony merely
identified possible sources of arsenic and explained the contexts
in which Beatrice's statements arose. The statements themselves
were partially (that of 15 February) or entirely (those of 11 and
14 March) kept out of the public record. That, however, would
soon change.

'One has heard so much': friends and acquaintances

A great deal of testimony was supplied by people who had seen Harry in hospital or at home. Those who had been in the Infirmary emphasised Harry's depressed mental state. Fellow patient Arthur Smith told the inquest Harry had been despondent and convinced that he was a 'cripple'; he had spoken many times of 'doing himself in' if there was no improvement.[25] Harry Winter confirmed Harry had been 'intensely depressed'.[26] Edwin Morgan had chatted with Harry every day, and he testified that he had suffered from frequent outbursts of crying, convinced he would never improve: it had been 'impossible to cheer him up'.[27] Charles Fletcher, an unemployed collier, had known Harry for some fifteen years and been in the Infirmary with him. He sometimes fed Harry, who had told him he had neuritis or rheumatism, which Fletcher blamed on overwork and getting wet.[28] Harry had not talked about suicide in his presence, but he had been 'very depressed'. The letter from a fellow patient that Beatrice handed to Cornish on 14 March stated: 'Harry has told me in the Infirmary he would do himself in, as he could not stick it much longer.'[29]

Harry had continued to receive visits from friends at home. Fletcher called twice a week to shave him, and, on one visit, Harry surprised him with the revelation he had arsenical poisoning and it might take two years for him to be able to 'get about'. (Experienced with sheep dipping, Fletcher explained it was normally done in a fenced-off 'bath': he had heard of sheep being dipped in a tub – as the Paces had done – but never seen it done.) Fred Thorne, a miner who had also developed expertise as a masseur, met Harry at the Infirmary while visiting Fletcher. Harry's mother had approached him about helping her son. Thorne thus visited Harry at home and – refusing any recompense for his services – massaged him nearly every day up to Christmas.[30]

There was also testimony about Harry and Beatrice's financial situation. The Pace family was convinced that Harry had 'put by' a large sum of money. Two years before, he had 'made out' he had enough to buy a house; Leah Pritchard said that Harry had suggested he had about £450 and was thinking of buying a small farm: until his illness, she considered him 'well off'.[31] (Harry's mother told police that Harry claimed to have had £150 – more than a year's wages – in 'ready money' in a box in the room where the children slept.[32]) Dr Du Pré said Beatrice had told him Harry 'had a few pounds by him', though he was unsure what this meant. A discussion with the doctor had been 'instrumental', however, in Harry deciding to make out his will.[33] He sought out George Mountjoy, a local 'teacher of commercial subjects' who also styled himself a 'journalist'. Mountjoy (who will play an important role in post-trial events) was executor of Harry's will and testified at the inquest. He had been called to Rose Cottage in late July 1927. Mountjoy had expected Harry would quickly recover, but Harry thought it would take a long time to 'kick over' his illness. At first, he testified that Harry had spoken of arsenical poisoning; however, he took this back under cross-examination, suggesting he had picked it up elsewhere. 'One has heard so much', he said, provoking courtroom laughter, 'that one hardly knows where one has heard it.'[34] Harry's intention was to leave 'everything he had' to his wife.[35] 'Everything' consisted only of sheep, furniture and 'implements', and, at the time, the Paces had not had a bank account. The will was completed the next day. Mountjoy never again saw Harry alive.

Mountjoy had read about Harry's death in the papers and, like others, had been surprised by the delayed funeral. Waiting to be contacted by Beatrice, he heard somehow that some of Harry's sheep had been sold. As executor of the Pace estate, he should have been involved in any such transactions. Thus, a few weeks after Harry's funeral, he went to Beatrice, who told him that all but about ten sheep had been sold in the months before Harry's death for nearly £75.[36] Mountjoy engaged in what he described as a 'battle royal' with Beatrice about the money and, as he stated, he had to 'use all the emphasis in my being' to get her to give him the money.[37] He also rounded up the ten remaining sheep and put them on his own property. He forgave Beatrice's 'oversight', and he emphasised that his sole concern had been paying off any potential creditors who might emerge. There was also a life insurance policy that Beatrice had taken out in December 1924. The policy had cost a shilling a week and the amount due on Harry's death was £69 12s.[38] (Beatrice was not able to receive the money without a final death certificate, which would mean waiting at least to the end of the inquest.)

Along with Harry's mental condition and the Pace's financial situation, testimony focused on how Beatrice had cared for

Harry. Several witnesses said she had devotedly tended to him. Thorne said she had done all she could: as he put it, 'She left nothing undone.'[39] Fletcher thought Harry had improved 'a lot' under Beatrice's care, so much so that by 23 December he had been able to hold a newspaper and a 'periodical' in his hands. Alice Sayes said Harry had so improved that he 'cut out football coupons, and pictures for the children, hit little Leslie when he was naughty, cut a piece of metal to improve a smoky chimney, and opened the push-on lid of a tin of some specific for cattle he had sent for'.[40] (Leslie confirmed that his father had become well enough not only to cut tin 'with scissors and a hammer' but also to 'spank' him.[41])

Other circumstances were also illuminated, such as Harry's precipitous decline after Christmas. When Fletcher shaved Harry on 23 December, he had been in 'very good spirits' and 'better that day than he had been for a month or two'; however, in early January, Harry 'constantly retched' and complained of not being able to keep his food down. Joseph Martin visited Rose Cottage almost every Sunday after Harry's release from the Infirmary. Two days before Harry's death, he was 'quiet and looked thoroughly ill'; however, he was 'not suffering from retching, vomiting or diarrhoea during his stay' and could 'move about in the bed'.[42] Martin confirmed being summoned by a panicked Doris on Christmas Day, but said that when he arrived at Rose Cottage it was 'calm' and there was no mention 'as to a razor, or to a quarrel, or to threats of murder'. Asked, however, if he would discount claims that Harry might have taken his own life, Martin gave what the *Dean Forest Guardian* called a 'notable reply':

> Well, I should have a doubt on that, because he was a very funny man.
> What was there peculiar about him? – Well, he was a very funny natured man.
> In what way? – Well, he seemed to me a very one-sided man.
> What does that mean? – His chief object seemed to be his sheep. He did not talk of anything else much at all. You could not seem to get into proper conversation with him. I attributed it to his illness. I never heard him say he would like to take his life.

Harry had a 'gusty' temper, he thought, but Beatrice had nursed him well, and Harry never complained: 'I thought he was being very well done by'. Thorne saw Pace four days after Christmas, when 'he found him very much altered and very ill', complaining of pains and a burning sensation in his stomach and throat. Harry was too ill to massage, and subsequently he was only able to massage his arms and ankles. On 9 January Harry said 'he was suffering "Hell"' and 'he had a thumping in his head and his heart was beating terrible'.[43]

As Harry's friends and acquaintances gave their views, the local and national press was taking an increasing interest in the case, publishing sometimes extensive reports. Their sympathies were clear, as is suggested by considering the coverage in the *Daily Mail*. On 20 April, it reported that 'throughout this part of Gloucestershire there is unmistakable sympathy for Mrs. Pace, the widow, because of the long ordeal to which she has been subjected'.[44] A week later, it referred to Beatrice's 'persecution': her 'piteous' police statement had drawn 'exclamations from other women in court', and the paper criticised the inquiry's duration. 'Every responsible person in this part of the Forest of Dean to whom I have spoken', the correspondent wrote, 'is of the opinion that the time has come to comment openly on the protracted nature of the inquest into the death of Mr. Harry Pace.' 'Local sympathy with Mrs. Pace … has changed to indignation at the long ordeal to which she has been subjected.'[45] The article also focused on Beatrice's domestic difficulties, particularly caring for a sickly infant in the midst of the inquest. By early May, the *Mail* editorialised in more urgent terms: the 'protracted inquiry … raises issues of great public importance quite apart from the determination of the cause of death'.[46] Citing Beatrice's 'bad health owing to continuous worry' and 'abject poverty', it demanded action from the Home Secretary: 'It is very unsatisfactory and unfair that any citizen should be the victim of such torturing delays.' But as 'unsatisfactory' as it may have been, the inquest still had some way to go.

'I let the jury draw their own inference': medical and forensic testimony

The final category of evidence related to medical views on Harry's illness and forensic analysis gleaned after his death. Much of the testimony of the doctors who treated Harry served as the basis for the description of his illness outlined in Chapter 1. During the inquest, Dr Nanda asserted that Beatrice was 'quite willing' for Harry to be hospitalised.[47] Dr Mather recounted how Harry's stomach problems had subsided by his admission to the Infirmary, but the 'numbness and loss of power' in his feet and hands had thereafter gotten worse; when he left, he 'could only stand upright with support, and had only a little use in his fingers'.[48] Du Pré recounted a visit a few days after his release: Harry's stomach problems had disappeared, but his paralysis was as bad or worse. Up to Christmas, Harry improved, and he could move unaided around his bedroom.[49] Du Pré agreed with Wellington's claim that Harry had made 'a vast amount of progress' under Beatrice's care.[50] However, when the doctor saw Harry on 27 December, he found him in bed suffering from stomach pain and unable to keep his food down. The doctor did not associate Harry's problem with a recurrence of his previous illness; diagnosing gastric influenza, he prescribed sodium bicarbonate and sodium salicitate. 'From that time until death he saw him about twice a week', the *Dean Forest Guardian* reported, 'and until 48 hours before death his condition was about the same.'[51] Although he had certified a natural death on the morning of 10 January, Du Pré testified that the results of the post-mortem had convinced him that he had been wrong.

Forensic testimony was vital to any poisoning case; however, that issue was causing some disagreement behind the scenes. As discussed, Cornish's report discounted the possibility of suicide. 'Naturally', the detective wrote, Beatrice wished people to believe Harry had taken his own life; however, he admitted that she was not alone. 'That is the theory of many people,' Cornish stated, 'including Doctor Du Pré and Professor Walker Hall.' He pointed out to his superiors that the medical evidence at the inquest 'will be very conflicting', with the two key medical experts – Walker Hall and Ellis – disagreeing about the dose that killed Harry. Walker Hall believed Harry had received one large fatal dose, whereas Ellis thought he had ingested several smaller doses.[52] Their conflicting opinions led the Director of Public Prosecutions, Sir Archibald Bodkin, to call in a further expert to help settle matters.[53]

The man he called upon, Sir William Willcox, was a pioneer in forensic analysis. Although Willcox had resigned his Home

Office appointment in 1919, he had retained the title of Honorary Medical Adviser, a position he held for another twenty years. He had testified in dozens of murder trials, including those of Dr Crippen and Armstrong. Describing the 'great Home Office pathologist', the *Sunday News* claimed his 'very name is dreaded by the murderer', noting he had 'sent Crippen to the scaffold'.[54] He was known for his slow, careful manner of speaking and the deliberate manner in which he gave evidence.[55] Willcox tried to smooth over any disputes between Walker Hall and Ellis at a 'conference' on 13 May. G. R. Paling (from the Department of Public Prosecutions) also attended. They discussed the probable source of the arsenic and sought to 'clarify the likely periods in the illness when arsenic had been administered'. The men achieved a 'considerable conformity of opinion'.[56] There was, in any case, little sign of disagreement suggested in the forensic testimony given at the inquest on 14 May by Walker Hall, Ellis and Willcox. (Ellis had given some testimony the preceding week and was also recalled the following day.) Dr Charles Carson, who had conducted Harry's post-mortem, had already given the inquest a detailed description of the body. Ellis noted that over nine grains of arsenic had been found in Harry's body, more than four times the minimum lethal dose of two grains.[57] Wellington, cross-examining, sought to suggest that the large dose of arsenic itself suggested a suicide:

> And you may have heard the saying that 'it is the suicide who uses a huge dose and the double-shotted pistol?' – I have not heard of that. And it sounds common sense, doesn't it? Are you aware of any case in which so large a quantity as this has been found – I cannot recall a single case.[58]

(There were suggestions that this was the largest amount of arsenic hitherto found in a homicide case; however, while large it was not unprecedented.[59]) Professor Walker Hall, 'grey-haired, and bespectacled', also testified that Harry showed signs of both chronic and acute poisoning.[60] He thought the organs' condition suggested that the last dose had been taken within six and forty-eight hours of death. Another had been absorbed between fourteen and twenty-one days before death (a time span that would have included Christmas Day) and another between three weeks and six months.[61] Cross-examined, Walker Hall agreed that Harry's improvement after returning home suggested that there had been no administration of arsenic during that period; however, he was sceptical that enough arsenic could have been absorbed through the skin (say, accidentally through sheep dipping) to cause a fatal illness. He and Wellington also sparred about medical details involving the rate at which arsenic is absorbed or excreted by the body, the conditions which affect those rates and the speed with which the symptoms of arsenic poisoning appear or fade.

Willcox's testimony was seen as a highlight by the press, not least because of his fame and connection to previous cases: 'Whilst he was in the witness-box ghosts of past tragedies flitted to and fro, intensifying the atmosphere which surrounds the as yet unsolved problem of the dead sheep farmer.'[62] Willcox agreed with the post-mortem diagnosis of acute arsenical poisoning and found the timing of doses offered by Walker Hall largely correct. One, he thought, must have been taken within forty-eight hours of death and another 'within a few hours of the onset of the symptoms on Christmas Day': at least one was taken 'in the intervening time' between them. He described Harry's symptoms in late July 1927 as acute arsenic poisoning and doubted enough arsenic could have been absorbed during sheep dipping to cause them. Willcox also made the second reference during the inquest to the Armstrong trial, at which he had provided decisive testimony and about which he had written a pamphlet. He observed in Coleford, for example, that only about one-third as much arsenic had been found in Mrs Armstrong's body as in Harry's. Willcox carefully responded to cross-examination. Questioned regarding the possibility of suicide, he said Harry's situation was 'possibly' a 'time when a man might be likely to translate threats into actions'. Asked whether a murderer would leave poison lying around, he said he would 'rather not answer': 'In agricultural districts there were poisons about houses. In some cases people were very careful and in others extraordinarily careless.'[63] Although evidence suggested that Harry had had sheep dip in his room (in the 'sheep box' Leslie had brought up) Willcox refused to speculate about whether he had taken the poison himself.

Questioned by Paling, Willcox noted what would become a crucial point: had a large dose of sheep dip been taken in a powdered form shortly before death, one would expect to find quantities not only of arsenic but also of sulphur in the intestines. (Sheep dip was actually about twenty per cent arsenic and sixty-five per cent sulphur.[64]) This was not so in Harry's case. While questioning Walker Hall and Willcox, Wellington referred to a reference work, *Taylor's Principles and Practice of Medical Jurisprudence*, sometimes reading sections aloud that – in his view – suggested possible alternatives. In particular, Wellington argued that Harry could have absorbed a sufficient dose of arsenic the previous July to cause the symptoms that had led him to the hospital. Walker Hall agreed with some of the statements in the book, but questioned Wellington's use of them: at one point he tartly referred to one of Wellington's conclusions as 'the translation put on medical words by a layman, a lawyer', a comment that 'was much enjoyed by an amused court'.[65] Interestingly, with regard to the timing, Willcox had given similar testimony during the inquest into the death of Mrs Armstrong six years earlier, concluding that she had taken two grains of arsenic in the two days before her death, and 'a quantity corresponding to a possibly fatal dose must have been taken within 24 hours of death'.[66] Willcox had then also emphasised how difficult it could be to clearly identify the symptoms of arsenic poisoning in a sick patient.[67]

Along with testimony on the timing of doses, that on the source of arsenic was crucial. As noted, it was determined that Harry could not have ingested powdered sheep dip, because of the lack of sulphur in his body. Ellis demonstrated, however, that it was possible, by mixing sheep dip with water and letting the sulphur settle, to create a clear, arsenic-rich liquid. If the sheep dip was the source of what killed Harry, it would have to have been treated – Ellis argued – in some similar way. The only other item found at Rose Cottage that contained arsenic or traces thereof was the 'dusty bottle' found in the kitchen on 11 March.[68] Ellis said the contents of the bottle were similar to a solution of sheep dip in water 'from which the greater part of the sulphur had been removed, and to which had been added potassium permanganate'. In court, he demonstrated how such a solution could be created by removing the sulphur from sheep dip in water and mixing in the purple-coloured permanganate. Recalled the following week, he also produced two examples each of a mixture of cornflour, milk and sugar ('as would be given to an invalid'); a bottle of egg white; and a flask of tea. In each case, one sample contained arsenic drawn off from sheep dip and the other did not. They looked identical. Wellington gently mocked Ellis's demonstrations and questioned their relevance:

> Mr. Wellington: You are showing those interesting experiments with a view to showing that in each case in the cornflour or tea there is no evidence that arsenic was being administered – Yes.
> You are asking us to infer that Mrs. Pace had sufficient scientific knowledge as to have possibly produced that form of poison without her husband being aware? – I let the jury draw their own inference.[69]

It was, thus, possible to remove sulphur from sheep dip; however, would Harry have been capable of doing so himself? Evidence was far from conclusive on this issue, as shall, at a later point, be discussed.

A number of other questions remained. Testimony from 'disinterested quarters' – as Willcox put it – claimed Harry had talked about suicide. But would a man who wished to kill himself have bothered to remove the sulphur from arsenic-laden sheep dip? Would Beatrice, on the other hand, have had the knowledge to draw off the colourless arsenic from the sheep dip, and, if so, the opportunity to do so without being discovered? What was the purpose of the arsenic solution in the 'dusty bottle'? There was no conclusive evidence at the inquest that could answer these questions. However, all witnesses – with the exception of the Pace family – were emphatic that Beatrice had devotedly nursed Harry: she had urged him to go into hospital, resisted his efforts to leave the Infirmary and tended to all his needs upon his return, leading to a great improvement in his condition. But as the proceedings drew to a close, the woman at the centre of the investigation would finally have the opportunity to answer questions herself.

The 'tragic widow' speaks

Beatrice was the last witness called (except for the briefly recalled Ellis). On Tuesday, 15 May, 'there was a stir in Court' when she went into the witness box.[70] Beatrice was assured by the coroner that she was not appearing as an accused person, but he also cautioned that any evidence could be used against her. Wellington first stated that his client wished to make clear that she had been treated 'with great consideration and kindness' by Scotland Yard. She also confirmed that her statements were accurate as entered into the record. She asserted that the life insurance policy had been taken out at Harry's request and that he had been aware of the premiums being paid out of his wages. She said she had passed on any relevant information or evidence to investigators, had not destroyed any bottles or powders contained in the 'sheep box' and had given the police any assistance she could. She did not know the contents of the bottle with the purple liquid or how long it had been there; she did not know what 'permanganate of potash' was and could not recall ever using it. She did not even know, she said, that sheep dip contained arsenic. She confirmed that Harry rarely drank alcohol and was 'thrifty' and a non-smoker. She had been concerned about his mental state. Before Christmas, Harry had wept and been depressed: 'He cried all one afternoon and said he would never be any good to her or to the children, and he went to the window to throw himself down through. She caught hold of him and got him on to the bed, and told him he would soon be better.' Harry was convinced he would never walk again. She tried to cheer him up by saying she could get a chair to 'wheel him about'. 'On several occasions', she said, 'he was like this.' She had been the only one to prepare Harry's food, 'including the tea he had'.

Toward the end of her testimony, she was asked pointed questions: '"I want now to give you the chance if you can – if you can," repeated the Coroner, "to tell the members of the jury how your husband managed to get nine grains of arsenic in his body."' Beatrice, with 'a slight quaver' in her voice, replied, 'I cannot tell you, sir – I cannot tell you.'[71] After describing her trek through knee-high snow to fetch Du Pré on Boxing Day, her testimony concluded with a question from Wellington: 'The doctor knew that arsenical poisoning had been diagnosed, and left you to nurse him? – Yes, and I did nurse him.' She 'broke down' at this point, burying her face in her hands, and a policewoman offered her smelling salts. Since her 'tear-filled' eyes prevented her from reading the written transcript of her testimony, it was read to her. Afterwards, she seemed to improve and spoke to at least one reporter. 'I feel', she said, 'that a great weight has been lifted off my mind. I could not have rested if I had not done so. I knew that I had nothing to fear from telling the truth.'[72] Thus ended not only Beatrice's testimony but also the inquest's evidence-gathering stage. The court was adjourned till the following week, when the jury's deliberations would begin.

A dramatic verdict

On Tuesday, 22 May, the inquest resumed for what was to be the last time. There was some brief, final testimony from Ellis, with regard to his analysis of the tub in which Beatrice and Harry had dipped lambs in July 1927. He had analysed the water it contained and that in an old beer bottle lying in it. Both contained arsenic but no sulphur. Cross-examined, Ellis admitted that his findings were consistent with Beatrice's claims of having dipped sheep, even if he would have expected rather more arsenic to have been washed away. It was, however, 'conceivable', in the words of the *World's Pictorial News*, that more arsenic should remain.[73] Then, the paper described the coroner's summary of the evidence:

> In view of the vast mass of evidence which had been given, the summing up was one of the shortest on record, lasting considerably less than an hour. He pointed out that the result of the post-mortem examination was to show that there was no natural disease to account for death, and that the view of Dr. Carson, that Pace had died from poisoning, was borne out by the findings of Sir William Willcox, the great Home Office pathologist, Professor Walker Hall, of Bristol University, and Mr. Ellis, the county analyst. Then, speaking very solemnly, he again urged the jury to put out of their minds anything they had read or heard, and just put it to themselves whether, in the circumstances, they thought there was ground for suspicion, and whether they thought there was need for some further investigation.[74]

While Beatrice 'toyed nervously with her handkerchief', the coroner also explained to his jury the significance of their decision:

> The Coroner explained the Coroner's Act in relation to a murder issue, and emphasised that the jury's finding on that point amounted to nothing more than the finding of a True Bill by a Grand Jury. It had the effect of putting persons upon their trial, and it led to further investigation by another court. 'In other words,' he said, 'you have to consider whether a case has been made out against a person or persons, which they have to answer, not before you but before another court.'[75]

The court was then cleared and the jury sent off to reach their verdict.

Beatrice, accompanied by Alice Sayes, went across the street for tea. Nearby, 'little knots of people stood at the street corners discussing the case'. After about an hour, 'there was a sudden stir outside the court':

> Women fought their way up the stone steps, clinging to the railings on either side in order to maintain their foothold. A hefty sergeant of the police held them back and ordered them to 'make way'. Mrs. Pace, a frail figure in deep mourning, mounted the steps. Shortly afterwards she was seated in her usual seat just behind Inspector Cornish. The policewoman was at her side. The jury, grave and solemn-looking, never once glanced at the widow.[76]

After the court had settled, the jury foreman delivered the verdict: Harry Pace had died from arsenical poisoning 'administered by some person or persons other than himself' and the case called for further investigation. There was some confusion in the court as to what the verdict actually meant. Carter consulted a legal manual before responding. Referring to the laws governing inquests, he explained that if there was 'some person' whom the jury suspected they must be named: 'No person can be committed by a coroner's inquisition and so bring about a further inquiry into the case unless some person is named.'[77] 'In some cases', he stated, 'it may be possible for the finding to be murder against a person or persons unknown, but if you find there is a person, that person has to answer a charge in another court. It is, therefore, necessary for you to name that person.'[78] 'We are not agreed upon that', the foreman responded. Sensing that the jury might have someone in mind, Carter suggested that they again retire to reconsider the issue. The crowded court was again cleared.

Within thirty minutes, the jury returned. Its foreman – a grocer 'whose normally ruddy features were pale' (and who may have had tears in his eyes[79]) – rose to his feet when asked by the coroner whether they were agreed. The jury had 'revised' their verdict, he said: they concluded 'that Harry Pace met his death by arsenical poisoning administered by Beatrice Annie Pace'. His words triggered a shocked reaction in the packed court: 'There was a wail of anguish from the black-clad figure as, with quivering lips, she uttered her denial "No, I didn't." She slumped in her chair ... and was borne, weeping, from the court, protesting her innocence.'[80] From the back of the courtroom, a woman's voice declared 'it is wicked', and the room was cleared.[81] Two hours later, Beatrice was brought back to face two magistrates (one man and one woman) to be charged.[82] Still in shock, she was 'supported at the waist by the hands of a policewoman' and was 'crying and moaning' as she was formally charged with murder.[83] When asked whether she had anything to say against being sent to prison to await trial she stated simply 'No, nothing'; she then 'sank back again weeping and shaking and sat pathetically with her head on her knees until an escort came forward and removed her from the dock'.[84] She was taken to Cardiff prison and placed in the hospital wing. 'She was in a distracted condition when admitted', the *Dean Forest Guardian* reported, 'and spent a restless night without any sleep.'[85] This is hardly surprising: the jury's verdict meant that she would inevitably face a trial for premeditated murder, the punishment for which was hanging.

The next regular assizes for Gloucestershire were at the beginning of June, but it seemed unlikely that all of the pre-trial procedures would be completed by then. (She would still have to face the formality of a magistrates' court to decide whether there was a prima facie case against her and to take the depositions that would be used at trial.) The delay of holding the case till the next regular assizes in October was, however, undesirable. Two options remained: a recent change in the law allowed the case to be dealt with at another county's assizes (adjacent Monmouthshire and Herefordshire were mentioned as possibilities). Alternatively, a judge could convene a special session in order to deal with the Pace trial alone. 'This was actually done', the *Dean Forest Guardian* pointed out, 'in the celebrated Armstrong case at Hereford.'[86] As she awaited her fate, this is not likely a comparison that Beatrice would have found encouraging.

4

'Easing the burden of the tragic widow': the making of 'Mrs Pace'

From the beginning, the Pace case was more than simply a legal (or local) matter. Up to the inquest verdict, most of its key events took place within a few miles of Rose Cottage yet were followed throughout Britain and beyond. Press coverage created a figure known to millions of newspaper readers: 'Mrs Pace'. The inquest verdict charging her with murder made her not only a more sensational but also a more complex figure. Women went to the gallows far less often than men; still, between the turn of the century and spring 1928, eight women were hanged in England and Wales, two of them in the 1920s.[1] Poisoning was seen as one of the most cold-blooded crimes, and, if convicted, Beatrice might face a difficult battle for mercy. Examining the Pace case as a national sensation, the following chapters also locate it within British culture and society. Beatrice's ascent from obscure farmer's wife to celebrity murder suspect set the stage for one of the most eagerly awaited trials in inter-war Britain.

Human interests: murder in black and white

The 1920s and 1930s were a golden age for press spectacles: increasing literacy, advances in printing technology and expanding consumer opportunities (and the advertising they brought) gave newspapers unprecedented social, political and economic influence that would only be challenged (especially by television) after the Second World War. Newspapers had been around in some form since the seventeenth century. But it was the emphasis of nineteenth-century 'new journalism' on melodramatic 'human-interest' stories

– pioneered by the *Daily Telegraph* (founded in 1855) – and the later growth of tabloids such as the *Daily Mail* (1896), *Daily Express* (1900) and *Daily Mirror* (1903) that created the modern mass press. Crime stories drove the newspaper 'revolution' led by Lord Northcliffe, founder of the *Mail* and *Mirror*, under the motto 'get me a murder a day'.[2] In 1921, daily metropolitan newspapers had a circulation of nearly five-and-a-half million. By 1939, this figure had nearly doubled.[3] Harry Pace's mysterious death and the travails of his widow possessed exactly the kind of 'human interest' that sold papers.[4]

There was nothing unprecedented about an interest in murder, as centuries of woodcuts and pamphlets testify.[5] But the mass press enabled a new level of fascination with sinister demises. As Martin Pugh notes, inter-war newspapers treated crime as 'popular entertainment', depicting 'a society in the grip of violent crime of all kinds'.[6] But despite a menagerie of social fears – returning war veterans, foreign gangsters, 'hooligans', 'motor bandits', 'razor gangs' and 'dope fiends' – homicide rates remained at or near the historic lows of the turn of the century.[7] Nonetheless, murder dramatically affected the period's social imagination and became a crucial ingredient in its celebrity culture. An editorial in the *Daily Herald* in 1927 pondered the 'strange and exceedingly widespread fascination of the sinister and the macabre': 'Why do nine people out of every ten follow the meagre official details and the billowing rumours of an actual murder mystery more eagerly and breathlessly than the most devoted detective story "fan" ever stumbled from clue to clue in the encouraging company of Sherlock Holmes or Sexton Blake or Dr. Thorndyke?'[8] As this suggested, this was not only the age of newsprint sensations but also the classic era of the fictional 'whodunit'.[9] The narrator in Agatha Christie's archetypal mystery novel *The Mysterious Affair at Styles* (1920) – centring on the poisoning death of a society lady – captures the mood: 'The papers, of course, had been full of the tragedy. Glaring headlines, sandwiched biographies of every member of the household, subtle innuendoes, the usual familiar tag about the police having a clue.' 'Screaming headlines in every paper in the country', one character complains: 'damn all journalists, I say! Sort of Madame Tussaud's chamber of horrors business that can be seen for nothing.'[10] Rather than country houses, by far most of the real-life 'chamber of horrors business' took place in provincial villages, urban working-class neighbourhoods and middle-class suburbs. But the appeal was the same.

One of the models here was the case of American-born Florence Maybrick, convicted in Liverpool in 1889 of murdering her husband with arsenic derived from fly-papers. The public was later fascinated by cases such as Kitty Byron's fatal stabbing of her lover on a London street in 1902 or the international spectacle of the 1910 trial of Hawley Crippen for the murder and dismemberment of his wife.[11] In the same year as Major Armstrong's arsenic murder trial, 1922, Edith Thompson and Frederick Bywaters were sensationally convicted of murdering Edith's husband.[12] The 1924 trial following the fatal shooting of Egyptian prince Fahmy Bey by his English wife was a scandal of another sort, marked by titillating suggestions of 'foreign' sexual practices.[13] The intimations of madness, brutality and infidelity during the Pace inquest thus fit a common pattern, and female suspects were particularly fascinating to the press.[14] This interest derives partly from novelty: woman kill other adults far more rarely than do men.[15] But there was nothing automatically sensational about female killers, some of whose cases received comparatively cursory press coverage. In 1911, for instance, Fanny Gilligan, having long tolerated her partner's cruelty, poured paraffin over him and set him alight.[16] In 1925, Laura Lynn slit the throat of her violent, womanising husband after nineteen years of marital torment.[17] Though reported upon, neither case blossomed into a media spectacle as did those of Florence Maybrick, Edith Thompson or, as was becoming apparent by May 1928, Beatrice Pace.

What made the Pace case different? One reason may be the vigorous debate about gender roles in the late 1920s. Discussing the pros and cons of 'the modern woman' – and her younger incarnation, the 'flapper' – had become a press obsession.[18] Beatrice, as Chapter 7 will discuss, had a rather ambiguous position in this debate. But men's behaviour, too, was under increasing scrutiny.[19] Family violence remained widespread, but its acceptability had been receding since the nineteenth century.[20] Beatrice's exceptional popularity was also a result of the multi-layered narratives her case offered: the Pace case could be seen to be 'about' different things. There was, prominently, the mystery of Harry's death. However dramatic, Fanny Gilligan's lit paraffin or Laura Lynn's razor blade left few loose ends. Other cases were in a different category. The stabbing inflicted upon Percy Thompson by Frederick Bywaters may have meant there was no question about the cause of the former's demise; nonetheless, there was plenty of room for speculation about the role played by Thompson's wife Edith, which was fuelled by the reading of her and Frederick's love letters in court. Similarly, in the Fahmy case, although Prince Bey had unmistakeably died from a gunshot wound inflicted by his wife, the circumstances leading to that fatal act were anything but clear. With regard to Harry Pace's death, it was not even apparent whether 'foul play' was involved. To some, then, the Pace case was a real-life mystery of the sort being popularised in this period by Agatha Christie, Margery Allingham or Dorothy L. Sayers. Other readers might be fascinated by the 'tragedy' of Beatrice's own life as she was left widowed, impoverished and responsible for five children. 'Mystery' and 'tragedy' were already a potent mix of themes, but to them we can add 'injustice'. As Chapter 8 will discuss, critiques of the police, justice system, poverty and domestic violence accompanied the 'human interest' angle, helping to ensure that the 'ordeal' of 'Mrs Pace' was covered by sensationalist tabloids and serious broadsheets alike.

Mrs Pace and the magistrates

The inquest verdict meant that Beatrice would be tried for murder at the 'assizes', the ancient legal institution that, until 1972, was the main British court for trying serious crimes. First, however, evidence would be presented before a magistrates' court (sometimes called a 'police court'). Despite the presence of counsel for the accused and prosecution, this would not be a 'trial' but rather a 'committal proceeding' to confirm whether there was sufficient evidence to justify sending it to the assizes. Although in some sense the hearing was redundant (the inquest verdict meant her case would proceed regardless of the magistrates' decision) this was standard procedure.[21] Unlike at the inquests, the rules of evidence generally valid in English courts would apply. The proceedings were held in Coleford before five magistrates (one of them a woman).[22] The Crown was represented by G. R. Paling (who had assisted the coroner at the inquest). Beatrice was defended in court by Dr W. G. Earengey, who was instructed by her solicitor, Trevor Wellington. The magistrates' chairman referred to a 'great number' of witnesses and a 'mass' of evidence: 'however wearisome some people might consider the process to be', he said, 'the evidence had to be taken down in writing, in long hand' (thus producing the written 'depositions' that could be referred to at the trial). The hearing was, however, relatively brief: starting on Thursday, 31 May, it concluded the following Monday evening. Accounting for the Sunday break, it took up four days.

Following the chair's warning to the public gallery that no 'demonstration of any kind' would be permitted, Paling outlined the Crown's case, distilling what – in his view – was a clear case of murder. He portrayed Harry as a 'very robust, strong and healthy, hard working man', though he admitted he was 'a man of certain peculiarities of temperament and was no doubt a very restive man'. He described in detail the course of Harry's illness and the large amount of arsenic found, highlighting the forensic experts' conclusions regarding the timing of the doses. This was all well known, but, as the *Dean Forest Guardian* put it, his 'most interesting' comments dealt with how the poisoning occurred. The inquest had been, at least officially, an open-ended procedure; now, the Crown's suspicions were stated directly. Paling dismissed the possibility of accidental absorption ('no case was on record to support such a theory, nor could so large a quantity of arsenic in the body be reconciled with this theory') and disparaged the plausibility of suicide. Was it possible that Harry, 'lying helpless in bed and in a dying condition', could have retrieved sheep dip from the drawer in his room, separated the sulphur in water, imbibed it and disposed of the sulphurous sediment? Moreover, why should Harry keep trying to kill himself with arsenic 'which had failed him already more than once, and which he knew to be a painful form of suicide?' Why were his alleged threats to kill himself not mentioned until after the funeral was stopped? Paling argued that homicide was more likely, and he used one of Beatrice's comments – that nobody could have given Harry anything without her knowing it – against her: indeed, the prosecution would argue that 'no one else could have given him the arsenic'. Ignoring the issue of motive, he said she 'was the only person who could say why she did it, and he was not going to suggest any reason why she should. That there was at the moment no very definite or apparent motive made it none the less a crime, if in fact a crime it was.' Instead, he focused on the 'nasty water' incident, drew attention to claims that two whole packets of sheep dip had been seen in the house in August 1927 and highlighted the presence of the 'dusty' bottle's arsenic mixture.

What followed Paling's opening argument was, in essence, an abbreviated version of the inquest evidence, with some variations. The Pace family again aired their suspicions. Harry's visitors testified as to his condition and state of mind. Joseph Martin, like others, commented that Harry never complained about or seemed suspicious of Beatrice, and 'she did everything she could for him'. Fred Thorne's testimony described certain features of Harry's room – such as the fact that the chest of drawers could only be reached by getting out of bed – and a map of the room was created to be entered as evidence.[23] Attention was focused on young Leslie's comments that what remained of one packet of sheep dip had been put back into the 'sheep box' he had later brought to his father. Describing Harry's Christmas outburst, the boy noted that he previously 'had threatened to shoot them all'. Details regarding the purchase of the sheep dip or Harry's life insurance were entered into the record. Cross-examined by Earengey, Inspector Bent agreed that Beatrice had cooperated fully, 'behaved perfectly frankly, and answered every question without hesitation'. There had not appeared to be 'concealment or destruction of anything relevant to the case'. All of her statements, when checked, had proven to be true.[24]

In an intriguing moment, Sergeant Hamblin had trouble identifying a green bottle labelled 'Butter of Antimony' that Dorothy had found in the fireplace in Harry's room. He eventually settled on a large green bottle: its label, however, did not state 'Butter of Antimony'. ('No one', Earengey quipped, 'is going to suggest, are they, that the police have changed the labels?') He also confirmed that Beatrice had complained two years before that Harry 'had threatened to shoot her and the children'. Dr Du Pré retraced the stages of Harry's illness and explained how Beatrice, about a month before Christmas, had asked him to get Harry into another hospital, concerned he was not getting better quickly enough. He said he had told Beatrice that Harry had arsenical poisoning before he left the hospital, a comment Earengey picked up on: was it believable, he asked, that 'she was continuing to administer arsenic when she knew that you knew he was suffering from arsenical poisoning'? Importantly, Du Pré thought, contrary to prosecution claims, that Harry could have walked to the dressing chest 'unaided' from late November 'until within 12 hours of his death'.[25]

The final day, 4 June, saw crucial testimony. Public attendance, 'principally women', had increased greatly.[26] (Still, the *Dean Forest Guardian* noted that the court 'was by no means full'; the *World's Pictorial News* may thus have exaggerated in claiming it was 'packed to suffocation'.[27]) Analyst Rowland Ellis restated his forensic findings and noted that the only apparent sources of arsenic were either the sheep dip or the 'dusty' bottle containing 'just over 2 ozs. of dirty looking purple liquid, consisting of potassium permanganate, insoluble permanganese compound, sulphur and arsenic compounds' amounting to about three quarters of a grain. Asked by Earengey whether he found 'potassium of permanganate' in Harry's body, Ellis first said that would be 'impossible' due to the rapid breakdown of colouring materials in the digestive tract. Pressed further, he said different 'salts in the body' could not be distinguished, but he admitted he had not done any such experiments. He also agreed that, while there was no apparent purpose to adding the permanganate, it was possible that an arsenic solution – one that 'could be used for destroying sheep maggots' – might simply have been added to an old bottle containing some left-over potassium permanganate.[28]

The most dramatic moments involved the reading out of Beatrice's statements from 15 February and 11 March. The former had been read aloud at the inquest (except for passages regarding Harry's infidelities), but the second had only been given to the jury to read. Despite some references to Harry's violence at the inquest, it was not until Paling read out what the *World's Pictorial News* called her 'secret statement' that details emerged.[29] Beatrice's 11 March statement contained dramatic claims. Harry had beaten her, threatened to murder her with a razor, struck at her with a hatchet and menaced her with a pistol. He had once tied her to the bed, and when she fled to her father's house he followed and threatened her with a shotgun. He had set the family's blankets alight, buried one of his children's clothes, locked his family out of the house and brutally killed two pet dogs. He also destroyed household objects during periodic rages. She questioned Harry's mental state and detailed his affairs (specific names were omitted during the reading) while asserting her own fidelity. She could not account for the arsenic poisoning except through suicide.[30] Beatrice remained largely composed, but when Paling reached the claim that Harry had 'thrashed' her while pregnant, she 'burst into tears' and 'wept for some time, despite the efforts of the attendant to calm her'.[31]

Newspapers gave the abuse allegations prominent, even front-page, coverage, and the 'sensational new disclosures' (*Sunday News*) and 'astonishing scenes of passion and cruelty' (*The People*) were recounted in full.[32] The *World's Pictorial News* referred to the 'secret statement' as 'one of the most amazing human documents ever read aloud in a court of law', and devoted substantial space to lengthy, verbatim sections, as did the *Daily Mail*, then Britain's largest-circulation paper.[33] As was typical, particular passages were highlighted by being off-set from the main text. The 3 June issue of *The People*, for example, emphasised details from the February statement about Harry's cruelty and alleged intentions to kill himself. Dr Du Pré's comments that Beatrice, with 'great difficulty', had persuaded Harry to see him and that she was a 'devoted nurse and left nothing undone that should have been done' were similarly stressed.[34] The *World's Pictorial News* displayed the claims of abuse in a prominent box just under the headline.[35] Thus, with regard to the reading of her first two statements, Beatrice, although on trial as a perpetrator, was mainly depicted as a victim. Her third statement, from 14 March was not read aloud. It was handed to the magistrates to read, 'for obvious reasons' as Paling put it.[36] (He must have meant 'obvious' to the magistrates, as no public explanation was given.)

Professor Walker Hall testified again that the final dose that had killed Harry was taken within forty-eight hours and that others had been taken between forty-eight hours and fourteen days, fourteen and twenty-one days as well as between two to three months prior to death. The onset of symptoms on Christmas Day was consistent with arsenic having been taken a few hours before. Interestingly, Walker Hall seemed to suggest under cross-examination that one would *not* necessarily find sulphur in the intestines if sheep dip ('either in powder form or mixed with water') had been taken, since it 'would have disappeared normally within 24 hours'.[37] The prosecution's claim was that Harry could not have killed himself simply by ingesting powdered sheep dip since no sulphur remnants had been found. When asked the question again, the professor said he *would* have expected to find sulphur. Earengey, however, insisted that his first answer be included in the record.[38]

As was usual, the defence had the final word. In summarising the evidence, Earengey denied that even a prima facie case had been made: there was merely a 'suspicion' based on the fact that Beatrice had prepared Harry's food. 'We do not even know', he pointed out, 'how the arsenic was administered.'[39] Suggesting that Harry's illness in July 1927 may have been caused by accidental poisoning, he emphasised that 'Mrs. Pace's whole conduct was consistent with her having taken the interest in her husband that was to be expected from a wife, and thoroughly disproved the theory of the prosecution that she administered arsenic to him': 'It was devotion carried almost to excess in her desire to get her husband well. Nobody could suggest a single thing she could have done more than she did.' The police agreed that she had been cooperative and concealed nothing, and Earengey stated it was only due to 'suspicion and antipathy by the immediate relatives of this man' and 'rumours' that the case had gotten so far. He insisted suicide remained a possibility, pointing to Dr Du Pré's testimony that Harry could have reached the 'sheep box' up to twelve hours before his death. 'There goes', he underlined the point, 'the whole fabric of the case of the prosecution.'[40] And if Beatrice had killed Harry with the arsenic in the 'dusty bottle', why did she not destroy it? 'Do you think she was mad enough to leave evidence of her guilt if she were guilty?', he asked: 'I think you will give her credit for a modicum of common-sense, and I cannot conceive the veriest [sic] baby taking such a line of conduct as that.'[41] He urged the magistrates to decide that the prosecution had failed to make its case.

Earengey completed his plea shortly after 6.15 p.m. When the court reassembled some forty-five minutes later, Beatrice was so overwrought that she needed assistance to take her seat. She then 'bowed her head on the ledge of the dock' and struggled to stand when asked to do so as the verdict was read. 'The Bench has carefully considered all the evidence brought before us', the chairman stated, 'and are unanimously of opinion that it is sufficient to put the accused upon her trial.' Beatrice fainted as the clerk began to read out the committal order. 'It was some moments before he noticed', observed the *World's Pictorial News*, 'that the woman in the dock was senseless – incapable of hearing a single word he was saying.'[42] The clerk paused, and a doctor was sent for. On behalf of his unconscious client, Earengey pleaded 'not guilty', and the magistrates committed her case to the next assizes in Gloucestershire.

'The scene was a painful one for all in Court', the *Dean Forest Guardian* stated: 'The police-woman and wardress applied smelling salts and flicked their handkerchiefs in her face in the effort to bring her back to consciousness.'[43] Their efforts were fruitless, except for a moment when Beatrice wailed piteously, 'Can't you take me home?'[44] She was carried to an anteroom and attended by a doctor until she recovered sufficiently to depart. The Coleford street leading from the court toward Cardiff was 'lined with people', and the appearance of the police car 'was the signal for a remarkable demonstration': '"Here she comes," was passed along the crowded pavement, and as the car was driven slowly by, handkerchiefs and hats were waved vigorously.'[45] Beatrice was seen to lean forward in the car and waved her handkerchief in return. Perched on the shoulders of a family friend, Doris Pace watched her mother once again depart for prison in Cardiff. 'She threw kisses to her mother and waved her little handkerchief', it was reported, 'until the car had passed from view.'[46]

Two days later, the assizes were opened in Gloucester by high-court judge Mr Justice Horridge, who met with the grand jury. There were three cases to deal with: Beatrice's murder trial, six charges against an engine driver for 'forging and uttering postal orders' and a 51-year-old tin worker 'indicted for an alleged serious offence against a girl of 15'.[47] Because of the short notice, Beatrice could not immediately be tried; however, the case was considered by the grand jury. Horridge had received the magistrates' depositions only the night before. He spoke briefly, summarising the prosecution and defence arguments. He mentioned the prosecution's claim that Beatrice was the only one who had prepared Harry's food and drink as well as their contention that a suicidal man would not have poisoned himself multiple times. For the defence, he observed that doctors knew by the time he was released from the Infirmary that he was suffering from arsenical poisoning: 'You may think, said the Judge, that has some important bearing on the case, because you may ask yourself whether the woman, knowing that the poisoning was discovered, would have continued poisoning him in those circumstances.'[48] Horridge told the jurors that their sole responsibility was to find whether there was a prima facie case and gave them the magistrates' depositions, stating that they were 'extremely well written, and nothing like so lengthy' as those from the inquest. 'It is', he observed, 'a case I know you will go into carefully, although it may take you some time.'[49] Within an hour, however, the jurors found a 'true bill' against Beatrice for murder, formally sending the case to trial. Horridge agreed to return to Gloucester for a special sitting to deal with that case alone as his schedule allowed. At the latest, the trial would take place in early July.

The tragic widow in prison

Between her arrest and trial, Beatrice was jailed on remand, being moved from Cardiff to Birmingham on 5 June after the magistrates' hearing. She was kept in the prisons' hospitals, a not uncommon practice with some murder suspects, allowing closer observation and (not incidentally) the prevention of suicide attempts. Beatrice was 'in a state of absolute collapse' when brought to Cardiff, but the *World's Pictorial News* reported that she made 'a slight progress towards recovery' under the 'kindly attention of the women officers'.[50] She could mix freely with the other patients, received a special diet and did not have to sleep in a cell. The paper described Birmingham's prison as 'very beautiful' and 'very like a castle in appearance with its turrets and battlements'.[51] An unnamed visitor stated: 'No doors were locked behind me as I had entered, as might have been expected, and when I entered she greeted me with a glad smile and a warm hug.' Beatrice was sitting before a 'cosy-looking fire' and was 'knitting away'. 'Everyone', she said, 'is so kind to me', and well-wishers had sent her money so she could have the food she liked brought in. While in Birmingham, a black cat belonging to the prison slept every night on her pillow. Beatrice said that she welcomed the company, coming to see the cat as a good omen.[52]

She wrote many letters. 'All her letters', reported the *World's Pictorial News*, 'are full of passages concerning her children and express the longing that she may soon be with them.'[53] Insight into Beatrice's experience in prison is gained from six letters she wrote to Alice Sayes. The first was written the day after she had been charged. Although 'fairly well', she felt 'awfully upset and worried': 'I never thought they would have brought me here. But never mind. I have never done any wrong and that is why I am so broken hearted over it.' She hoped to get out on bail 'just to be with the children' and was relieved Sayes was taking care of Jean; she urged her to ensure the other children were being cared for and had 'enough of food'.[54] The separation from her family preyed upon her. She praised Leslie's testimony: 'I saw Leslie, he done well. Not a word of untruth did he say. I had a good mind to give him a kiss.' She was less pleased about Dorothy. Someone had told her 'that Dolly rides all day on the back of motorbikes while I am here worrying myself to death'. She asked, 'Do you ever see Dolly? Does she ever ask you how I am? I expect she has forgotten me.' She was also concerned about her in-laws going into Rose Cottage: 'I hear that the Pace people goes [sic] down there. I hope it is not right. I hope they won't get in the house. Tell Les [Sayes] to go to Mr. Bent. Also tell him to nail up the windows [and] also the door leading out of the back kitchen into the kitchen.'[55] She wrote fondly of visits by her brothers, solicitors and friends as well as the gifts she received, from the 'lovely bunch of flowers' sent by an unknown admirer to the chocolate the Sayeses had brought: 'I was longing for a sweet as I had not seen one since I left Coleford.'[56] She also mentioned visits from her Member of Parliament.[57]

Beatrice's letters testify to her close relationship with her 'dearest friends', Alice and Leslie Sayes. She signed all her letters as 'your ever-loving friend'; one claimed they would 'soon be together again never to part'.[58] In another, she quoted (approximately) a popular song written two years earlier: 'I am longing to come home and sit in that cosy armchair of yours and hear that record of mine, "Are you lonesome tonight, do you miss me tonight, do the chairs in your parlour seem empty and bare. Do you stand on your doorstep and picture me there." I hope I shall soon be there, as I am getting rather fed up.'[59] She planned to leave the district, telling Alice on 6 June she was ready to 'sell it all' if she got home again. Two weeks later, she thanked Alice for offering to rent her two rooms at their house. But she had other plans: 'I shall go back to the Fetter Hill just for a week to clear up the few things that is there and then I shall leave it for good.' Her gratitude was plain: 'I shall never be able to thank you and Les enough for all you have done for me. I shall never forget you both.'

Her outlook teetered between optimism and despair. 'Things will be bound to come right', she wrote on 23 May, but by 12 June she was thinking 'there is nothing in life for me now', complaining that 'this case has made me an old woman'. On 20 June, although 'ever so pleased' to hear that her children were doing well, she wrote, 'this case is worrying me to death because I am suffering for nothing'. A week later, she admitted to being 'fed right up with one thing and another', and her doubts were apparent in her use of the phrase 'if I live to get home again'.[60] But she made an effort not to let the strain show.[61] In his report to the Director of Public Prosecutions, the prison medical officer advised that Beatrice had been 'under close and constant observation'. He had seen her every day since she arrived from Cardiff and had 'a number of long interviews with her'. Other than a 'slight degree of enlargement of the thyroid gland' her physical condition was quite good. As to her mental state: 'She was somewhat depressed on the evening of her arrival here, after the railway journey. But since then she has been quite cheerful. She takes food well. She is reported to sleep very well at nights. She converses readily, rationally, and with apparently excellent memory.' She was, the report concluded, 'quite fit to plead to the Indictment at her trial'.[62]

The making of 'Mrs Pace'

Outside prison walls, interest in the case was growing. Throughout the investigation and inquest, the press had emphasised the suffering of the 'tragic widow': her separation from her children, her anxieties and fears and her impoverished family's struggles. *The People* had profiled itself as one of Beatrice's defenders by mid-March, alleging harsh treatment by Scotland Yard. In April, its headlines signalled its take on the story: 'Help for Mrs. Pace: widespread sympathy for Dean Forest widow', 'Widow Pace's terrible ordeal is prolonged' and 'Widow Pace's despair'.[63] The *Daily Mail*'s approach that month was similar: 'Widow's ordeal at inquest', 'Child's witness box ordeal', 'Mrs Pace's long suspense' and even 'The persecution of Mrs. Pace'.[64] The *World's Pictorial News* was running stories with titles such as 'Suspense of tragic

5 Beatrice Pace with the family's sheepdog, 'Rover', at Rose Cottage, in an undated press photo from 1928. Although many images of Beatrice and her children appeared in the press, only one very indistinct photo of Harry was printed.

mother of ten' and 'Easing burden of the tragic widow', describing the courtroom in Coleford as 'the scene of her prolonged agony'.[65] The *Sunday Express* called the murder charge 'the climax of the long series of ordeals endured by the tragic widow since the death of her husband more than five months ago'.[66]

In May and June, the public persona of 'Mrs Pace' became more clearly contoured. The magistrates' court hearing allowed a rapid, press-friendly recap of the events in the case just as Beatrice's incarceration and impending trial created a dramatic human-interest angle. Attention was also given to those around Beatrice who were 'straining every nerve and sinew to help', such as her brothers (Arnold and Fred Martin), Mrs Paddock ('the kindly proprietress of the King's Head Hotel' who was taking care of Doris), and Leslie and Alice Sayes ('two of the staunchest friends that ever a woman could have').[67] (Nesta Ryall, in an article titled 'The benevolent plain people of England' – which highlighted the assistance Beatrice was receiving from friends, neighbours and even strangers – singled out Alice Sayes: 'In a countryside of kindliness and good nature, she is a conspicuous example of the best type of womanhood.'[68])

It was not unprecedented for the press to portray an accused murderer positively. Press and public reactions to accused (and even convicted) killers were often unpredictable, sometimes surprising and occasionally mercurial. Those who killed for base motives, such as material gain, or whose acts were especially grisly were, unsurprisingly, vilified. However, killings committed in the heat of passion, in response to serious provocations or victimisation or as a result of insanity might be treated with a striking degree of understanding. The killer's methods and motives as well as the respective characters of the accused and the victim were decisive, as earlier cases showed. Although Kitty Byron had publicly stabbed her lover, for instance, she was seen sympathetically after details of his cruelty emerged.[69] Some commentators even expressed sympathy toward Hawley Crippen, depicting his late wife (and victim) as slovenly and sexually unrestrained.[70] Press opinion of Edith Thompson swung from sympathy to condemnation and, following her death sentence, partially back again: childless and with a career, she embodied the 'modern' woman, which may have worked against her, as did, certainly, her adultery.[71] Because Marie Fahmy was seen as the victim of her Egyptian husband's 'deviant' sexual practices, public opinion moved her way, possibly contributing to her acquittal.[72]

Beatrice's case was absorbed into this media world, and, despite her perilous situation, she had some advantages. Though poor, she embodied a respectable and traditional ideal of femininity and was consistently depicted as a devoted wife and mother. Beatrice benefited greatly from the decision by reporters (nearly all of them, most likely, men) to cast her story in a particular way.[73] Journalistic selectivity not only emphasised the suspect's positive features but also depicted her accusers negatively. Although the Pace family's criticisms were reported via transcripts of inquest testimony, they were dismissively lumped together with the 'gossip' surrounding the investigation. *The People* labelled their evidence 'insinuations and rumour' that had added 'little or nothing concerning the actual cause of Harry Pace's death'.[74] The *Daily Mail* highlighted Beatrice's 'outward composure' in facing 'what her solicitor ... described as a campaign of insinuation on the part of her relatives'.[75] Thus, no hostile counter-narrative about Beatrice ever emerged. This was perhaps crucial: one factor in the shift in public opinion against Edith Thompson in 1922 may have been criticism by her brother-in-law Richard published in *Lloyd's Sunday News*.[76] Elton Pace never gained (and may never have sought out) a similar platform. It is important to note the contingency of the journalistic consensus in her favour. Different depictions had been possible, and Cornish's report made clear that there were some in the Forest unfriendly to Beatrice. Their voices, however, remained local.

Beatrice's public persona also benefited from press attention toward her children, of whom numerous photos were printed. *Thomson's Weekly News* wrote that behind the Pace case 'lies the story of a shattered home and of a plucky girl who acted as "little mother" to her four younger sisters and brothers'.[77] This referred to Dorothy, who explained that before friends and family had stepped in to take care of the children 'plans were being made to remove us to the workhouse'. (The *Daily Mail* had even assured readers that the three remaining animals in the house – Harry's sheepdog Rover and a ewe and a lamb named Blossom and Tinker – were being taken care of by 'a farmer in the district'.[78]) Dorothy emphasised not only the family's poverty – there was often 'scarcely a penny in the house' and frequently the 'larder was empty' – but also her mother's tragic press image, stating that 'tragedy has played a big part in her life' and describing the deaths of five Pace children.[79] 'Mother never complained' during the inquest, asserted Dorothy, 'Her sick baby came before everything else.'[80]

Dorothy's younger sister Doris attracted particular attention. The *World's Pictorial News* described her as a 'pretty eleven-year-old girlie' who, at the inquest, had 'so won the hearts of all present that the jurymen gave her a bag of sweets'.[81] After Doris was reported to have sent money to her imprisoned mother that she had been saving up to buy a doll, strangers began sending her replacements: 'They came from all parts of the country, and range from tiny, plainly-dressed dolls, obviously sent by poor people, to large, handsome dolls, beautifully dressed, with eyes that open and shut.'[82] Doris and her dolls became a press fixation. The *Sunday Express* carried a very similar story on its front page the same day; two weeks later, another front-page article dubbing Doris 'the most tragic child in England' included a photograph of her pushing a doll in a stroller and reprinted a letter to her mother.[83] The *Daily Mail* described her room as 'like a well-stocked toyshop'.[84] *The People* even published an article 'by' Doris – whether cobbled together from conversations with a reporter or fully invented is unclear – with a heading in what was alleged to be her own handwriting.[85] Beatrice was described as particularly close to Doris, and *Thomson's Weekly News* highlighted the 'poignant little scene' every morning and evening during the magistrates' court hearings, as Beatrice was driven to and from Coleford from prison in Cardiff: 'Doris always contrived to get a place in front of the crowd lining the streets, and immediately the prison car came in sight commenced to wave vigorously and blow kisses to her mother, who responded with fervour.'[86] Doris's place in 'the crowd' brings us to the important role played by the broader reading public.

Growing support

What effect did the press coverage have? The large, supportive crowds outside the magistrates' court were one result. Rose Cottage itself became a tourist destination. Though 'locked up and deserted' it was visited by 'an extraordinary number of morbidly minded people': 'many photographs were taken and mementoes (such meaningless trifles as a forget-me-not or a chip of wood) were carried away'.[87] It was reported that 'charabancs [were] making detours from their ordinary trips to allow their passengers to see the place, whilst cars in scores make special journeys, their occupants taking cameras in order to take snap-shots of this little homestead, the picturesque surroundings of which seem so far removed from tragedy'.[88] There were precedents for this sort of behaviour. Crowds, for instance, had gathered outside Edith Thompson's home after her execution and some people made off with souvenirs, even 'stealing leaves from her privet hedge'.[89] But given the isolation of the cottage, its role as a magnet for sightseers and souvenir-seekers is all the more remarkable.

There are other signs of the popular response to the case. Dorothy referred to the arrival of 'hundreds' of letters since January, whereas before her father's death, a letter was 'something of an event'.[90] During the inquest, there were as many as twenty a day, along with parcels containing gifts or small amounts of money.[91] In O'Donnell's words, Beatrice 'was the recipient of shoals of letters from people in all classes of society, sympathising with her': 'There were letters from the occupants of lowly cottages and members of exclusive West End clubs. Each time I went to see her she would bring forth sheaves of these letters to show me.'[92] In April, it was reported that 'numbers of people' moved by the family's troubles had 'sent Mrs. Pace postal orders, and she has received several offers of assistance'.[93] Someone had even sent her dog Rover seventy-five pounds of dog biscuits. In addition, at least six marriage proposals arrived during the inquest 'from places as far apart as Dundee, Didcot, Peterborough and Ireland'. 'Some people have strange ways of expressing their sympathies', Dorothy observed: 'Naturally', she explained, 'mother did not reply to any of these letters.' Dorothy received her own proposal from a man in Detroit, Michigan. 'My answer to that letter', she said, 'is that I am only eighteen, and that, although my mother was a year younger when she married, I have no intention of following her example.'[94]

Public support took a more tangible form after a legal defence fund was set up by A. A. Purcell, MP (Labour) for the Forest of Dean. Physically imposing and a combative speaker, Albert Arthur ('Alf') Purcell had held a variety of positions in the trade union movement and had been affiliated with versions of socialism rather to the left of mainstream Labour politics, even participating in the founding congress of the British Communist Party.[95] Although he soon left it, he remained associated with the cause of Soviet Russia (which he visited twice in the early 1920s). He had sat for the Forest of Dean since 1925, having earlier sat briefly for Coventry. He took an avid and personal interest in the Pace case, attending the magistrates' hearing and visiting Beatrice twice in prison.[96] Before both prison visits, he had, as was required, sought permission. The Home Office had qualms: 'Mr. Purcell is a Communist', wrote a senior official, but, gesturing toward Beatrice's popularity, he concluded: 'I doubt the expediency of giving any M. P. any grievance *in this case*.'[97] The visits were approved on condition that they not be publicised.[98]

As Purcell told a reporter 'the plight of Mrs. Pace and her children had moved him very deeply': her case was one 'calling for support'. Noting that Beatrice's brothers had exhausted their own limited resources, he asserted that she should 'have the means at her disposal of securing counsel equal to the man engaged for the prosecution'. This would be a 'matter of several hundred pounds at least'. Although a 'poor man', he continued, he 'would be glad to contribute £10 10s', asking for further donations to be sent to him at the House of Commons.[99] Any money remaining would go to supporting the family, particularly the children.[100] Purcell urged people to send what they could. The fund grew quickly. By the end of May, about £80 had been collected.[101] This had increased to £190 by 3 June, and five days later that sum had risen to £700.[102] On 10 June, the total was £950.[103] The donations varied widely:

> Mr. Purcell says that many sums of £5 and £10 have been received and promised, while there are others of one shilling and two shillings and even stamps have been sent. The contributions come from old-age pensioners, unemployed men, widows, farmers' wives, a Covent Garden porter, and working girls.[104]

'Rich men subscribed their guineas, poor women their shillings, and children their coppers', the *Sunday News* reported: 'The great heart of humanity throbbed into action on the impulse of this wretched woman's plight.'[105] The donations provided further opportunities for the press to highlight poignant aspects of the case:

A contribution was sent by six Dutch working girls in Amsterdam, who, in a little note in broken English, said they had heard of Mrs Pace's case through a wireless message, and wanted to help her. A nine-year-old boy in Cardiff sent 1s. in penny stamps. With his subscription was a note in big, bold schoolboy writing, in which he said: 'I am sending you twelve penny stamps for Mrs Pace. I got this money for running an errand for the lady next door.'[106]

The rapid rise in the defence fund between 3 and 8 June, however, was largely down to a single cheque, the background to which takes us far from the Forest of Dean.

The money, £500, had been received via the *Daily Mail* from Barbu Jonescu, a Romanian businessman and associate of Prince Carol of Romania. In 1927, the prince had renounced his country's throne in favour of his six-year-old son.[107] Accompanied by much press interest (the prince was regarded as something of a glamorous playboy), he came to Britain in the spring of 1928, residing at Jonescu's mansion in rural Surrey. Claiming to have come for unobjectionable reasons – 'I want to play cricket and to see it played, and I also want to stock myself with English clothes'[108] – he soon fell afoul of the government amid accusations of intrigues aimed at regaining his throne. In early May, coinciding with a large demonstration of Transylvanian peasants, two airplanes reportedly chartered by the prince had been waiting to take off from Croydon carrying 120,000 manifestos announcing his return to power when they were stopped by police.[109] The manifestos were seized by Scotland Yard, and on 8 May police told the prince he must 'depart immediately'.[110] Jonescu insisted that 'these things had been done without [the prince's] knowledge', but Carol decamped to Belgium, followed by Jonescu.[111]

On 4 June, the *Daily Mail* received Jonescu's £500 cheque from Brussels. In a letter, he said he had read in the paper that 'a certain M. P. – I forget the name for the moment' was raising a fund and he felt compelled to act: 'As this unfortunate lady has been under a terrible ordeal for months past owing to the long-drawn-out proceedings of the inquest', he wrote, 'I am enclosing my cheque … in order that she will be represented worthily at the trial.' Interviewed in Brussels, he said he had done no more for Mrs Pace than he would have 'for any other poor person in a similar position'. His answer as to why he had sent the cheque to the *Mail* had more than a touch of intrigue. 'Other newspapers', he said, 'would accuse me of propaganda or of having some sinister purpose': 'So unscrupulous are my enemies that I receive through the post documents, letters, and replies to letters I have never written which, if they fell into strange hands, would lead to the inevitable conclusion that I am engaged in conspiracy.'[112] Purcell found the cheque 'magnificent' but emphasised that a total of at least £1,000 was needed. By the trial, he had gathered some £1,250 but still appealed for more.[113]

All things considered, Beatrice was in an ambiguous position on the eve of her trial. She not only faced a capital charge but, since Harry's death, had endured grinding poverty, hostile gossip, a police investigation, an extended coroner's inquest and weeks in prison. Three legal proceedings (the inquest, magistrates' court and grand jury) suggested she had committed a cruel, premeditated killing. Even with a largely circumstantial case, the prosecution appeared confident. On the other hand, she had attracted competent and influential supporters. Journalists were writing sympathetic stories about her, and her solicitor and his colleagues were chipping away at the Crown's case. Her MP's efforts ensured she would be capably defended in court. Finally, she was the beneficiary of a striking degree of public support, one that adverse legal decisions did nothing to diminish. 'Mrs Pace' had powerful forces arrayed against her; nevertheless, by the time she faced her final trial, she was far from alone. Indeed, it would seem she had a nation behind her.

5

'Every wife in the country has opportunity': the 'tragic widow' on trial

Within a few days of the committal proceedings, Purcell announced he was 'in touch with a first-class KC' (i.e., 'King's Counsel').[1] It was then declared that, alongside the continuing efforts of Wellington's firm and of Dr Earengey (assisted at the trial by his wife Florence, who was also a barrister), the defence would be led by Norman Birkett, one of the brightest rising stars in the British legal profession.[2] Birkett – described as 'lanky' and with 'untidy red hair, angular features and spectacles' – was forty-four when he agreed to defend the 'tragic widow'.[3] The son of a prosperous draper in Ulverston, Lancashire, Birkett had left school at fifteen to work in his father's shop. Six years later, having frequently preached at local Methodist churches, he began studying for the ministry. His mentor recognised his intellect and suggested he attend Cambridge. Birkett read history and theology at Emmanuel College, where, however, his interests shifted toward law. (In a letter to his disappointed father, Birkett explained that he might 'find the ministry rather cramping'.[4]) Called to the bar in 1913, he practiced in Birmingham before moving to London in 1920 to enter the chambers of renowned barrister Edward Marshall Hall. Only four years later Birkett 'took silk', joining the elite rank of barristers known as 'King's' (or, when appropriate, 'Queen's') Counsel. He also represented Nottingham East as a Liberal in the Parliament of 1923–24.

As a teenager, Birkett had reportedly told a family friend, 'I'm going to help women who are alone in the world. There are so many who are alone.'[5] Indeed, in his 'maiden speech' to the House of Commons he supported a backbench Labour proposal to give state pensions to widows with children. He backed it, as he put it, 'with all my heart': 'A widow is left, and she has to shift and fend for herself, to go out to work, or, to use a common phrase, "to manage somehow". In such a case the children have no father or mother at all.'[6] Birkett went beyond the Labour motion, arguing consideration should also be given to unmarried mothers as well as deserted – and even divorced – wives. Such sympathies may have contributed to him agreeing to take on the Pace case (as a biographer put it) for the 'most reasonable fee which he could in the circumstances, namely 100 guineas in addition to the "special" fee of 100 guineas on the brief, with no "refreshers"'.[7] ('Refreshers' were daily fees in addition to the charge for accepting the 'brief'.)

Despite an unimposing appearance, Birkett reportedly possessed a 'golden voice'.[8] It had 'a sort of Northern "burr" in it', observed the *World's Pictorial News*, which he used 'very effectively, either in opening or closing speeches'.[9] His eloquence had served him well as a youthful preacher and marked him out during his Cambridge years. Combined with his willingness to work on his cases 'often to the point of nervous exhaustion', it had also become one of the keys to his success as a barrister.[10] His specialty was cross-examination. Although 'slow and deliberate', there were moments when he addressed the jury in which 'the flood-tide of his eloquence overflows, and his face becomes alive with the earnestness of a zealot pleading his case'.[11] Beatrice was fortunate to have a man of Birkett's skill on her side.

A long-awaited trial

After weeks of growing suspense, the trial of *Rex* v. *Beatrice Annie Pace* began on 2 July 1928 at the Shire Hall in Gloucester. The twelve jurors (ten men and two women) had been chosen from parts of Gloucestershire outside the Forest of Dean.[12] As the *Manchester Guardian* reported, 'so keen is public interest in the trial that the principal hotels in Gloucester have been booked up'.[13] Thus, the jury members were lodged in a Diocesan Church House where, it was noted, they would be 'under constant supervision'.[14] Mr Justice Horridge was provided with a 'special guard': 'Mounted police', the *Daily Express* explained,

> under a superintendent who was formerly in the cavalry, will ride as
> escort to the judge's carriage when he drives to and from the Shire

Hall. Plain clothes police will watch the judge's lodgings, and an extra staff of sixty of the county constabulary have been drafted into the city for duty to control the crowds on the streets.[15]

Lady Horridge took an avid interest in the case and sat to her husband's left on each day of the trial.[16]

Like Birkett, Sir Thomas Gardner Horridge was both a Lancashire native (born in Bolton) and a former Liberal MP (for East Manchester). As a lawyer, he had been primarily concerned with commercial issues, and, in 1910, he was appointed to the King's Bench Division. He was seen as 'sound, competent, dignified, and expeditious', though also 'somewhat brusque' in his dealings with counsel and witnesses.[17] The *World's Pictorial News* described him as having a 'deep, resonant voice, not ponderous in any way, but rather musical'. 'Whilst he is listening to the evidence', it noted, 'he sometimes has a peculiar habit of wrinkling up his face so that it looks very much as though he is smiling.'[18]

Birkett had pleaded before Horridge several times. In what was popularly known as the 'Green Bicycle Case', tried at Leicester in 1920, Birkett appeared for the Crown in the prosecution of a schoolmaster charged with the fatal shooting of a young woman in a country lane. Witnesses had seen her in the company of a man with a green bicycle (later found in a nearby canal) that belonged to the defendant; however, the prosecution was unable to directly prove his guilt or suggest a motive, and the case remains officially unsolved.[19] On another occasion, Birkett appeared in Horridge's court to defend a man charged with forgery. At a time when most judges required defendants to stand throughout the proceedings, Birkett believed that – except for pleading or hearing the verdict – they should be allowed to sit. During the long trial, Birkett asked whether his client might take his seat:

> 'Why?' inquired his Lordship sharply.
> 'I think the prisoner is under some strain', Birkett replied.
> 'Not unless there is some special reason', the judge rejoined. 'We are getting really too delicate in our habits towards people who are being tried.'[20]

If nothing else, the exchange puts into perspective the observation, made on the eve of Beatrice's trial, that Horridge was 'one of the most humane judges on the Bench'.[21] He was not entirely inflexible, however, and was later convinced on the same point by one of Birkett's colleagues.[22]

The prosecution was led by Sir Frank Boyd Merriman, KC, the Solicitor-General. Merriman, forty-eight, was Conservative MP for Rusholme, Manchester. He was 'a slightly built man with rather impassive features', the *World's Pictorial News* observed, who 'never gets in the least bit flustered': 'He is undemonstrative in his methods, and there are none of the fine gestures or eloquent rhetoric which serve many counsel so well. He appeals rather to the logical side of his hearers.'[23] He was assisted by St John Micklethwait, KC, and H. M. Giveen, a junior counsel for the Treasury. (Micklethwait had participated in the prosecution of Major Armstrong, who, the *Daily Express* reminded its readers, 'was executed at Gloucester Prison for the murder of his wife by poisoning'.[24])

The press predicted a 'wonderful legal battle' – even a 'battle of legal giants' – between Merriman and Birkett.[25] They had been on opposing sides before, notably in a high-profile case the preceding year arising from a collection of essays in which it had been claimed that former Prime Minister William Ewart Gladstone (who had died in 1898) had been a hypocrite and womaniser. Two of Gladstone's sons (themselves of advanced age) had publicly questioned the author's character and honesty; he, in turn, sued them for libel and was represented by Merriman. But Birkett so successfully defended the sons of the 'Grand Old Man' of nineteenth-century liberalism that the jury not only decided in their favour and awarded them costs but also asserted that 'the evidence that has been placed before them has completely vindicated the high moral character of the late Mr W. E. Gladstone'.[26] Alongside the many pre-existing connections among the prosecution, defence and bench, added drama was provided by the 'record number of famous medical men' called as witnesses. As at the inquest and committal proceeding, Sir William Willcox – described as 'the foremost authority on poisons in the world' – and Professor Isaac Walker Hall appeared for the prosecution. Dr Robert Bronte ('the eminent pathologist') was the defence's forensic expert.[27] (Famous Home Office pathologist Sir Bernard Spilsbury was named in the press as a prosecution witness, but, while he may have attended the trial, he was not called.[28])

The trial was a sensation. One of Birkett's later biographers was a young reporter in Cardiff at the time, and he later commented on 'the anguished apprehension in everyone's mind'. 'Day after day', he recalled with some exaggeration, 'the newspapers were full of little else' but the case.[29] Not only curious strangers flocked to Gloucester but also 'villagers who have known the Pace family for many years'.[30] As the trial opened on Monday, 2 July, the *Liverpool Echo* reported, 'what seemed to be the whole population of the little village of Fetter Hill today journeyed by motor omnibuses' to view the trial.[31] 'What all these people hope to do or see', remarked the *Daily Express*, 'is doubtful. The public space in the court is small, and only those who have privilege tickets will be admitted to the other part.'[32] Fewer than one hundred public spaces were available.[33] The police struggled to keep order as long queues – one each for women and men – formed on the first morning of the trial at seven o'clock.[34] The court had been 'inundated' with applications for places in the public gallery, and among the successful applicants were 'novelists and dramatists', some of whom were 'well-known' (though, sadly, unnamed).[35] Despite sporadically poor weather on the first day, crowds of as many as 2,000 people gathered, the majority of whom were women.[36] A *Daily Mail* reporter stated: 'Never have I seen so many women at a murder trial.'[37] On the second day, the crowds returned by bus and 'obtained the foremost places in the separate queues of men and women outside the Shire Hall'.[38] ('Among the crowd that surged about the hall', it was noted, 'were a number of American women tourists, who, having read of the case, halted in their motoring tour of the West Country to take part in the women's demonstration.'[39])

The *Liverpool Echo* thought the courtroom reminiscent of 'a chapel of the Puritanical days': 'Semi-circular in shape, the well of the court is fitted with high-backed oak pews, while the floor is of stone. In addition to the pews there are low forms, on which people sat with strained backs.'[40] Beatrice sat toward the front of the court in the dock, accessed via a winding stairwell leading up from below. During the trial, *The People* described her as 'a pathetic figure in black, plucking nervously at the flesh beneath her rounded chin, while her feet tattoo incessantly upon the wooded floor of the dock – tap – tap – tap': 'Eerie', the reporter observed: 'compelling'.[41] She was flanked by a 'silk-stockinged wardress and a blue-clad nurse', and, when not in court, was held in Gloucester

6 The scene in front of the Gloucester Shire Hall at the opening of
Beatrice Pace's murder trial.

(©The British Library Board, *Daily Sketch*, 3 July 1928, p. 1)

Prison. Although the prison did not normally accommodate
women, special arrangements had been made to avoid the necessity
of a daily journey to and from Birmingham.[42] She was kept in a
detached part of the prison 'under the care of a female officer' and
travelled to the Shire Hall each day by car, a distance of only some
300 yards.[43] Her arrivals and departures were eagerly anticipated
events for those outside the court, who cheered or jeered various
figures in the case as they came and went. The *Liverpool Echo*
described the scene as people collected to await Beatrice's arrival:
'The appearance of her taxi, preceded by mounted policemen was
the signal for a great outburst of shouting. People [were] waving
their hands and showering remarks on the tragic widow as she
drove into the small courtyard.'[44]

Three Pace children – Dorothy, Doris and Leslie – also attended.
Doris, the papers noted, always carried one of her many dolls,
and her arrival 'invariably evokes sympathetic comments from
the women there'.[45] But even well-meaning enthusiasm could
turn frightening. Crowds 'besieged' the children at the local

hotel where adult minders took them for meals, calling out their names and cheering wildly when they appeared in the entrance 'to satisfy their curiosity'.[46] As the first day's proceedings adjourned, 'crowds of women' followed 'a little party of Coleford people' – including the children – to a nearby hotel where they went for tea. 'Women climbed to the windows of the hotel and forced the door. Nothing would satisfy them until Mr. Smiley, the landlord, appeared, holding Doris Pace with one hand and Leslie Pace with the other.'[47] Their emergence, however, did not calm matters: 'The crowd cheered uproariously. "Where's the doll?" they called to Doris, and the little girl had to hold up the toy that had been given to her by a sympathiser.' The children were taken inside, but the crowd blocked the street, and some admirers pressed into the hotel. The police finally appealed to 'keep the girl out of sight as much as possible and to get her away quickly'.[48] Then, they sought to restore order: 'The mounted police had to ride the crowd back before it was possible to bring Mrs. Pace's children out to the motor-omnibus which was waiting to take them back to Coleford. Even then, women followed the omnibus in an attempt to get a sight of them.'[49] Beatrice was sometimes brought in and out of the court via a back entrance so as to avoid the thousands who waited to see her, but such ruses were not always effective.

On Tuesday, the 'extraordinary demonstrations of women sympathisers' continued, and 'sentiment ran riot' when Beatrice left the court to be greeted by 'many thousands': 'There was a solid jam of people, mainly women, on each side of the roadway.'[50] The *Manchester Guardian* estimated that nearly 3,000 people thronged the narrow streets. 'A contingent of fifty police', it reported, 'standing two deep, made a solid wall, thus preventing the crowd from mobbing the car.'[51] The *Daily Express* described the scenes along the route from the court to the prison: 'Every window held its spectators. Men climbed trees and telegraph poles, and others were on the roofs of houses, and indeed at any vantage point from which the motor-car could be seen in which Mrs. Pace was sitting.'[52] When Elton and Leonard Pace, accompanied by their sister Leah, left the court to return to Coleford, a different sort of demonstration began. 'A number of women raced after them', the *Daily Express* reported: 'There were booes [sic] and hoots.'[53] There were also threats: 'Amidst shouts of

"Kill him", "Lynch him", a woman who tried to strike Pace in the face was knocked down by a policeman's horse.'[54] Elton remained unperturbed by the 'menacing crowd': 'An unforgettable picture – Elton Pace swinging sturdily along upon his stick, chewing doggedly upon his gum, pausing to raise his hat ironically to the angry mob, waving away the protecting police and later standing upon the steps of the Coleford bus to bow to the jeerers.'[55] The police responded: 'The mounted police rode forward to keep the people away from the witnesses, and a number of foot constables doubled up to form an escort around them.'[56] The next day, Harry's kin were brought out by a side door to a waiting car without the crowd noticing.[57]

Despite the presence of 'scores' of constables, maintaining access to the court was a challenge.[58] On Wednesday 4 July, matters seem to have come to a head: 'There was a demonstration against the police, whose task was one of great difficulty. The superintendent of the mounted police, in trying to clear the pavements, was almost thrown from his horse, and even the tactful efforts of the constables on foot aroused much resentment.'[59] There was another 'wild demonstration' when Beatrice left the court:

> Mounted police, riding into the thick of the crowd, forced hundreds of excited people out of the street behind the Shire Hall before Mrs. Pace's car drove out. The throng was pressed back, inch by inch, until they were massed at each end of the street. When the car came out, headed by mounted police, the crowd burst the police cordon, and surged forward, cheering wildly. From the windows of the houses fluttered handkerchiefs.[60]

A smiling Beatrice reportedly 'bowed to the crowd as she sat between her two wardresses and waved her hand'. The police were so alarmed at the temper of the crowd that 'a police guard' had been assigned to protect Elton Pace, and Doris's guardian was ordered to keep her 'in the background'.[61] By ten o'clock Friday morning, 'the crowd waiting to watch the arrival of Mr. Justice Horridge was far bigger than on any other day since the trial began':

> Once more, Mrs. Pace was loudly cheered by sympathisers during the journey from the gaol to the Shire Hall. In contrast was the reception given to the brothers and relatives of the dead man. As they drove up in a closed motor-car the crowd began hooting, and

continued their jeers until these members of the Pace family had disappeared into the hall. [62]

It might have been a small comfort to the Pace family had they known that Friday would be the last day on which they would have to run the hostile gauntlet.

The prosecution's case

Unaffected by the chaotic atmosphere outside, the trial proceeded in typically decorous fashion. The room was silenced on 2 July as Horridge – wearing a red robe and traditional wig – entered the court and bowed before taking his seat.[63] Flanked by two wardresses, Beatrice was composed as she entered the dock. But when the charge was read to the jury and the words 'wilful murder' were spoken, she 'gave a little gasping sob, and smothered her face in her two hands'. [64] After she pleaded 'not guilty', the first substantive part of the trial was a summary of the prosecution's case, delivered by Merriman. Despite a few shifts in emphasis, the prosecution's approach remained the same, though Merriman admitted that the case against Beatrice was circumstantial.[65] As it had previously done, the Crown argued that Harry had ingested a large quantity of arsenic administered in at least three doses over the few weeks prior to his demise, and it claimed he would have been too paralysed and weak to have poisoned himself. While the sheep dip packets were the likeliest source of arsenic, the absence of sulphur in Harry's body suggested someone had drawn the arsenic off to remove it. Addressing the jury, Merriman sought to make the suicide option sound as flimsy as possible:

> [I]f you are satisfied that arsenic was administered in such a form that there was no sulphur with it, and you are satisfied that that man was not in a position, at any rate during those 48 hours before death, to get rid of the sulphur himself, there is an end of the theory of suicide.[66]

If the separation of the sulphur, the timing of the doses and Harry's allegedly helpless condition made suicide implausible, it followed that – in the absence of other likely suspects with access to Harry – his wife had poisoned him: by her own account, she alone had prepared Harry's food.

For the first time, the prosecution directly discussed the issue of motive. Beatrice's claims of abuse had been aired at the inquest and committal proceeding. Merriman now observed that these had given her plenty of reason to wish Harry dead. 'At times when a husband should be more attentive than usual', he said, referring to Beatrice's many pregnancies, he had treated her 'with great brutality, and on more than one occasion had threatened real violence'. Testimony would also suggest, he claimed, that she had expressed the wish to do him in on more than one occasion. 'It may be', Merriman admitted, 'that these were mere words of bravado uttered under provocation of some incident of brutality, but it cannot be entirely overlooked that she has used such words.'[67] Beatrice's victimisation – whatever public sympathy it brought her – was now turned against her.

Perhaps in an effort to emphasise the scrupulousness of the Crown's treatment of the defendant, Merriman did not fully close the door on alternative arguments, not least since in poison cases, 'you cannot overlook the possibility that it may have been self-administered': 'Here it is not merely a possibility which has to be negatived, there is a suggestion plainly made by the prisoner in a statement which will be read in due course that her husband poisoned himself.'[68] However, here too, Merriman sought an advantage. 'The real significance attaching to these suggestions [of suicide]', he claimed, 'lies in the anxiety of Mrs. Pace to put them forward.'[69] The testimony of Harry's kinfolk would contradict her popular image as a doting wife. There had been 'curious' incidents, such as the glass of water which tasted 'salty and nasty': 'It answered', Merriman emphasised, 'to the description of the fluid which could be extracted from sheep dip if the sulphur were allowed to settle and the liquid drained off.'[70] Merriman alleged that neither of the two packets of sheep dip Beatrice bought had been used in July 1927. Only one had been found, and he dismissed Beatrice's suggestion that any remaining sheep dip had been burned. As he saw it, the claim of suicide was nothing more than an attempt to cover up a cold-blooded murder.

Defence by cross-examination

Despite the new emphasis on motive, the most striking element of the trial was not the reiteration of the prosecution's case but rather the defence's response. Birkett's strategy centred on a searching cross-examination, under the pressure of which – gradually but relentlessly – the framework of the Crown's arguments would buckle. One of the first witnesses called was young Leslie Pace, who testified to the sheep dipping in July 1927. Describing the procedure and agreeing that his father was, as the *Liverpool Echo* put it, 'fairly well wetted with the liquid', Leslie also noted that some of the sheep dip had been left over; his father had 'screwed it up in a piece of paper' and placed it in the 'sheep box' kept in the kitchen. He then repeated his earlier claim that, around Christmas, he had brought the box to his father's room. Cross-examining, Birkett asked Leslie what Harry had found. 'Something wrapped up in paper', he replied.[71] The possibility that Harry had this 'something' from the sheep box close to hand clearly made the suggestion of suicide more plausible.

Birkett also sought to undermine the testimony of Harry's family. He raised doubts about Harry's mother's statements regarding how often she had seen her son or Beatrice's unwillingness to leave visitors alone with Harry. When Porter claimed she had visited a month before Harry's illness began, Birkett pounced, recalling her statement at the inquest that she 'had hardly been' to Rose Cottage before July 1927 and compelling her to admit that she was not aware that Beatrice had taken Harry to the doctor in 1926 while he was suffering from stomach pains.

> Mr. Birkett (sharply). – You realise the immense importance of being accurate if you can?
> Mrs. Porter. – I am saying the truth.
> Do you say you never saw your son alone? – Not when he was ill.
> When did you see him alone? – I cannot remember.
> Did you ever ask to see him alone? – No, sir.[72]

He also critiqued her lack of assistance during Harry's illness:

> Is it a fact that you, the mother, never rendered one moment's assistance in nursing the son? – No, she did not want me.
> Did you ever stay the night and nurse? – I don't remember.
> She had had a baby, and the baby was sick. That was enough for one woman, was it not? – Of course it was.

What followed was one of the trial's most dramatic moments. Birkett had prepared an uncomfortable surprise. Having picked up a birth certificate from the defence table, he forced Porter to make a 'tight-lipped reluctant admission' that, twenty years previously, she had borne an illegitimate son that she had later given away for adoption.[73] In itself, that was hardly relevant. 'You are trying to hurt me', she said. 'I am most anxious to avoid it', Birkett replied.[74] However, he posed a further, surprising question: 'Do you know if your son is dead?' Porter, visibly distressed, stated she refused to answer any more questions, but the judge told her, 'however painful it might be', she must. Birkett then revealed his purpose. 'Do you not know', he asked, 'that he shot himself while of unsound mind?' Porter professed to know nothing of the inquest into the death of her son – a Grenadier Guardsman – in 1927, saying: 'That is the first I have heard of it.'[75] Facing Birkett's 'terrible whip-like' questions, she 'shrank, her face flushed and paled, her lips set in a straight line, and her eyes glowed resentfully'.[76] The issue was dropped, but Birkett had successfully implied that suicidal despondency might run in the family. He also managed to generate a rare note of sympathy in the press toward one of Harry's family. The *Daily Mail* saw two women 'on the rack' that day: not only Beatrice but also her mother-in-law.

Turning to Harry's brother, Birkett questioned Elton's version of key events and depicted him as a 'bully' with a grudge against Beatrice.[77] Elton was vividly described by *The People* as, 'no ordinary man': 'black-headed, cheeks wind-whipped and red, his door-like shoulders placed firmly against the wall of the crescent court'.

> His close-knit hair shows jet black against the vivid red of the square wall column that supports him. A carelessly knotted tie blows down over crumpled white shirt, belted at the waist.
> The heavy, rounded jaw works incessantly, the strong teeth chewing. For days Elton Pace has chewed [gum] without stop – chew – chew – chew.[78]

He repeated his claims that Beatrice had expressed a wish to kill Harry and behaved suspiciously. Beatrice had even 'tried to get him out' of Rose Cottage on the day before his brother died.[79] During Elton's testimony, 'Mrs. Pace began weeping, and asked for a glass of water which was given her.'[80]

The cross-examination was described as a 'sharp duel', recalling Wellington's own heated exchanges with Harry's brother at the inquest. Elton's voice, 'at times a big-throated bellow, seemed to shake the walls of the building'.[81] Birkett questioned Elton's claim to have been 'on friendly terms' with Beatrice, asking whether she had forbidden him to enter the house some four years ago. 'She told me that very often, sir', Elton replied, asserting, 'We made it up again very often.'[82] Birkett called that a 'deliberate untruth', which Elton denied. However, he admitted being banned from the house at least half a dozen times.[83] He had not visited for about six months prior to Harry's illness, but he testified that Beatrice had frequently said she could poison Harry over the preceding six years. She complained about Harry never going 'out for pleasure' but always 'scrapping' with the sheep. Elton explained to the confused judge that this was a Forest expression meaning 'spending time with' his flock. There was laughter when Birkett said 'you must have got a little tired of that conversation' and further amusement when he asked Elton whether he had informed Harry of Beatrice's threats. 'Certainly not', Elton said, 'He'd have gone down my neck, he would that.' 'He was over-seeing in her', Elton explained. 'What do you mean by over-seeing?' Birkett asked, 'Do you mean something that was not there?' The public gallery's light-hearted reaction brought a sharp rebuke from the judge: 'I won't have this laughter here. If anyone does this again, I will have the court cleared. This is not a laughing matter, and you ought to be ashamed of yourselves for being such idiots as to laugh in a place like this.' Harry 'was devoted to her', Birkett clarified, and Elton agreed: 'he could see no fault in her'. Birkett questioned that evaluation on the basis of Beatrice's assault charge against Harry. 'No it would not look right', Elton admitted, but he insisted: 'I know it is a fact.' He dismissed Beatrice's concern for Harry, on the other hand, as 'play-acting'.[84]

Birkett hammered away at such claims, asserting that they were fiction. Elton, 'at the top of his voice', insisted otherwise. As to Beatrice, he commented 'she can stand more than that': 'she has got a bad reputation around there'.[85] Birkett asked whether he said that 'to injure her while she sits in that dock on her trial for murder'. 'Well, facts are facts', Elton replied. During this exchange there were 'muffled expressions of sympathy' from the women in court and a 'wail' from the defendant: Beatrice began 'sobbing convulsively' and was attended to by a nurse.[86] She soon resumed listening to her brother-in-law, who proudly recounted how he had stopped Harry's funeral. 'I can see now', he concluded, 'that I had good cause for saying what I did.'[87]

Other members of the Pace family were closely questioned by Birkett. Leah Pritchard and Leonard Pace restated key elements of their inquest testimony, with Pritchard complaining about 'unpleasantness' with Beatrice preventing her from seeing her brother. However, prodded by Birkett, she admitted that Beatrice 'gave the impression' of 'trying to do her best' for Harry. Leonard repeated his claim that there had been two full packets of sheep dip in the house in August 1927 when he dipped some sheep for Harry. He had not used the dip from Rose Cottage, so the vital question of what had happened to one full packet remained.[88] However, under cross-examination, Leonard could not recall the shape of the table he had seen the packets on, and he admitted that they might have been empty: the 'missing' packet might never have existed.

Birkett also cross-examined Inspector Bent. Describing his investigations, Bent referred to 'a dark blue bottle' that Beatrice handed Sergeant Hamblin. Later, Bent referred to the 'brown bottle half full and covered with dust' that he had found in searching Rose Cottage on 11 March. This again raised the confusion about them: as noted, Sergeant Hamblin had had difficulty identifying which bottle Beatrice had handed him. The judge intervened:

> Mr. Justice Horridge: Is there any relevance in any of these bottles except No. 7 (the green bottle)?
> Sir F. Boyd Merriman: There is some confusion as to the number of the exhibit.
> Mr. Birkett: I reserve the right to comment on the use which has been made of these bottles hitherto. I shall have a good deal to say in particular about the green bottle. While I am anxious not to prolong this trial, I am not going to give any points away.[89]

Having signalled that the bottles would be an issue when the defence had its turn, Birkett moved on to Bent's taking of Beatrice's first statement at her home on 15 February.[90] The statement was read in court by the clerk, and, once again, when the section describing Harry's 'intimacy with other women' was reached, names were kept secret. Bent agreed that Beatrice had 'been ready and willing' to give him 'every information in her power' and that 'throughout she has been perfectly frank', answering all his questions 'without hesitation'.[91]

Birkett's cross-examination of Chief Inspector Cornish was more combative, and, at points, the Scotland Yard detective's face 'flushed' and 'his fingers plucked at his collar'.[92] After Beatrice's long statement from 11 March was read out, Birkett began by suggesting that – far from making a 'voluntary statement' – Beatrice had been 'cross-examined' and 'interrogated' in an intimidating manner.[93] Cornish, Birkett implied, had pre-judged her as guilty and asked leading questions. The extent to which her statement had been shaped by the detective's queries was important. Police guidelines for taking statements from suspects (the so-called 'Judges' Rules') prohibited 'cross-examination', and Birkett argued that Cornish had overstepped these boundaries.[94] For example, Beatrice had stated, 'I don't think it is possible for any person who has visited him to have given him any poison to take.' Birkett insisted that Cornish had tricked her into making an incriminating comment.

> What you were doing was to eliminate everybody else except Mrs. Pace? – No, I was trying to get from all the others as much as from Mrs. Pace by what means the arsenic got into the body.
> But you said to her, 'Nobody else has been nursing him? Nobody else has prepared his food?' Is not that cross-examination. – No it is examination.
> You had cautioned the woman and then you cross-examined her. – No, sir, I asked her questions.[95]

Birkett observed that Cornish had 'cautioned' Beatrice that her statements might be used against her, something typically done with suspects the police expected to charge. Cornish said this was because of the rumours he had heard. 'From Elton Pace!' Birkett exclaimed, asking 'Did you caution him?': 'No.' Birkett implied that the detectives had been unduly influenced by the Pace family and had pressured Beatrice when she made her statements.[96] He did not directly refer to 'third-degree methods', but – given the heightened concerns about police powers in 1928 discussed in Chapter 8 – perhaps he did not have to. 'You had cautioned her and then for three hours without a break interrogated her?' Birkett asked. 'Yes', agreed Cornish, though he thought 'interrogated' the wrong word. 'I asked her questions', he said, denying any 'unpleasantness'. 'If anyone is unpleasant', Birkett replied, 'I am afraid it is myself. Mrs. Pace is not complaining, but I am trying to do something in this trying, anxious, and terrible time.' One of his concluding questions – 'She tried to do her best to answer all your inquiries?' – elicited a cool response: 'Up to a point.'[97] It may be that Cornish, here, gestured to Beatrice's mysterious 14 March statement which, at trial, was not introduced.

Birkett also followed the press in idealising his client as a caring wife who had done everything possible for her husband while also nursing a sick infant. Regular visitors confirmed Beatrice's devotion and observed that Harry had never complained or expressed any suspicions about her.[98] Du Pré thought Beatrice had been 'a devoted nurse and wife' and had appeared 'to do all she could to get him better'.[99] He also confirmed that Harry's first medical examination in 1927 had been entirely a result of his wife's persuasion, and she had been pleased when he agreed to go into hospital.[100] Birkett emphasised that when Beatrice fetched Du Pré on Boxing Day, she had 'trudged through snow knee-deep all the way to the surgery, a distance of nearly three miles'.[101] 'Higher than her knees', the doctor corrected.[102] He had no doubt that Harry's improvements were due to his wife's care, and he revealed that she had sought to have him re-hospitalised.[103] Birkett moreover, was not above using sentimentality to make his point, such as when Leslie was questioned:

> Mr. Birkett asked him: 'Your dad was very unkind sometimes?' – 'Yes,' the lad replied. 'A long time ago he said he would shoot us with a gun.' – Your mother has always been very kind to him? – Yes. – Do you love your mother? – Yes. – Has she looked after you well? – Yes. – And your brothers and sisters? – Yes.[104]

Birkett also questioned Harry's mental state. Thorne referred to him as being 'hopelessly despondent', and Martin said he thought Harry 'had a very peculiar side to him'.[105] Fellow patient Charles Fletcher said Harry 'did not want to get better' as he 'did not seem to have any hope'.[106] Birkett dismissed the life-insurance issue. The agent who had sold Beatrice the policy admitted that he had tried to get her to increase the amount; however, she had refused, 'as she could not afford it'.[107]

Finally, and crucially, Birkett confronted the forensic evidence provided by Ellis, Walker Hall and Willcox. He had already elicited testimony from Dr Du Pré contradicting the prosecution's claim that Harry would have been too ill to have handled sheep dip himself in the later stages of his illness. Between 27 December and 8 January, Du Pré said, Harry would indeed have been able to move about his room unaided. Birkett asked about the crucial 48-hour period in which a final, large dose of arsenic had been consumed:

> Between your visit on the 8th January and your visit on the 9th, could he have walked about the room unaided? – I had not the means of proving it, because I did not see him do it, but I judge he would have been able to do it.[108]

This contributed to, though it did not prove, the defence's suicide alternative.

Ellis, the county analyst, once again presented his findings about the arsenic found in Harry's organs, described the contents of items found in the Pace home and explained how arsenic could be separated from the sulphur in sheep dip. He cleared up the matter of the bottle Dorothy found in her father's room: the bottle, he said, was blue. It had, furthermore, contained 'butter of antimony' (antimony trichloride, 'an extremely corrosive poison', as Ellis put it) but no arsenic. A *green* bottle found in the 'sheep box' was empty. The only bottle remaining that might be relevant was the 'dust covered' one that 'contained a solution of sheep dip and some sulphur (the greater part of it having been removed), to which had been added potassium permanganate'. As the *Dean Forest Guardian* noted, 'much importance was attached to this bottle' during earlier investigations and at the inquest. Having been challenged by Earengey at the magistrates' court, he provided a 'supplementary report' at trial: the amount of manganese in Harry's body was, in fact, less than normal. The bottle, 'which at one time appeared of vital importance, ceased to be of consequence'.[109] Merriman, certainly aware of what was coming, had noted as much in his opening statement.

However, Birkett suggested that the collapse of that evidence undermined much of Ellis's earlier testimony about how sheep dip could have been processed to create a colourless, arsenic-rich liquid that 'could be added to brandy, or water, or cornflour'. It was only after the inquest jury had seen these suggestive experiments (and after the magistrates' hearing) that Ellis had even looked for traces of manganese in Harry's organs. Ellis agreed that the solution in the 'dust covered bottle' was no longer relevant to the case; however, he reiterated that no sulphur had been found in Harry's body, and that had sheep dip been taken in powdered form (as, it was suggested, a suicide would do) it would have been present. Birkett, having already raised useful doubts, moved on. (It was suggested after the trial that the dust-covered bottle's contents were, in any case, common 'amongst sheep farmers for the killing of maggots in sheep'.[110]) Walker Hall repeated his testimony about the timing of the arsenic doses: Harry had been the victim of 'chronic' and 'prolonged' arsenical poisoning, possibly since 1926.[111]

The final prosecution evidence came from Willcox, who re-summarised the findings of Ellis and Walker Hall. Harry had been suffering from acute arsenic poisoning from 24 July 1927: the acute symptoms lasted for seven to ten days after which, 'as often happened', peripheral neuritis developed.[112] Between 25 December and 10 January his symptoms were 'entirely consistent with acute poisoning by arsenic administered in more than one dose': probably one within a few hours of the onset of illness on Christmas Day, one within forty-eight hours of death and another at some point in between. It was impossible that Harry's later illness (from Christmas to 10 January) could have been caused by unintended exposure to arsenic. Harry, after all, had been almost entirely bedridden. But Birkett raised the possibility that Harry's poisoning in the summer of 1927, and implicitly his occasional symptoms stretching back to 1926, had been the result of accidental absorption of sheep dip solution. Willcox himself, Birkett pointed out, had written a pamphlet warning of the dangers of 'accidental poisoning through arsenical preparations such as sheep dip, and also that the danger existed of suicidal effects'.[113] Willcox stated that a person who did not wash his hands before eating or biting his nails, or who had a cut or sore might ingest some arsenic. In struggling with sheep during dipping, some of the solution might be splashed on clothing or even get into the mouth.[114] He thought it 'inconceivable', however, that so much arsenic had found its way into Harry's body this way. But Birkett had raised the possibility that Harry's *initial* illness had been the result of careless handling of sheep dip. (Du Pré had also agreed that there were 'many ways in which arsenic could get into the human body'.[115]) Beatrice's statement to Bent had claimed that Harry was 'careless' with sheep dip, leaving, for example, the unused solution in the tub after use.[116]

Those inside the courtroom were thus witness to a series of duels in which Birkett sought to raise doubts about the prosecution evidence in preparation for the defence's second stage. The prosecution case had indeed been weakened. The widow's main accusers seemed vindictive, and some of their factual testimony was questioned. Beatrice's role as a caring nurse and a cooperative witness was highlighted. Crucially, Birkett had made it seem plausible that Harry – plagued by painful symptoms resulting from accidental poisoning with sheep dip – had become despondent and suicidal, a possibility reinforced by the revelation of another suicide in the Pace family and Dr Du Pré's claim that Harry would have been physically capable of poisoning himself. Even before the defence presented its own case, then, Birkett had made 'self-administration' seem more plausible. He had not proved that scenario, but, for the defence, making it seem possible was perhaps enough.

A sudden vindication

Following four-and-a-half days of testimony, the prosecution rested its case before the lunchtime adjournment on Friday, 6 July. The 'protracted nature of the proceedings', it was reported, had caused a severe drain on Beatrice's resources: costs were reported to be running at about £220 per day, and Purcell described the defence fund as 'almost exhausted'. It had also taken a toll on the defendant herself, who showed signs of strain when she arrived at the Shire Hall on Friday:

> Mrs. Pace, still wearing the same black dress and hat, displayed distinct signs of weariness, as she walked heavily up the stairs leading to the dock. She appeared languid and did not seem to take her usual interest in the people in court.
> The women friends from Coleford, who have sat near the dock each day, were there again to-day, but Mrs. Pace did not have her usual cheery smile for them.[117]

Elizabeth Porter and Leah Pritchard also sat directly behind her; however, the women exchanged no apparent signs of recognition.

After the court reconvened after lunch at about 2.30 p.m., Birkett rose to open the defence, the overture to what the *Dean Forest Guardian* called a 'dramatic closing scene'.[118] There was, he

said, 'no case' to go before the jury and no evidence of administration of arsenic by the prisoner. Judge Horridge demurred,
suggesting Birkett was exaggerating the weakness of the prosecution's case. Birkett retreated somewhat but insisted 'there is
scarcely a case to go to the jury' before launching a frontal attack
on Merriman's evidence.

> The Solicitor-General in opening the case said he must produce
> evidence to prove that the dead man was poisoned by arsenic
> obtained from sheep dip and administered by the prisoner with
> intent to murder, but a possibility not to be overlooked was that
> the arsenic might be self-administered ... There is no evidence of
> administration of arsenic by the prisoner. None. The fact that there
> is arsenic in the body, the fact of the quantity of arsenic in the
> body, and the effect on the organs – all those matters of science are
> consistent with self-administration. The burden is on the Crown
> and they must prove administration [by Beatrice Pace].[119]

This, he said, they had not done, and he mocked the prosecution's
emphasis on the opportunity she had for poisoning Harry by
preparing his food: 'Every wife in the country has opportunity',
he declared: 'If it is said the prisoner alone prepared the food,
that will not do. There was no one else to prepare the food, and
that kind of argument would lead to this – that every innocent
thing the ordinary person may do becomes some evidence of
guilt.'[120] Since no convincing evidence had been offered, he said,
no defence was necessary: the trial should be ended. Horridge
turned to Merriman. 'I am inclined to agree with Mr. Birkett',
he stated, 'that there is nothing stronger than suspicion in this
case.'[121] Merriman insisted that he had proved much of what he
had outlined in his opening statement. The judge subtly disagreed,
specifically doubting whether there even was a 'missing' packet of
sheep dip and noting Du Pré's view that Harry could have gotten
out of bed during the later stages of his illness.

Merriman must have realised where things were headed.
According to the *Daily Express*, the Solicitor-General 'saw the
current of reasoning in the judge's remarks' and he 'said quite
openly that he was not prepared to press the case'.[122] His own
thoughts remain a mystery, but in any case, a curious exchange
followed:

> Sir Boyd Merriman: What I was going to say was this – I did not

speak lightly when I said, not once, but twice [in the opening argument], that 'suspicion and guesswork will not do'.
The Judge: That is what I feel so strongly in this case.
Sir Boyd Merriman, continuing: It is very difficult in advocating the case to be quite sure that one's views are not coloured to some extent by advocacy. If I understand your Lordship rightly – that you have some doubt as to whether there is more than suspicion, more than guesswork – I have nothing more to say.

The legalistic nods and winks concluded, and Horridge briefly praised the fairness of the investigation and prosecution. He then turned to the jury: 'In my opinion', he said, 'it would not be safe to ask any jury to find a verdict of guilty on the evidence you have heard. I shall advise you to return a verdict of not guilty.'[123] This was a so-called 'directed verdict', which a judge could order when a minimum standard of proof against the defendant had not been satisfied. In short, it implied that no reasonable jury could have convicted the defendant based upon the evidence given.

In the dock, Beatrice remained unmoving, and it seemed to observers that she had little idea what was happening. She later explained that prolonged anxiety had badly affected her hearing and eyesight: she had only been able to follow a portion of the trial and the judge had been simply a 'red blur'.[124] She knew what Birkett had planned, but she also knew that if his gambit failed she would have to testify, something she obviously dreaded. The jury was told to rise, and the foreman was asked the usual questions: 'Are you agreed on your verdict – what is your verdict?' After the briefest of pauses, he responded: 'Not guilty.'[125]

At first, there was silence. Then, the defence's medical expert, Dr Bronte, turned to Beatrice and said, 'You're free.' Birkett followed suit: 'And that's that, Mrs. Pace.'[126] Word quickly spread. One reporter stated, 'In the court we heard the big roar of cheers from outside.'[127] The courtroom remained orderly, but after the judge had bowed to the assembled barristers and retreated 'with almost magical swiftness' through a curtained door, 'the whole decorum of the court went to pieces' as wild cheering burst out.[128] (Several of the jury members were said to have joined in the applause.[129]) A woman raised a cry, 'God Bless Her!' which was soon taken up and repeated 'until it was a thunderous echo in the crescent-shaped court'.[130] Beatrice blew kisses to her friends. Unable to believe what was happening, she sought confirmation from the wardresses guarding her. As the result dawned upon her, she exclaimed 'Thank God it is over!' before retreating to the privacy of the grand jury room. There, she was visited by Birkett and Purcell, whom she thanked profusely. She then immediately asked to see her children. Dorothy, Leslie and Doris came into the grand jury room for 'a happy reunion of tears and smiles'.[131] O'Donnell was approached by a messenger and also asked to join the 'glad party', and he emphasised that he was the 'only Pressman admitted to that reunion party following the dramatic climax of her trial'.[132] After a short time, Beatrice left the Shire Hall, a departure accompanied by the dramatic scenes already described in the Introduction. The legal 'martyrdom' of the 'tragic widow of Coleford' had, it seemed, at long last come to an end. Her story, however, was far from over.

6

'The matter is dead': a new life and some old shadows

Leaving behind the crowds in Gloucester, Beatrice was driven to Coleford and greeted at every village, as 'women and children and men as well came to their garden gates to cheer her passing. Her journey was a triumphal procession.'[1] 'It was a mad, joyous ride', one reporter wrote:

> From cottages at the wayside the men and women folk, and their children, came out to cheer and wave, to cry 'God bless her!' And Mrs. Pace leaned out of the window, and threw kisses back. On through the forest where the sheep farmers left their bleating sheep to cheer, where the quarrymen waved their picks, and flung their hats into the air to prove their joy. We swept through villages where the inhabitants were out to man, woman and boy.[2]

In Coleford, a crowd appeared 'like lightning and stood cheering outside the hotel'.[3] Her friends, 'fearing a breakdown', pressed her into the King's Head Hotel:

> There she ran excitedly from room to room, at times laughing almost hysterically, then burying her face in her hands while the tears that would not be denied trickled between her fingers. She was taken upstairs to a room fronting the main street. She could not stay still a minute. She ran her fingers over the piano keys and played a snatch of something that told of triumph and joy.[4]

The crowd appealed for her to appear at the window, and she did so, waving, blowing kisses and calling down, 'Thank you so much. I am so glad to be home with my babies.'[5] Beatrice was severely exhausted.[6] She relaxed at the hotel with her friends and children, possibly reading the many letters and telegrams that had arrived. There was a celebratory party at the hotel 'till the early hours of the morning'.[7] The upheaval continued the next day. 'Joy', it was reported, 'has run riot in Coleford': 'Housewives have no time for shopping, or for housework, this morning. They stand in groups at their doors discussing the acquittal. They talk of what the widow suffered, and tears run unheeded down their cheeks.'[8]

Birkett was widely praised in the press for his efforts on Beatrice's behalf. The acquittal, the *Daily News* commented, 'adds to the laurels which cluster thickly round the brows of Mr. Norman Birkett, K.C. He is perhaps the greatest legal discovery since the war.'[9] The busy barrister had immediately left Gloucester to deal with other cases. Wellington, of course, remained, and although eclipsed by Birkett during the trial, his months of work were locally admired. The Forest of Dean Miners' Association congratulated him: 'Though your role in the latter stages of the case was over-shadowed by an admittedly great and distinguished legal luminary ... the results of your agile mind could be plainly traced throughout the case. You may be interested to learn that the workpeople in the Forest of Dean speak most highly of your services.'[10] The Transport and General Workers' Union praised his 'splendid achievement on behalf of Mrs. Pace'.[11] Wellington responded that credit was due equally to his staff, adding, 'I do not think that has been sufficiently recognised.'[12] The West Ward Women's Section of the Gloucester Trades Council and Labour Party unanimously resolved that 'hearty congratulations' should be sent for 'the splendid brief prepared by yourself and Staff'. 'The result is a great credit to you', they continued, 'and will ever be remembered by the working-class women and men of Gloucester and the Forest.'[13] A fellow solicitor remarked: 'Gloucestershire is a lovely county, but there are certainly some here who could be well placed elsewhere. Fortunately, however, there are those who are well worthy of their residence therein, and who serve as an excellent antidote to those who do not bring a good reputation to the county.'[14] (Those 'who could be well placed elsewhere' were not named.) Along with such letters of congratulation, Wellington had reportedly also received, the press noted, several that offered 'authentic examples of arsenical poisoning contracted whilst dipping sheep in arsenical preparation'. There had also been an 'extraordinary number of letters from medical men, some of considerable repute, supplying information on many scientific

7 The King's Head Hotel, Coleford. In 1928, it was run by friends
of the Paces. Journalist Bernard O'Donnell regularly had tea with
Beatrice here during the inquest. Doris resided in the hotel while
her mother was in prison awaiting trial. After her acquittal,
Beatrice stayed here for some weeks.

(Courtesy of Barry Martin)

questions, which would have had to be discussed fully had the
case for the defence been heard'.[15]

Fortunately, a few letters from Wellington have survived.
'Everyone in this office', he wrote on 11 July, 'had the strongest
opinion from the early days of the investigation, not merely that
no charge could be established, but that this poor woman was as
innocent as we were ourselves.' He had, however, a nagging regret
about the trial's premature conclusion:

> Perhaps the one disquieting thing is that her defence has never yet
> been heard. We are convinced that the production of numerous
> witnesses and the development of the case foreshadowed by Mr.
> Norman Birkett's cross-examination would have left it impossible

for anybody to suggest that all that had happened was that the Crown had failed to bring home guilt.[16]

He also had a more prosaic concern: getting paid. A few days after the trial, he quipped, 'I find gratitude in clients a very real thing until the bill goes in. The only anxiety I now have is that this case shall not be a mere *success d'estimate* [sic].'[17]

Beatrice began building a new life. She gave notice that she would quit Rose Cottage, telling *The People* that she 'could not possibly live here after what has happened'.[18] Already run-down, the depredations of souvenir-seekers had made the cottage 'quite uninhabitable'.[19] She made a final visit there on the day after her acquittal. Coincidentally, Elton Pace was working in his own quarry nearby when she arrived.[20] 'Mrs. Pace saw him, smiled and nodded', reported the *News of the World*, but he 'showed no sign of recognition'.[21] As *The People* described it: 'Elton rested on his pick and looked stonily at his brother's widow, then resumed his work. Mrs. Pace wiped the tears from her eyes and got back into the car. "Aye, she did a bit of smiling," Pace said, "but I have no smiles for her!"'[22] She set off for a holiday (in Windsor, though other destinations were reported) accompanied by a few friends, among them Alice Sayes.[23] The *Daily Herald* reported that Beatrice was seen off by a crowd gathered at the village crossroads.[24] (The *Sunday Express* later printed a holiday photo.[25]) Rose Cottage was again visited by 'thousands of tourists', many of whom 'held picnic parties under the trees surrounding the farm yard. Many snaps were taken and all manner of things were taken away as curios.'[26]

One vital matter had been handled before Beatrice's departure: the sale of her 'life story'. There are suggestions that the issue had caused tensions. On 26 June, Purcell had gone to the Home Office, seeking permission to visit Beatrice in prison. Her solicitors, he stated, were 'anxious to get her to sign away through them her rights in her life story for £400, the £400 to be applied in payment of their costs in the trial'. Purcell was appalled by the 'monstrous proposition': not only did his friends 'in the newspaper world' think the story would be worth far more, he believed any proceeds should benefit her and the children rather than the solicitors.[27] He thus wanted her to sign over to him the right to negotiate the sale of the story. Purcell's visit was allowed, but not the document he wanted her to sign, which violated rules regarding people on trial for murder.[28] Purcell's confidence in the story's saleability would, however, prove justified, as Bernard O'Donnell later recalled. Wellington invited newspaper representatives to his office on the day after Beatrice's acquittal: the story would go to the highest bidder. Much to his regret, O'Donnell was outbid by the *Sunday Express*, who paid slightly over £3,000 for the story.[29] Although difficult to calculate precisely, the amount would be a substantial six-figure sum today, perhaps somewhat over half-a-million pounds.[30] On 9 July, Wellington wrote to a fellow solicitor that 'arrangements have been made which will, we trust, assure this poor woman's future'.[31] The *Daily Herald* gave Purcell credit for having 'secured a very considerable sum of money' for the widow.[32] As his defence fund reportedly covered nearly all of the legal costs, most (and possibly all) of the money raised by the sale of the life story may have remained in Beatrice's hands. A somewhat updated memoir also appeared in *Peg's Paper*, but any payments related to that are unclear. The money from the *Express* certainly helped Beatrice to rebuild her life and to put the preceding months behind her. (As Beatrice put it, it helped 'to make a fund that will keep me from want as long as I live'.[33]) However, dramatic developments were soon to reawaken the 'Fetter Hill mystery'.

Dark suggestions

On 17 August – a week after the last instalment of Beatrice's *Sunday Express* memoir – the name 'Pace' returned to the headlines.[34] New 'documents' had been sent to Scotland Yard ('in a bulky registered letter' one paper specified), and 'fresh statements' throwing 'a new light on events prior to the death of Harry Pace' were causing the Home Office to give the matter 'earnest consideration'.[35] Reportedly, 'a quarrel among persons concerned in the case' had led to a 'sensational and unexpected sequel to the Coleford poison case'.[36] Some downplayed the events. The *Daily Mail* maintained that 'in official quarters it is considered unlikely that there will be any developments', and the *Daily Chronicle* speculated that 'pique might be at the bottom of the whole affair'.[37] The *Evening News* even said the police 'do not attach much importance to the documents': 'it is known', it explained, 'that there is considerable ill-feeling regarding developments since

Mrs. Pace was acquitted. It is thought that the letters may have been written with an ulterior motive.'[38] (The *News of the World* pointed out that rumours had circulated since the acquittal, but 'while the local police have been cognisant of them they have taken no action'.[39]) What these documents contained and how they were handled can now be explained via the police and Home Office files on the case. But first: what was the perspective of newspaper readers in August and September 1928? Although aware that something sensational was occurring, they were given information that was vague, contradictory and sometimes plainly inaccurate.

A fresh wave of stories soon appeared. On 1 September, the *Daily Express* reported that Sir Archibald Bodkin, the Director of Public Prosecutions, had accompanied Paling and Willcox to the country residence of the Solicitor-General (Sir Boyd Merriman, who appeared for the Crown at Beatrice's trial) in Kington, Herefordshire.[40] There, they discussed 'the advisability of new legal proceedings in the Pace poisoning case'. No concrete information was forthcoming, but Cornish and Campion were said to have been recalled from leave to investigate.[41] (Many of the key figures – Cornish, Campion, Bodkin, Merriman and Inspector Bent – were on holiday as the wave of new stories broke in early September.[42]) Attention focused, the *Sunday Express* reported, on an alleged 'complete diary' concerning Harry's life and 'details of how poison could be administered and the effect of the poison on any person taking food so contaminated'. Beatrice Pace herself 'is, of course, quite removed from this new and most interesting legal development' and had not 'the slightest knowledge of the new phase of the case'. The matter was vexing: 'No problem like this question of the death of Harry Pace has ever confronted the Director of Public Prosecutions. Procedure is exceptionally difficult. Yet the issue involved is so serious that every effort possible will be made to ensure the course of justice.'[43]

The same day, *The People* made a front-page claim to reveal the 'truth' about the 'Pace case sensation': citing an 'unimpeachable source', it insisted there would be no new prosecution. The accusations were 'shown to have been actuated by malice, and were not substantiated by the facts'. The paper quoted Purcell: 'I regard it as most scandalous', he complained, 'that there should be suspicions concerning a person who has been tried by judge and jury and acquitted. It is an attempt to pursue the party concerned.' An effort to reopen the case based on 'suggestions and innuendoes' would be 'a distinct attack on the constitution of our law'. The Forest of Dean Police Superintendent – with, one hopes, deliberate wit – told *The People*, 'the funeral will take place without an inquest'. 'By that', the paper interpreted, 'he meant that the documents, being worthless, will be "buried" and nothing more come of them.'[44] But the *Sunday News* reported that Inspector Bent had gone to Gloucester to receive instructions. Interviewed, he said: 'The whole matter is one of great secrecy and one which it is impossible to make a statement on. The statement that inquiries are about to be made I cannot contradict, but I cannot disclose their nature at this juncture.'[45] Two people were said to be involved, and there were suggestions of 'conspiracy' and 'perjury'.[46] The *Herald* thought arrests were imminent, but the next day *The Times* and the *Telegraph* suggested 'the matter might come to nothing'.[47]

As the story broke in mid-August, Beatrice was still at the King's Head in Coleford. Journalists distanced her from the new developments, perhaps aware that she was again being advised by Wellington's office.[48] She told *Reynolds's Illustrated News* her conscience was clear: 'I am not the first woman against whom the tongues of slander have been directed.' The reporter noted that 'a good deal of the local gossip is declared to have its origin in envy of Mrs. Pace's financial situation':

> In the Forest of Dean, where there is much distress among the unemployed miners and their families, the money raised for Mrs. Pace is regarded in the light of a fortune.
> Despite gossip, there is still a good deal of sympathy for Mrs. Pace and her family.
> 'Poor dear, I wouldn't go through what she has for fifty times the money', said Mrs. Paddock, her staunchest friend, to me today.[49]

By early September, when Coleford was again 'full of the wildest rumours', Beatrice had moved to a 'trim little house' in Gloucester.[50] Purcell told the *Daily Herald* the widow was worried, but he had assured her 'that she had no cause to be troubled, and that the matter was ended as far as she was concerned'.[51]

The matter was far from 'ended' for the press, and the first half of September saw heated speculations about police interviews of local people and high-level meetings among the public prosecutor, Home Office and Metropolitan Police. A so-called 'mystery man' in the Coleford area was described, who 'might have been able to throw considerable light on the latest developments' but who had gone to London to seek work.[52] There was an erroneous story (later corrected) that a woman's 'long statement' and 'sensational story' at Coleford police station had led to the new inquiries; there were also claims that an overheard conversation in the Coleford marketplace had been called to the prosecutor's attention, but there is no evidence that this was true.[53] The *Evening News* suggested on 3 September, 'All kinds of stories about the new Pace development are being told in the Coleford district, but none of them gets near the truth of it.'[54] The *Dean Forest Guardian* complained that the matter had been 'most unproperly commented on very freely by the daily press'. 'Many wildly inaccurate statements have appeared', it admonished, 'one being that the Scotland Yard detectives who had charge of the case were arriving last Saturday. As a matter of fact, Chief Inspector Cornish is actually on a holiday, from which he has not been recalled.'[55] This was, in fact, wrong; moreover, the paper was not above some speculation of its own. While there was 'little probability' of reopening the case, it noted an 'astounding document' ('unprecedented in its character') prepared by 'a well known resident of the district' and given to the police:

> The utmost importance was attached to the contents of the document, and extraordinary measures were taken to test its authenticity and, at the same time, to circumvent the activities of the sensational Press who swarmed once more to Coleford on receipt of the intimation that the Pace case might be re-opened. The resident who prepared the document became, of course, the principal medium through whom the authorities attacked the new situation, and he was on more than one occasion whisked away from his house under cover of night in mysterious high-power motor cars to attend conferences at a distance.

No one was named, but the paper speculated that an offer had been made to publish the document 'at a price beside which the amount paid to Mrs. Pace for her "life story" ... fades into insignificance'. But while it contained an 'apparently unassailable vision of the true circumstances' of Harry's death, the 'legal difficulties confronting action by the Public Prosecutor' were most likely 'insurmountable'.[56]

No such obstacles, of course, stood in the way of a revival of the popular fascination with the case. The *Daily Chronicle* reported that hundreds again visited the Paces' abandoned cottage: 'They came by charabanc, motor-car, motor-cycle and on foot, and lingered for hours in the glorious sunshine around the homestead. The more adventurous entered the garden, picked fruit and twigs off the trees and even thrust their arms through broken windows to tear strips of paper off the walls for souvenirs.' The 'depredations' of the keepsake hunters had taken their toll: 'Holes in the walls of the house show where even bricks, stones and pieces of mortar have been prised out as keepsakes, and the garden bears signs of corresponding treatment.'[57] But in mid-September the stories about the 'new developments' in the case abruptly ceased. At the end of the month, the *World's Pictorial News* explained, vaguely, that the matter had been 'cleared up to the satisfaction of the authorities and everyone concerned'.[58] But what, actually, had been happening behind the scenes?

'This latest development has been extraordinarily interesting'

In late July, three weeks after Beatrice's acquittal, Cornish wrapped up the case by submitting a complete set of reports and statements to be evaluated and sent to the Home Office.[59] But on 11 August he received a letter from George Mountjoy. Mountjoy, the executor of Harry Pace's will, had testified at the inquest and seemed positively disposed toward Beatrice. However, in his letter to Cornish, he claimed he and the other 'Foresters' had thought she was guilty all along. More spectacularly, he claimed Leslie Sayes had been Beatrice's 'confederate' in a four-year plot, 'a horrible and callous affair'. He alleged the widow had promised Sayes half of the money from Harry's life insurance and her own life story: thus, Mountjoy concluded, '1½ thousands are due to them (after some fashion of course)'. But although 'saved from the scaffold' by her friends, Beatrice had offered them a paltry £20. The dispute meant 'the parties have broken up', and the Sayeses had told him the whole story. Mountjoy's interest was clear: 'I am asking newspapers to purchase the account of them through me', he explained, offering them '10 columns' – 'every sentence sworn to' – telling the whole story. 'Now', he declared, 'the crime must be revealed.'[60]

Indeed, Mountjoy had wasted no time. W. K. Bliss, from the *Daily Chronicle*, saw Cornish at Scotland Yard on 14 August with a similar letter.[61] Bliss found the offer intriguing, but he had thought it prudent to contact the police. In his letters to the press, Mountjoy emphasised the Sayeses' closeness to Beatrice: '20 hours out of the 24 were put in with Mrs. Pace', and they had told him their story 'for sale to any newspaper in the country'. Though Leslie Sayes had been an 'accessory before the fact', Mountjoy had been 'given to understand that no law can touch either of them for any crime now'. The story 'would make some of the most startling reading we have had for many years'.[62] Bliss was going to interview Mountjoy and Sayes; Cornish asked to be kept informed. Two other newspapermen got in touch with the detective after being contacted by Mountjoy: one was from the *News of the World*; the other was R. Gittoes-Davies, editor of the Cardiff *Evening Express*.[63]

Mountjoy had sent Gittoes-Davies various documents, copies of which the editor had forwarded to Cornish. He told Cornish that he and a reporter had 'motored over' to see Mountjoy. Informed that the paper 'was not interested in the matter in the absence of signed documents', Mountjoy 'thereupon volunteered to provide a statement' signed by Sayes.[64] Within days, Gittoes-Davies called Cornish again: Mountjoy wanted the documents back. In consultation with Deputy Assistant Commissioner Norman Kendal, Cornish decided the original documents should be kept. Kendal wired Gittoes-Davies and they arrived at Scotland Yard the next day.[65] They included several of Beatrice's prison letters to Alice Sayes, two undated notes signed 'Beattie' and a statement signed by Leslie Sayes.[66]

Bliss later told Cornish that he had spoken to both Mountjoy and Sayes. Mountjoy had not, of course, been able to show Bliss Sayes's original statement. (Though Mountjoy thought it was in Gittoes-Davies's possession, it was, in fact, on its way to Scotland Yard.) Undeterred, Mountjoy presented another statement. Bliss had also met with Sayes himself and enquired whether he was aware of the seriousness of his claims. According to Bliss, Sayes stated 'he did not mind what happened as long as he showed up that "Bitch", meaning Mrs. Pace'.[67] Bliss also had a letter from Mountjoy on the 'easy and reasonable understanding' he sought. Mountjoy expected that he would 'assist as a journalist to write it week by week'. Bliss would 'have power to *add* or *delete* – reasonably of course', and Mountjoy requested that any cheque be made out to him. Concluding, he insisted, 'Your firm to wire best offer [at] very-very earliest hour.'[68] The claims made by Mountjoy and Sayes were indeed sensational, describing not only a sinister, cold-blooded crime but also portraying Beatrice as a sadistic murderess who gleefully deceived police, press and public.

Before considering the plausibility of their claims, we must consider how the police and prosecutor responded. What, for example, could they do? Beatrice had been duly acquitted and could not be re-tried for murder. But there were other options. 'If the story were true', Kendal speculated, 'in theory I suppose one could prosecute Mrs. P. for perjury.'[69] Despite Mountjoy's assertions, Sayes could certainly be charged as an accessory to murder or as a murderer himself.[70] The authorities, however, were cautious. Kendal wrote to Chief Constable Clarke in Gloucestershire to suggest getting an official statement from Mountjoy.[71] Clarke responded that he had tried, but he had 'quite definitely refused to make any statement'.[72] On 20 August, Cornish wrote to Mountjoy with what may have been calculated nonchalance, thanking him for the 'interesting' letter and welcoming any 'fresh information'.[73] Three days later, however, the Home Office Legal Adviser, Sir Ernley Blackwell, told Paling to prepare a new case that could be submitted to Merriman for further instructions.[74]

Mountjoy seems to have been unsettled by events, particularly by Gittoes-Davies sending his original documents to the detectives. He wrote to the journalist to say he had expected the material to be handled confidentially so 'that no other eyes should see, or ears have heard one single syllable of this amazing story'.[75] But he still sought a lucrative deal, claiming (wrongly) that the police 'are dropping their side of it': 'as you were the first to be negotiated with, you will have the opportunity of offering me your highest price for this – the most arresting scoop of recent years'.[76] Mountjoy also wrote to Cornish, expressing surprise at the slowness of his reply and sounding uncertain about Sayes's legal position. How would police react 'if the whole thing was confessed', he asked.[77] Cornish replied that he was not in a position to say.[78] And then he went on holiday.

On 3 September, Arthur Locke, head of the Home Office's Criminal Division, recorded that he had been contacted by Kendal, who was seeking the whereabouts of Leslie Sayes and had asked for a warrant to intercept and inspect letters to Alice Sayes. A secret order, approved by the Home Secretary, was issued to the Post Office, authorising the examination of any correspondence addressed to Sayes and requesting that 'any indication of the address of her husband' be passed on.[79] The order produced a letter from Alice's sister that referred to Leslie having gone to London to seek work. (It remains in the case's file. 'There is people living here from Coleford that know the Pace[s]', she wrote, 'and they don't talk very good about them.')[80] How much this helped the police is uncertain: after all, the departure of Leslie Sayes – who was the newspapers' 'mystery man' – was reported in the press.[81] On 7 September, Kendal informed Locke that the surveillance was no longer necessary.[82] The next day, Locke thought the 'sensation' was 'likely to fizzle out', but he assured that 'as soon as tangible information is available it will be sent forward'. [83]

Cornish and Campion were ordered back from leave. On 4 September, they met Paling at Paddington Station before leaving for Gloucestershire.[84] He impressed on them 'the need for secrecy and the necessity to avoid our movements becoming known to the press'. They met Chief Constable Clarke 'in a secluded spot' near Kemble and arranged to meet Mountjoy at the police station in Tidenham. That evening and the next day, Inspector Bent brought Mountjoy to the station. Cornish found the meetings frustrating. 'Mr. Mountjoy is a very self-willed man of an extremely strange disposition', he wrote. He was reluctant to give the police any details and 'adverse to the Foresters thinking that he has been in any way instrumental in giving information to the police concerning this new development'. Mountjoy was 'undoubtedly of the opinion that Mrs. Pace is a guilty woman'; however, he sought to avoid getting Sayes into trouble, thereby allowing 'Mrs. Pace to go "scot free", and enjoy a fortune in the bargain'. He especially wished to spare Alice Sayes – 'an innocent party' – any difficulty. If the story were sold, however, Leslie, 'having shown up Mrs. Pace and provided for his family, would cheerfully admit his share in the poisoning drama and bring people and evidence to prove beyond doubt the truth of his allegations'. Mountjoy told Cornish things in conversation that he 'refused emphatically' to include in his official statement: 'he said he would say no more if they were written down even'. One was that Beatrice had told him some years ago that 'she wished her husband would get poisoned'; the other was that Sayes had 'led him to believe that he had actually assisted Mrs. Pace by mixing and administering the poison'. But if forced to testify, he would only admit to the information in the statement itself, 'and he is not disposed to assist in any way further'. Cornish tried to convince him otherwise but Mountjoy, he wrote, 'has that dogmatic temperament so often met with with the Foresters and my attempts were futile'. He had at least gotten him 'to promise that he would not influence Sayes to repudiate his statements if they were true'.[85]

The detectives returned to London and questioned Sayes. The East Ham Labour Exchange had informed the prosecutor's office where he could be found, and, on 7 September, a constable was sent to collect Sayes from his address in Manor Park. Cornish and Campion met him at the East Ham police station. It was, of course, not their first encounter: during the inquest, rumours of an affair between Leslie and Beatrice had been investigated. Cornish had then observed that Sayes was seen as 'a poor man' and recently unemployed. His problems had continued: Sayes told a journalist in August that he had been out of work a long time and suggested he hoped to find work 'at one of the big London docks'.[86] Cornish had earlier concluded that Sayes was 'regarded in the vicinity as a somewhat dangerous man, in as much as he is a political agitator, and is frequently to be found addressing very large meetings of the miners of the locality in an extreme manner'.[87] He had also discovered that Sayes had bought a lot of poisons, though he had denied that when first asked. Cornish questioned him, but none of the poisons contained arsenic, and Sayes had convincingly argued that he was not aware that they were poisonous. In London, Sayes was reluctant to speak. He was presented with the two statements Mountjoy had claimed he had signed and asked if he had 'any observation' to make. The 'intention', Sayes explained, had been 'to send them to the Press to try and make some money, but eventually I have not', saying 'I can write what I like, can't I?' The signatures were his, but he pointed to one document and said 'I did not see that written.' He refused 'to make any statement of any description about them' or to 'verify whether it is the truth or lies'.[88] The police let him go.

Cornish's superiors were beginning to doubt the case was going anywhere. Neither Mountjoy nor Sayes had offered any evidence for their claims or even indicated what proof might be forthcoming. Any new prosecution would be fruitless, and a false move could prove embarrassing (and costly). At least some in the police and the prosecutor's office seem to have thought the whole matter was simply an attempt to cash in on the Pace case's notoriety. As Kendal wrote in a memo on 14 September:

> This latest development has been extraordinarily interesting. The difficulties in the way of taking any action against anybody are obviously very great, but it is very annoying if Mountjoy and Sayes are to escape and it looks as if they will escape.
> Nobody can expect Mrs. Pace to be anxious to give evidence in a libel case. By far the most attractive end to this story would be for Sayes to be in the Dock and Mountjoy in the witness box, but I am afraid that the Attorney General will think it too thin.[89]

The head of the CID, Sir B. E. Wyndham Childs, replied, 'I do not think we shall get any further.' Metropolitan Police Commissioner Sir William Horwood agreed: 'Nor do I', he wrote: 'The matter is dead.'[90]

Shortly before, Mountjoy had asked Cornish whether the case had been 'officially dropped': 'If not,' he wrote, 'I have some damning evidence to produce, outside that of Sayes, I think.'[91] Upon return from his (interrupted) holidays five days later, Cornish asked for details, avoiding any comment on the case's status.[92] Mountjoy replied that that 'important omission' left him with the impression that the case had (in words echoing Horwood's) 'died a natural death'.[93] If so, he wrote, he failed to see the use of providing details, but if Cornish would assure him that the case was still open he promised to 'get to work to establish on safe grounds and simplify the evidence I referred to'.[94] Cornish assured him the case 'is not yet dead', and, as with any unsolved crime, they were open to new leads; however, he needed 'as many particulars as you can as to the effect and the source of the information'.[95]

Mountjoy's response, on 20 September, made a series of remarkable new accusations. First, he claimed that Charles Fletcher – who had testified at the inquest and trial – had suspected Beatrice of trying to murder her husband and 'pleaded with the family' to get Harry out of the house. Second, he said Leslie Sayes had convinced Dr Du Pré to change his testimony about Harry's mobility shortly before his death. Third, Mountjoy said that Fred

Thorne, Harry's masseur, had confronted Beatrice (in the presence of another, unnamed witness) and told her to stop poisoning Harry. Fourth, Beatrice had told him personally that 'she should like to see him poisoned'. Finally, in a hand-written addition to his typed letter, he wrote that he could prove Harry had £400 a 'few weeks before his illness'.[96] A week later, Cornish responded dismissively: he thanked Mountjoy for the information, stating, 'I shall be glad if you would let me know should you receive any further evidence that can be proved, but for the moment, the matter remains as it was.'[97] 'As it was' meant, effectively, that the case was closed.

An old crime revealed or a new one attempted?

Was there anything to the 'damning evidence' offered by Mountjoy or Sayes? It is difficult to be certain: many claims were based upon hearsay or involved material evidence that had allegedly been destroyed. True, Sayes made incriminating allegations about his own conduct (suggesting he would not have made them lightly); however, he appears to have believed (whether encouraged by Mountjoy or not) that he was immune from prosecution. It may be that both men thought they could sell their story while facing very little real danger. Neither Beatrice nor any of the other people mentioned by Mountjoy and Sayes were re-questioned – leaving a relatively thin evidentiary basis for evaluating their claims. Nonetheless, their story seems dubious.

Consider the statements that Sayes had signed. The one sent to Gittoes-Davies claimed Beatrice had told 'several persons' about her aim of poisoning Harry.[98] Sayes said he had seen her put sheep dip powder in Harry's butter on 23 July 1927, and the next day she had been 'somewhat elated over the fact that she had found out what to give him'. After Harry's return from the Infirmary, Beatrice had 'gradually' given him sheep dip 'in powder form' by 'sprinkling it on pancakes she made for him' and adding it to bread and milk. She gave him these at night so he could not detect their altered colour. On Christmas Day, Sayes claimed he had seen Beatrice put more sheep dip in the butter used for Harry's beef sandwiches. The final fatal dose was given on 7 January, '33½ hours before death'. Sayes even claimed to have organised the cover-up of the crime. She 'left it all to me': he had 'instructed Mrs. Pace what to do and say at the inquest and also what to tell the police'. She had gotten her children to lie about the sheep dipping in July – which never took place – and 'suggested to' Rosa Kear that they had dipped sheep when, in fact, they had only been 'attending to' them. Beatrice had given Harry, in all, a 'little less than half the packet' of sheep dip. She had become suicidal during the investigation, he said, and even planned to kill herself, but he and Alice had dissuaded her. In Windsor after her acquittal, Beatrice was 'so elated with it all' that she boasted how 'Les had beaten the best brains in the country.' But when he had seen Beatrice soon afterwards on the street in Coleford, she had had the 'impudence' to offer him £20 'to square it up' after having promised him half of the insurance money and half of her 'life story money'.

The other statements, dated 15 August, that were given to Bliss (from the *Daily Chronicle*) contain similar accusations.[99] The first claimed Beatrice had been 'trying and wishing' to get rid of Harry for nearly six years, and she had attempted to 'dispose of him by poison' three years previously; Beatrice had put powdered sheep dip in butter, bread, milk and cornflour. Sayes claimed that the whole sheep-dipping story was his idea; he could, however, 'easily prove' that Harry had not dipped sheep in 1927. The second statement additionally asserted that 'Mrs. Pace never at any time extracted arsenic *from* the sheep dip'; before Harry's death, the 'price of silence' had been half of the insurance money, but 'when it was known that a life story was possible', Beatrice had offered half of what she could get for it.[100]

There are good reasons to be sceptical about all of these claims. Sayes said Beatrice told 'several persons' about her murderous intentions; however, the only people who testified to such threats at the inquest or trial were Harry's blood relatives and their spouses. The vague and shifting chronology of the allegations is also suspicious: Sayes referred to poisoning attempts going back, alternatively, six or three years, Mountjoy to a plot 'extending over four years'.[101] However, no medical records were produced at the trial that would have suggested *years* of attempted poisoning, and even Harry's suspicious family thought he had been healthy until 1927. Sayes also claimed that Beatrice had resumed 'gradually' poisoning Harry after his return from the Infirmary. However, all the witnesses at the inquest and trial – including his doctor

– testified to a significant improvement in his condition between late October and Christmas. If, as Sayes claimed, the final poisoning took place '33½ hours before death', this would have placed it, at the earliest, in the early hours of 9 January (Harry died between 10.30 and 11.00 on the morning of 10 January); however, Sayes *also* said that it had been given to him two days earlier, on 7 January. Furthermore, in one of his three available statements, he stated that Beatrice told him Harry must have swallowed '1½ lbs.' of salts of lemon.[102] However, though the matter had been raised, there had been no forensic evidence that Harry had consumed this substance.

Did Beatrice and Harry really dip lambs on 23 July 1927, as testified to by Leslie and Doris Pace and Rosa Kear? Sayes stated that Beatrice had 'suggested' to Kear that sheep were dipped when they were merely being 'attended to'. Kear, however, had not only observed the Paces from a distance but had also gone out to 'remonstrate with' Beatrice for straining herself so soon after Jean's birth a month before (at which Kear had assisted).[103] Her testimony, of course, could have been in error, as might that of the Pace children. But there was another witness: Harry Pace himself. Dr Du Pré recalled that Harry had 'attributed his illness from dipping sheep ... just before I saw him'. 'Both the man and his wife told me this', Du Pré observed.[104] At the infirmary, Harry had told Dr Mather that he had been using sheep dip a few weeks before his admission.[105] This raises further doubts about Sayes's claim that no sheep had been dipped the previous year. Sayes said that a witness (who testified at the inquest to having bought 'sheep' from the Paces) *could* have testified that the 'sheep' had not been dipped.[106] But Beatrice had specified that they had only dipped 'lambs' (a distinction made at the inquest). Another witness had indeed bought 'lambs', Sayes stated, but he *had not checked* whether or not they had been dipped. Thus, the 'evidence' against the sheep dipping in late July amounted to claims that five witnesses (the two children, Rosa Kear, Dr Du Pré and Dr Mather) had perjured themselves and that a purchaser of the Pace lambs *did not know* whether they had been dipped or not.

Sayes's alleged motivation (Beatrice's offer of half of the insurance money and the proceeds of the 'life story') is also questionable. At the earliest, the possibility of selling her life story for a significant sum cannot have been seen as likely until at least after the inquest. Thus, the expected reward would have been half the life-insurance money. Would Sayes have taken a leading role in a long-term plot to murder a man – at considerable risk – and then organise its cover-up for, ultimately, £34 16s (somewhat over £6,500 today[107])? People, of course, have been killed for less, and Sayes clearly needed money. Nonetheless, it seems more likely that the new accusations were motivated by an effort to cash in on Beatrice's celebrity, especially if Sayes believed, as Mountjoy suggested, that no prosecution could result.

One of the greatest problems with Sayes's story, however, is his repeated claim that Beatrice had poisoned Harry with sheep dip in its powdered form. He said she had poisoned his butter, milk, bread and cornflour in dim light so that he could not see the poison. But presumably he would have been able to taste the sulphurous substance. (The whole purpose of the alleged extraction of the arsenic was to eliminate its tell-tale flavour.) Several experts had concluded that Harry could not have ingested powdered sheep dip. The police were well aware of this: Kendal suggested that Sayes's claims should be forwarded on to Sir William Willcox, 'because so far as I can see it is impossible to reconcile what [Sayes] now says with the evidence given by the doctors which was, unless I am mistaken, to the effect that beyond any doubt had the sheep dip been used in the state in which it was bought traces of sulphur must have been found in the body'.[108] Sayes's claims do not stand up to close scrutiny.

What about the allegations Mountjoy made after Sayes's refusal to speak to the police? He knew the authorities were losing interest, and he may have thought that new claims would revive the investigation and, therefore, press interest. His letter to Cornish on 20 September – in which he stated that several witnesses had given perjured testimony – is unconvincing. He claimed, for example, that Charles Fletcher knew Beatrice was poisoning Harry and approached the Pace family about the matter; however, this seems contradicted by Fletcher's inquest testimony (for example, Harry had 'never complained' about his treatment and Beatrice had given 'the impression that she was trying to save his life'[109]). Not even the Paces themselves ever referred to Fletcher having told them anything. Like Fletcher, Fred Thorne had not only refrained from criticising Beatrice, he had even praised her. Would such witnesses have repeatedly perjured themselves – at no benefit to themselves – if they believed Beatrice guilty?

The most spectacular of Mountjoy's new charges was that, at the trial, Dr Du Pré had changed his earlier testimony ('twice given' at the inquest and before the magistrates) that, in Mountjoy's words, 'during the last two or three days' Harry would have been 'unable to feed himself'. He claimed that an 'interview' between Sayes and the doctor had 'settled the point', and at the Gloucester trial 'the country was amazed' to see the doctor 'entirely altering the tone of his evidence' by stating that Harry could indeed have fed himself, undermining the prosecution's case.[110] There was, however, no alteration (let alone a 'right-about-face') in Du Pré's evidence. At the inquest, the doctor described Harry as 'helpless' on 9 January, about twelve hours before death.[111] But up to forty-eight hours before Harry's death, 'so far as his muscles were concerned and so far as I can say there was nothing to suggest a return of the peripheral neuritis'.[112] He gave similar testimony at the committal proceeding, stating directly that Harry *may* have been able to get out of bed unaided and walk to the dressing chest up to 'twelve hours before he died'.[113] At the trial, Birkett asked him whether Harry could have 'walked around the room unaided' in the period between his visits on 8 and 9 January.[114] Du Pré could not prove it, but he believed so. We also know from Cornish's first report on the case that by mid-March, Du Pré – apparently like Professor Walker Hall – believed that the case was one of suicide.[115] Whether Du Pré was right or wrong, his testimony remained consistent.

Finally, the evidence Mountjoy had offered Gittoes-Davies included two notes, signed 'Beattie', allegedly sent by Beatrice to Alice Sayes. They were undated, but Leslie Sayes claimed that they had been sent from the King's Head Hotel right after the trial. One note – though hinting at tensions between the widow and her friends – contains nothing obviously incriminating.[116] The other, Cornish observed, was 'couched in rather strange terms'.[117] It read:

> My Own Dearest Friends,
> Don't worry, keep quiet, let them have there [sic] say, we will have ours after.
> *Never, never, never* will I forget you, I will be yours as ever I have been, only do as I say, *keep your tongue quiet.*
> I will write you again. I am coming out one day and I am coming to see you and the children. I cannot write, I am not so well this

morning. Let me know by letter how things are going on with [you, and] you can write here. Let Myra address your letters, they won't know her writing. All I ask you I want you to do. You will never regret it. Love as ever.

Beattie xxxx

There *is* something mysterious here, but Beatrice had many reasons to want her friends to 'keep quiet'. She had had long experience with local gossip, which continued after the acquittal, and she had, moreover, just sold her exclusive story to the press. As explained in Chapter 8, she had secrets that were not, necessarily, related to Harry's death. One cannot even be certain that the notes are authentic. Mountjoy had sent nine of Beatrice's prison letters with them, and since none of them are remotely suspicious, their purpose must have been to enhance the authenticity of the accompanying notes and highlight Beatrice's close relationship with the Sayeses. Cornish at first described the 'Beattie' notes as 'undoubtedly' in Beatrice's handwriting; however, he later referred to them only as 'evidently' attributable to her.[118] The handwriting of the prison letters and notes are not unquestionably the same. Ultimately, the 'Beattie' notes prove nothing.

The claims made by Sayes and Mountjoy – while impossible to retrospectively dismiss outright – are highly questionable. If they were true, they would indicate perjury by several key witnesses: not only Beatrice herself, but also Leslie and Alice Sayes, Mountjoy, Thorne, Fletcher, Leslie and Doris Pace, Dr Du Pré and even Harry's kin (to whom Fletcher allegedly revealed his suspicions). Forensic analysis ruled out the alleged poisoning method and its timing. Finally, there is the context of the allegations' provenance: Sayes told police that he and Mountjoy wanted to 'make some money': when pressed, both men backed down. When it became apparent that his original plan was unlikely to succeed, Mountjoy's new claims were, if anything, even more fanciful. He may have believed in Beatrice's guilt, but he also wanted to sell a story. This was a risky game that could have led to prosecutions not only for perjury but, possibly, for murder. Perhaps Mountjoy was unaware of this. Perhaps he did not care.

Sayes was involved in at least one conspiracy. If his August statements were true, he had helped Beatrice kill Harry Pace and cover up the crime; if they were untrue, he had joined with Mountjoy to try selling a bogus story to the press and – possibly

– to pressure Beatrice into paying him. The police may have seen the latter option – blackmail – as more likely. But 'whatever Sayes may have threatened to Mrs. Pace', Kendal observed, 'it seems to me practically impossible to expect that she would go into the witness box'. [119] On 9 October, Chief Constable Clarke wrote to London to say that Sayes had returned to his home in Ellwood two days earlier. 'As far as can be ascertained', he observed, 'he intends remaining there indefinitely.'[120]

By then, Beatrice had relocated to Gloucester, and whether she ever spoke to Leslie or Alice Sayes again is unknown. In her new home, as a sympathetic reporter put it, Beatrice 'thought that peace would come to her and that, maybe, the public would soon forget all about her'.[121] She came closer to this goal when on 1 November Cornish wrote to his superintendent that he had been told that 'no further action is contemplated in this case' and 'the papers can be put away'.[122] The only subsequent additions to the file are the original documents that Mountjoy had sent to the *Evening Express*, where they remain to this day. For all official purposes, the 'Fetter Hill mystery', after many twists and turns, was finally dead.

7

'18 years of hell':
gender, marriage and violence

We have seen the rise of the Pace case as a media event, but the next two chapters take a closer look at its depiction and contemporary relevance. Much of the reporting that followed Beatrice's acquittal had little to do with the alleged crime: Beatrice and Harry became figures in an emerging culture of celebrity that was substantially fed by the criminal justice system. 'Once a man is involved in a murder case', wrote Kingsley Martin in the *Political Quarterly* in 1931, 'he leaps into the same newspaper category as the Cabinet Minister, the film star and the record breaker. Every detail about himself and his past, every story about his relatives and mistresses has news value.'[1] The same was equally true – perhaps even more than equally – when women were accused. Six years before the Pace case, stories about Edith Thompson and her murdered husband Percy had similarly filled the papers, as, in 1926, did articles about Louie Calvert, the second woman executed in England during the 1920s.[2] As noted, Beatrice sold her memoir to the *Sunday Express*, and later that year an expanded version appeared in the weekly periodical *Peg's Paper*. *Thomson's Weekly News* carried a four-part biography published under her daughter Dorothy's name. Meanwhile, Bernard O'Donnell wrote a detailed retrospective series for the *World's Pictorial News*. Their similar themes – Beatrice and Harry's courtship (discussed in chapter 1), their violent marriage, the suspenseful legal ordeal and Beatrice's post-acquittal life – offered narratives that would have been read in the context of changing marital expectations in the 1920s.

Gender roles were among the most contentious topics of press and public debate in the 1920s. Such tensions have been reflected in subsequent histories. Responding to earlier emphases on the emancipating effects of the Great War, some historians have stressed the subsequent 'backlash' that rolled back women's war-time gains. The post-war women's movement has been depicted as fragmented, and a 'new feminist' ideology that emphasised women's distinctive natures has been blamed for undermining arguments for equality.[3] It has been claimed that the 'only' acceptable images offered women were as housewives and mothers: they were sent 'back to home and duty' and other roles 'were presented as wholly undesirable'.[4] Other historians have, however, resisted seeing the inter-war period as a 'slough of feminine despond'.[5] They have, for instance, noted the continuing role of paid work in women's lives, and, alternatively, they have examined other areas of women's experience – notably leisure, consumption and the media – thereby highlighting that multiple images of acceptable womanhood were conveyed.[6] Despite the post-war backlash, by the second half of the 1920s, positive – even exuberant – images of the 'modern woman' were plentiful, if controversial.

But inter-war gender debates were not just about women and femininity: men, masculinity and domestic life also came under new scrutiny. There were many reasons for the concern with redefining masculinity, such as the carnage of the Great War (and the wounded, maimed and psychologically damaged veterans it left behind) and mass unemployment.[7] Other trends had begun earlier: a declining birth-rate (bringing smaller families), the equalisation of women's suffrage (partially in 1918 and completely in 1928), developing media (from newspapers to film) that sought to attract a female audience and, finally, diminishing tolerance for domestic violence.[8] Certainly, marriage and parenthood remained the assumed aspiration for both men and women, and marriage rates rose between the wars.[9] Although this period saw the clear emergence of the modern 'career' woman, the designation of the home as women's proper realm remained predominant. This was, in one sense, a constraint. On the other hand, Ross McKibbin has suggested that the 'sexual politics' of the inter-war period ensured that there was 'at least one ground, the domestic, where a woman might hope to approach a man at least as his equal'.[10] Some women embraced such roles; others resisted them. Expectations about family life, too, were changing. A more 'domesticated' masculine ideal was influencing the middle classes, among whom 'companionate marriage' was 'a matter of course' by the early 1930s.[11] It is harder to judge trends further down the social scale, but while traditional markers of male status endured (such as hard work and physical toughness) there was less tolerance for 'unreconstructed' and 'pre-industrial' masculinities.[12] Such trends coexisted, however, with fears of 'effeminised' men, leading to concurrent reassertions of 'traditional' male roles.[13]

Inter-war culture was thus marked by a garrulous cacophony of opinions – amplified by the press – about what 'modern' men and women should be, or even whether being 'modern' was in itself desirable. Opinions were shaded according to region, class, age, religious belief, political affiliation, occupational milieu and, of course, personal experience. Events such as the Pace case present opportunities to plumb the complexities of a culture that was obsessed with the 'place of private life and what it represented'.[14] In the context of the 'modern' 1920s, Harry and Beatrice may have seemed figures from another age. They had, after all, been born under Queen Victoria and married in an Edwardian age partly obliterated by the war. Moreover, they lived in provincial isolation, far from the urban centres of effervescent modernity. On the other hand, there were millions of couples who led similar lives: for them, the Paces may have been all too recognisable.

The cruelties of 'Silent Harry'

Harry's brutality and Beatrice's suffering shaped their respective press personae. Advertisements for Beatrice's *Sunday Express* series were headed '18 years of hell' and featured a photograph of Beatrice – 'the most remarkable woman in England' – writing her memoirs. More than a 'mere sentimental recital of domestic troubles', the result was sold as 'a simple and unadorned statement of a life story which, in its almost unbelievable tragedy, its horror, its revelations of wifely endurance, surpasses in its bare facts the masterpieces of passion, hatred and cruelty drawn from the primitive life of the countryside by an Ibsen or a Thomas Hardy'.[15] Dorothy called her mother's married life 'an unending tragedy': 'I do not think there is a woman in the world who has suffered more.'[16] 'Sympathy with her throughout the country was all the stronger', the *Daily Mail* observed, 'because she had been brutally treated by her husband during his life and was left in very poor circumstances at his death.'[17]

Such emphases came at Harry's posthumous expense. When the name 'Pace' first hit the headlines, he had been lionised as 'a well-known and highly-respected working man'. He would 'toil all day, working hard to bring up his children' and was a 'very fond father': 'everybody' spoke of him 'in the highest terms'.[18] He thus seemed to have exemplified the masculine expectations of his time and class.[19] But only two weeks after his death, *Thomson's Weekly News* offered a different image, observing that he was 'excessively reserved and quiet', appearing to 'resent any outside interference or interest in his affairs'. Earlier claims that he was 'a man of some considerable standing in the public affairs of the district' were false and, in fact: 'Not at any time did he take any active part in public matters.'[20] Despite a 'lifetime in the district', Dorothy later wrote, her father was 'difficult', 'morose' and 'preferred to live his life apart': 'The men with whom he daily worked were mystified by him and spoke of him as "Silent Harry" ... Conversation of any kind, except perhaps about his beloved sheep, bored him.'[21]

Although Beatrice had at first labelled her marriage 'absolutely happy', contradictions emerged.[22] 'I am bound to state', she told the *Daily Mail* in late January, 'that many times he threatened to murder me and the family and to commit suicide.'[23] In early February, she called him 'a good steady man' and insisted 'we were very happy' but admitted he had 'fits of temper sometimes'.[24] In late March, an article called Harry 'cruel'.[25] As we have seen, more information came out during the inquest, and the reading of Beatrice's 'secret statement' in the magistrates' court made Harry's cruelty one of the case's defining themes, transforming his image from that of caring father to bestial tormenter. Subheadings in an article in *The People* reflect the shift in emphasis by June: 'Widow reveals husband's conduct with other women', 'Mrs. Pace chased with a gun at 2 a.m.' and 'Widow tells how her pet dog was fiendishly killed'.[26]

Violence had long been associated with predominant forms of male identity, and a certain amount of physical coercion had been seen as legitimate within marriage as long as it could be seen as 'disciplinary' and responding to the victim's marital or domestic failings, such as adultery, drunkenness, slovenliness and forms of 'unfeminine' behaviour.[27] But through the nineteenth and early twentieth centuries, such excuses for violence were becoming less accepted.[28] Changing judicial attitudes, feminist campaigns and media attention had ensured that condemning and controlling the brutality of husbands was on the cultural agenda by the 1920s. Women's suffering at the hands of men – via infidelity, psychological abuse or physical brutality – was a mainstay of the popular press, even if it was sensationalised and official responses to it remained inadequate.

Beatrice had initially told police that Harry had beaten her 'from the first day we were married' and then 'occasionally the whole of our married life until he was taken ill'.[29] She later clarified that he changed about 'a week or two' after their wedding: he swore at her, his voice 'was new and frightening' and he 'seemed to have grown jealous and distrustful'.[30] A couple of months later, 'near Christmas', one of the case's iconic episodes occurred. Beatrice had visited a sister-in-law, despite Harry having forbidden it. They argued, and when Beatrice's dog started barking, Harry took up a hammer, ran outside and 'hammered its head in till it was dead'. The next morning, he tied her waist, wrists and ankles to the bottom of the bed, announcing, 'I'll see no one else touches you. No other man will come near you now!' She was left there in the cold ('I had on only my nightdress, and there was no fire in the room') until Harry returned from work ten hours later.[31] Beatrice fled to her father's house, where Harry showed up and threatened her with a shotgun. Dorothy also recounted the story, which she had often heard from her mother.[32] O'Donnell, typically, heightened the drama, referring to the 'savage delight' Harry took in the 'terror' on the face of his 'girl-bride': 'Hands, arms, legs and body he tied. Tightly – so tightly that it caused moans of anguish.'[33] Beatrice also claimed Harry's beatings had led to miscarriages and – in two cases – fatal birth defects.[34] He also beat Dorothy, and 'whenever I could I used to get in front of her. She did the same for me. I've had many a sore back for Dorothy, and she's had many a sore back for me in her time.'[35] Dorothy confirmed that claim: 'But for me', she speculated, 'I doubt if my mother would still be alive.'[36] She called her father 'a strange man' who took little notice of the children and often did not speak to them for days 'except to grumble and to growl'. (Despite statements that he had beaten her and the other children – though 'not often' – she contradictorily stated, 'father did not raise his hand against us'.)[37]

According to Beatrice, Harry would also get 'wicked, childish ideas' about their animals.[38] Years after hammering one dog to death, he killed another by 'beating its brains out against the wall of the cottage'.[39] He kicked his sheep and sheepdog, and he twisted and bit their ears. Once, 'he suddenly flew in to a temper' when Beatrice went out. She returned to find 'he had taken all the baby's clothes and buried them'. 'More subtle tortures' involved the family being locked out of the house.[40] Beatrice complained of Harry's 'meanness': she had to sneak food from the garden, and Harry would respond to requests for 'a little extra for myself or the children' with 'What you haven't got you must do without!'[41] Dorothy saw this differently: she agreed he had been 'the reverse of extravagant' and 'resented any expenditure which was not absolutely necessary'; however, 'I have never known him withhold from my mother the money essential for the home, nor have I ever heard my mother complain that he treated her unfairly in money matters.'[42]

Harry was 'insanely jealous', restricting Beatrice's contacts and sometimes following her.[43] 'It used to be awful', she told O'Donnell, claiming that after going into Coleford to sell eggs and chickens she would return to find Harry 'in a blind rage, and he would accuse me of having been talking to men in Coleford'.[44] (Such exaggerated jealousy and controlling behaviour are common in abusive relationships.[45]) Harry's jealousy coexisted with his own sexual insatiability. Beatrice wrote that after their wedding, she found Harry 'owed about £40 to another woman for a baby'; he was, she explained, 'a terribly passionate man' who 'never gave me any peace at all'.[46] She told the police he was 'a very lustful man' and detailed his 'immoral associations with other women'.[47] She had once received a letter from the father of a seventeen-year-old girl, alleging that Harry had sexually assaulted her. Beatrice paid him 'to say nothing more about it'.[48] There was also, she told readers, 'trouble with my young sister, who was only twelve' (a revelation that had caused a 'thrill of horror' to run through the courtroom at her trial).[49] During one pregnancy, Beatrice told detectives, she had caught Harry with a girl at their home in a 'very compromising position': 'she had her knickers down and he had his trousers open'.[50] She did not describe the incident in her memoir; however, O'Donnell, quoting her, did.[51] Beatrice spoke to the girl's parents, and, apparently moved by Beatrice's condition, they dropped the matter. She vaguely referred to other deviance. Harry 'began to do other dreadful things that no ordinary man would do, and that I can't tell of': 'When I first found him out it nearly made me faint. He got sort of sheepish, and made me promise I wouldn't tell anybody. I expected a beating, but I reckon he felt a bit bad about it himself, and was ashamed.'[52] The 'dreadful things' remained unspecified.

Harry Pace was not depicted as entirely without positive qualities. He was hard-working and, if ungenerous, a steady provider. He was also not a drinker, and Beatrice noted his careful tending of the graves of their deceased children. ('It made up to me for many of the thrashings', she commented.[53]) The notion that men should rightfully dominate their households was still widespread; however, far from a reasonable paterfamilias, Harry was portrayed as an unfeeling brute who ruled his family through terror. His infidelities were other strikes against him: while the 'double standard' in sexual matters endured, it had narrowed.[54] As a result, he received little public sympathy. It must be noted that the only evidence for some of the specific incidents noted came from Beatrice herself; however, Harry's cruelty was confirmed by his children, and acquaintances testified to Harry's temper.[55] Chief Inspector Cornish highlighted Harry's strange behaviour and believed that he had been 'cruel to his wife since soon after they were married'.[56]

Unlike in some other murder trials from the same period, Harry's cruelty did not become a legal issue. Four years earlier, Marie Fahmy's allegations of her husband's deviant, 'Oriental' sexuality generated sympathies that most likely encouraged her sensational acquittal for his murder.[57] Women convicted of murdering their abusive partners sometimes gained official clemency by emphasising their partner's persistent abuse.[58] Beatrice, of course, did not seek to justify a killing, and her defence was that none had occurred. Nonetheless, depictions of domestic violence were central to the Pace case's press coverage and the public's reactions to it. Harry's violent, controlling behaviour motivated by sexual jealousy fits a common pattern across cultures and eras; however, assumptions about gender, marriage and violence were changing in the inter-war period, and press stories (whether fictional or real) of wives' suffering at the hands of deceitful, unreliable or violent husbands were commonplace.[59] As Alison Light has observed, 'the 1920s and '30s saw blistering attacks upon older versions of domestic life and made questions of the conduct of home life public property as never before'.[60]

An ideal victim?

Commenting on the crowd's reaction to Beatrice's arrival at the court during the trial, the *Daily Chronicle* enthused that rather than 'a woman on trial for her life' she 'might have been the central figure of a civic welcome'.[61] Upon her acquittal, the *News of the World* remarked that the public had 'all along shown sympathy on Mrs. Pace's behalf'.[62] It is impossible to quantify that claim, but the press had unanimously been on her side. Praised as a 'model wife and mother' and drawn as a 'tragic young widow', positive press accompanied her throughout her months in the public eye.[63]

The press, for example, emphasised Beatrice's attractiveness. The *Daily Mail* at first described her simply as a 'slight ruddy-complexioned woman ... with wavy brown hair',[64] but it later noted that she was 'still good-looking'.[65] O'Donnell emphasised this angle consistently: 'She is a pretty little woman,' he wrote, 'slim with rather rosy cheeks and a pair of blue grey eyes.'[66] Hers was a natural beauty, unadorned by cosmetics, which, although increasingly acceptable, retained an ambiguous respectability.[67] Her beauty was, however, under siege: as the inquest opened, *Thomson's Weekly News* noted that 'her face was drawn and haggard' and, by May, she was 'a pathetic careworn figure in deep mourning'.[68] In June, Dorothy stated, 'She is only 36, but she looks more.'[69] Journalist Vincent Wray had managed to get close to Beatrice's car before it departed after her acquittal: 'I looked into gentle brown eyes, sunken deeper into their sockets, and marked that deadly pallor of the formerly rosy cheeks. I was reminded of the words of Ovid in his immortal "Tristia": "You see her, and know that she was once beautiful."' There was, however, 'beauty still in this pitiable tragic figure', he thought: 'Her face is alight with mother's love, and her frail form bears the dignity of martyrdom.'[70] *The People* hoped that the 'acquittal has given her a new lease on life that will swiftly obliterate the marks her trials put upon her'.[71]

Alongside the tension between 'pretty' and 'haggard' was that between frailty and strength. Beatrice's emotional fragility was emphasised from the beginning.[72] 'She has never enjoyed robust health', claimed *Thomson's Weekly News*, 'having for some years been subject to fainting fits.'[73] 'I was a strong woman once', she told the *Daily Mail* in April, 'but I can hardly see you now, sir. My eyes are failing through worry and I am nearly blind. I cannot sleep.'[74] In early May, attention was drawn to 'her tear-stained face, and the manner in which her hands trembled as she nervously clutched a bottle of smelling salts'.[75] She fainted or was emotionally overcome at various points during the inquest.[76] When she testified, her initially strong voice had become strained, culminating in the 'anguished wail' in which she protested her innocence.[77] After the second inquest verdict, she 'fell forward, her head reaching the level of her knees' and 'was on the verge of collapse'; the police 'half-carried' the sobbing woman from the room.[78] There were similar scenes in the magistrates' court.[79] Dorothy wrote that such episodes were 'a daily occurrence'.[80] While Beatrice was in prison, one paper referred to her as a 'frail little wisp of a woman'.[81] This sort of emphasis was common in crime cases involving women.[82]

Nonetheless, Beatrice's 'courage' and 'fortitude' were also emphasised.[83] The *Sunday Dispatch* highlighted the strength of the 'stoic girl wife'.[84] One journalist recounted an interview shortly after detectives had questioned her. She repeated the phrase 'They will not break me': she was 'slender enough, fragile to look upon', he wrote, 'yet somewhere within her was the strength that helped her make good the vow'.[85] O'Donnell captured this duality through two impressions that would 'always remain distinct and vivid in my memory'. In one, she was 'the very embodiment of calm courage, her slim, rather pathetic figure absolutely refusing to bend beneath the cruel and relentless wave of slander and innuendo which threatened to hound her to the gallows'; in the other, he saw 'her helpless wilting body crumpled under the sudden shock of ... the amazing second verdict of the coroner's jury'.[86] After the trial, reporter Anthony Praga dubbed her 'the woman who endured', praising her grandly (if not entirely comprehensibly): 'She has reserves of strength and reserves of weakness, and those qualities she exhibited through her trial.'[87] John Valentine Holland argued Beatrice's fortitude came from being 'a child of the forest' and recalled a March evening when he had stood with her at the door of Rose Cottage looking out 'over the whispering Forest of Dean': 'She drew strength from the primitive place that bred and reared her, a strength that had its roots in the very soil of the Forest of Dean, a strength that fortified her to successfully battle the tearing anguish throughout the long months that she was on the rack.' Harry could not 'break' her, as 'he was really pitting his strength against that of the forest'.[88]

As this suggests, Beatrice's rural simplicity was seen as one of her important virtues. As O'Donnell put it, she had been a 'girl-bride' who was 'ignorant of life', an 'unsophisticated girl' with a 'simple mind' who 'knew so little of life that the mysteries of marriage and motherhood were as a sealed book to her'.[89] Beatrice claimed that if she had not been an 'ignorant child' when Harry proposed she 'would not have married him at all'.[90] Her ignorance extended to sex: 'I still believed that the doctor brought babies. My mother had told me nothing.'[91] Considering Harry's later behaviour, her assertion of sexual naivety was particularly poignant. It was also not implausible. Certainly, her claim of ignorance was typical of working-class women who wished to be seen as 'respectable'.[92] Beatrice's rural simplicity was part of her image as a 'dutiful wife and doting mother'.[93] Praga observed: 'It was for the great commonplaces that she was striving – decent home life, self-respect, the enjoyment of her children's affection, untainted by suspicion or divided loyalties.'[94]

Beatrice's marital devotion was emphasised. She professed to having developed an enduring (if inexplicable) love for Harry only after their marriage, one that mixed themes of innocence ('I was a great fool') and loyalty ('He was my man, whatever he did'). [95] After Harry's death, Dorothy wrote, Beatrice would 'not listen to a single word against the man whom she had taken "for better or for worse", only to find that the "worse" heavily outbalanced the "better"'. Her love for her tormenter was, in this view, a sign of virtue: 'Most women, I am sure, who had suffered only a tithe of what my mother endured as a wife, would have shed no tear when the end came.'[96] Such commitment was not seen as unproblematic; nonetheless, her uncomplaining endurance was praised.[97] Beatrice herself claimed she was comforted by her duties as a wife and mother. Describing her marriage as 'week in, week out, month in, month out, year in, year out – nothing but work, meals, rows, and beatings', she conceded that she 'wasn't unhappy the whole time': 'There was, first of all, Harry – I always tried to do my best for him – and after that came the children, and then myself.' 'I felt', she wrote, 'I was keeping my love for Harry alive by sticking to him and putting up as best I could with the things he did.'[98]

Unsurprisingly, her role as mother was most emphasised: she had, after all, given birth ten times over eighteen years. In an era in which birth rates were declining, this was remarkable, though far from unique. (Around the turn of the twentieth century, the average mother had six children, by the 1930s two; however, there were significant regional and class variations.[99]) As O'Donnell observed, 'the occasions when she was not in a condition of approaching motherhood appear to have been very rare indeed'.[100] 'What used to make things worse', Beatrice stated, 'was that year in and year out I had babies. I would hardly have one old enough to sit up, when there was another in my arms.'[101] In the *Sunday News*, Nesta Ryall described Beatrice as 'one of the most industrious, unselfish and hard working women I have ever met': 'I don't think she was ever inside a picture-house in her life. Her whole existence has been centred in her children.'[102] Of course, that fact that five of her children had died in infancy only increased the tragic aspect of her maternal identity.[103]

Beatrice reached out to her readers *as* a mother, being certain 'that every mother in England will understand and forgive' her for an inability to express all she felt: 'I wanted my children, and I wanted them all the time. They were with me in my sleepless nights, and they were in my thoughts while I was on my trial listening to the words I could not understand and sometimes could not hear.'[104] Dorothy emphasised that despite the family's poverty her mother had the domestic skills – keeping her children clean, well fed and appropriately dressed – that were key markers of working-class respectability.[105] Dorothy thought that her mother 'forgot her own troubles in the troubles of her children', a self-sacrifice becoming less unquestionably assumed by a younger, self-consciously 'modern' generation of women.[106] O'Donnell's article on the last day of the inquest highlighted Beatrice's single-mindedness. Even after being charged and sent off to prison 'in a terrible state of collapse', he wrote, 'her thought was for the children whom she was compelled to leave'.[107] In prison, when not writing letters 'full of passages concerning her children and expressing the longing that she may soon be with them', she was 'knitting socks and little garments for her baby Jean and little Doris, whose family of dolls continues to increase.'[108] She also knitted clothing for the children of other female inmates.[109] Dorothy quoted one of Beatrice's letters in which she even describes herself as an ideal mother: "'You know, Dolly," she wrote, "I have always been one of the best of mothers and I shall always be the same, as you know we have always had it very rough."'[110]

Support for 'Mrs Pace' was broad-based and encouraged by characteristics that clearly remained the key ingredients of respectable womanhood, especially her devotion to her children. But her image was also shaped by contradictions. She was beautiful, but her youthful good looks were threatened by the stresses she faced. Displaying appropriate feminine frailties, she was nevertheless praised for her strength and endurance. Despite hard-won experience, she exemplified provincial simplicity. Even the awestruck admiration she generated as a wife suggests that her devotion was considered excessive. Beatrice's public persona was, ultimately, more than a little ambiguous.

Advice and ambiguities

Beatrice's memoir series employed narratives that had already dominated press coverage of the inquest and trial; however, it also offered a more complex and, ultimately, ambiguous story. In two articles – 'A talk to wives' and 'A talk to those about to marry' – she gave advice to young women. This type of article was common. In seeking to expand their female readership, inter-war newspapers, as Adrian Bingham observes, 'created spaces where women spoke directly to other women about their lives'.[111] Beatrice's suffering was the source of her authority: 'Many persons claim to have undergone an hour, a day, a week, a month of bitter agony', her memoir's advertisement proclaimed: 'Mrs. Pace has come triumphantly through eighteen years of hell.' Her 'long married life of tragedy' was sold as edifying: 'No wife or husband; no one who intends to become a wife or a husband should miss reading Mrs. Pace's astonishing story.'[112]

Despite the enduring celebration of marriage, escaping it was becoming easier in Britain. For centuries, divorce had been limited to the aristocracy, and even they had endured a series of legal manoeuvres culminating in a special Act of Parliament.[113] Divorce was 'officially legalised' in 1857 but remained difficult.[114] In 1923, grounds for divorce were equalised: previously, a husband only had to prove his wife's adultery; wives required additional grounds. Proving adultery remained essential until 1937, after which divorce could be granted due to cruelty, desertion, habitual drunkenness, incurable insanity, rape, sodomy, non-consummation, bestiality or venereal disease.[115] Legal 'separation' had also been available since 1878 in magistrates' courts, which could also award 'maintenance' – support payments for wives and children.[116] Originally intended for abused women, legal separation's legitimate grounds were broadened and financial support increased, creating a system that would endure long into the twentieth century.[117] Faster, easier and, above all, cheaper, separation was more important than divorce for the working classes, even if, unlike divorce, it did not grant the right to re-marry.[118] Obstacles to dissolving unhappy marriages remained: some were financial (though maintenance payments were increased in 1920 and 1925) and others were cultural (involving fears of lost respectability).[119] But Beatrice had stayed with Harry, as she put it, not because she had to but because she wanted to.[120]

As described in Beatrice's memoir, her marriage recalls the 'cycle of violence' proposed by psychologist Leonore Walker.[121] The 'cycle' has three phases: tension-building, actual violence and, importantly, a period of reconciliation.[122] While not all abusive relationships fit this model, many do. Beatrice described many 'contrition' periods, in which Harry expressed regret and promised to change. In such phases, it has been observed, an abusive man appeals to his partner's 'optimism and her nurturance', highlighting his 'vulnerability, desperation, loneliness, and alienation' and providing 'added hooks that keep the woman in the relationship'.[123] In response, she attempts 'to placate the batterer, doing what she thinks might please him, calm him down, or at least, what will not further aggravate him'.[124] As Beatrice put it, Harry came first and had 'the best of anything that was in the house'. She 'was always on the watch to please him', for instance, making him pancakes ('the great things to put him in a good temper') when she sensed a bad mood.[125]

She tried to conceal her suffering from friends and family, which was also common.[126] One brother 'never dreamed' of what she suffered, saying, 'I did not know anything about the terrible thrashing which he used to give her, or I would have thrashed him till he couldn't stand.' Indeed, Beatrice feared her brothers 'would have killed him had they known'.[127] Her family was, however, at least partly aware. Harry had, after all, shown up at Beatrice's father's house and threatened to shoot her.[128] When one of Beatrice's brothers briefly lived with the couple, Harry threw his clothes 'all out on to the green', and Beatrice told O'Donnell that her family 'often told me that if I went back to him I deserved all I got, and that, if I was not careful, he would murder us all in our beds'.[129] One brother had offered 'a home with him if I would leave Harry'. She did so, but, feeling herself 'drawn by him', she returned. 'I had to go back to Harry', she wrote, 'no matter what he did to me.'[130] Some neighbours and friends must also have known of her suffering. Beatrice told police that Harry had been seen beating her with a stick, and she had sometimes sought help from neighbours.[131] Dorothy said her father once dragged her mother to a deep well in the yard, but a neighbour responded to Beatrice's cries.[132] After the funeral of one of his children (during which he had remained 'sullen and brooding' in bed), Harry – a 'wild-eyed, raging figure' – emerged from the house and threw a bottle at the returning mourners.[133]

To an extent, the police and courts appear to have been responsive when Beatrice sought help. But she did so rarely. After being beaten 'more cruelly than usual' while pregnant she fled to her father's house and summoned Harry for assault. He was fined, and he (and his mother) entered into recognisances to guarantee better behaviour. Beatrice returned when he promised to be kinder.[134] She told detectives that after Harry had threatened to shoot her and the children in early 1927 she had reported it to Sergeant Hamblin 'who came and saw' him.[135] She spoke to Hamblin on another occasion about Harry's threats, but when the officer came to check on her, she sent him away, wary of provoking Harry. She feared not only Harry's anger but also that 'the neighbourhood would get to hear of the disgrace in my home life'. She dreaded 'the gossip round about almost as much as the stick'.[136] It was not uncommon then (as now) for abused women to make complaints and then refuse to press charges.[137] Beatrice's financial dependence certainly made leaving difficult, which may also have motivated her efforts to cover up Harry's sexual assaults. In February, she told the police the payment given to one young woman's father came 'at the request of my husband'; after her acquittal, however, she wrote she had taken the initiative: 'I would do anything to save us from disgrace', O'Donnell quoted her, 'and I made him come with me so that we could talk it out with the father.'[138] As Beatrice put it, 'of course, I had to do all the talking': 'in the end I managed to get him to agree to take 7s. 6d. to say nothing more about it'.[139] As noted, her intervention in another case also prevented legal action.[140]

Her life with Harry was 'sometimes hell', but she found 'some happiness in sticking to it, and in not losing my love for him'. Addressing 'those about to marry', she said that if given the chance again, 'I would not marry a man of his type for all the money in the world.' Nonetheless: 'I have said it before, and I say it again – I loved Harry, and I would have stood by him whatever he did, and for another eighteen years, if he had lived.'[141] This loyalty contributed to her media idealisation; however, it also attracted critical letters from some women. A week after stating 'He was my man, whatever he did', she somewhat defensively reasserted her commitment: 'I am sure you will all say that if Harry was mad, I must have been madder to stay by him and put up with it, but as I said at the beginning, Harry was my man, and I had to stick to him.'[142] In 'A talk to wives', she responded further. At first dismissive – 'I do not believe that the women who say they would have run away would really have done so' – she explained: 'There are things in married life which unmarried women cannot understand and which even married women who have kind husbands cannot understand. There are things deep down in us that only experiences like mine can make us realise – feelings and ideas that a happy life doesn't bring out.' Among these feelings was the conviction that she had been right to stay. 'When you are poor and married and trouble comes', she continued, 'you begin to realise that you have got to fight the world together, even if you are fighting each other at the same time': 'You feel that you mustn't just turn your back and run away from things like a coward.'[143] Sufficient devotion, she suggested, made even an abusive marriage worthwhile. (Although she also expressed doubts: 'I don't know whether I am stupid or not, and perhaps all the women who have written to me are right, and I should have left Harry.'[144]) A 'fairly happy marriage', she wrote, is based on 'making allowances' for each other's 'bad points'. On this principle, her husband's remorse – 'he was nearly always sorry after he had been cruel to me' – was 'the best thing in Harry's character': 'Harry's regret made up to me for many a sore back. It was his best quality, and I knew it, and it helped me to allow for his bad qualities.'[145] (Dorothy judged her father differently. 'Dad was never regretful afterwards', she wrote, 'or if he was he never betrayed it. Never in my life have I heard him utter one word of apology for all the suffering he brought upon my mother.'[146])

Beatrice thought it had been a mistake to marry Harry, but once married she saw no way out. 'There was the sort of love in her heart', O'Donnell believed, 'that is often felt by a woman for a bully.' The 'strange bond which held her to him', he thought, had been her 'mother-love for the children' and 'an affection which sprang from the fact that he was the father of those children'. She had been under a 'hypnotic spell'.[147] Beatrice urged girls to be choosy about husbands, critiquing a popular notion of desirable manhood: 'I have read about "strong, silent men" in stories, and how women are supposed to love them, but let me tell you that whenever I hear about that kind of man I think of Harry, and I wonder why people write such nonsense. Poor Harry was strong and silent enough, and I do not advise any woman to marry such a type.'[148] She urged women to doubt men's promises and to observe their behaviour closely. Should they choose poorly, however, they had to stay; but far from seeing herself as a helpless victim, Beatrice emphasised her active role in holding her marriage and family together.

Beatrice was not simply idealised, or, perhaps more accurately, her idealisation was not simple. Although praised for her marital and motherly devotion – key components of 1920s womanhood – the critical reactions of some women emphasise how she exceeded contemporary expectations. She was not alone in this: as Anette Ballinger has shown, Laura Lynn – convicted of murdering her abusive husband three years before the Pace case – had also 'gone *further* than dominant expectations dictated, for she had maintained her love for her husband, despite her abuse, had actively pursued him when he strayed and had even dropped the summons for a divorce when he promised to change – a promise he immediately broke'.[149] Lynn's death sentence was commuted to imprisonment. In contrast to the 'emphasised femininity' of women like Lynn, Edith Thompson had epitomised the 'modern woman'. This, combined with her adultery and suggestions she had 'incited' her lover to kill her husband, worked against her.[150] Still, even an exemplar of traditional virtues such as Beatrice Pace had her limits: 'Marriage is over for me', she wrote: 'I have had one experience of it, that is sufficient for me for the rest of my life.'[151]

'A new frock and a new life'

After eighteen years of marriage, numerous pregnancies, the deaths of five children, shocking levels of long-term physical abuse, months of official inquires and relentless press attention, Beatrice could not have plausibly been depicted as inexperienced by July 1928. Nonetheless, her life story brought a different kind of innocence to the fore via her unfamiliarity with 'modern' ways. Her journey from rural isolation to a 'new life' recalls what Alison Light has referred to more generally as women's 'entry into modernity' in this period, 'a modernity which was felt and lived in the most interior and private of places'.[152] While decisive, such advances were controversial and countered by pressures toward more traditional forms of femininity. Even among feminists, issues such as motherhood, career, birth control and political allegiance were contested; however, Beatrice's 'arrival' in the modern world involved precisely those areas – leisure, clothing, consumerism – that were emblematic of the transformation of women's lives in this era.

Her memoir opened with her first visit to that quintessential symbol of inter-war modernity: a cinema.[153] The experience made her 'nervous': 'The dark, the music coming from somewhere I could not see, the bright, moving shapes on the screen, the noises they made somewhere to imitate the firing of guns or the galloping of horses, all frightened me a little. It was some minutes before I could settle down to enjoy myself.'[154] She admitted that that 'sounds silly in a woman of my age', but: 'it is because everything in my new life is so strange and unexpected'. On holiday after her acquittal, a friend asked whether she would like some coffee: 'I thought, "Well, now, I've never tasted it", and I said so. Everybody at table laughed and looked surprised.' 'I thought about it afterwards', she continued, 'and I decided to tell about it here, so that you will understand how different everything is for me now.' Such stories underlined a sort of 'make-over' narrative that is instantly recognisable today, even if its elements are period-specific. They included a fashionable new 'semi-shingle' haircut

Secrets of My Tragic Marriage

by Mrs PACE who was accused of the murder of her husband

PEG'S PAPER

2D.

No. 487. September 18th, 1928.

8 Title page of the women's weekly that reprinted a somewhat
updated version of Beatrice's 'life-story', which first appeared
in the *Sunday Express*.

(©The British Library Board, *Peg's Paper*, 18 September 1928, p. 1) that made her feel 'so much younger and lighter', 'almost as if a lot of dark memories had fallen off with each snip of the scissors'. 'I have also given up my black clothes', she admitted, 'I hope no one will think the worse of me for it.' This, too, was transforming: 'It is as if I had taken off an old, dingy self and put on a new one – as if I had changed the old clothes of myself.' Descriptions of her 'new self' were interwoven with old suffering, emphasising the contrasts. 'Now, I realise', she wrote, 'that what takes my breath away is only ordinary to other people.'[155]

The 'new life' angle was even stronger in the later version of the memoir, appearing in *Peg's Paper* between mid-September and the end of the year.[156] Unlike the family-oriented *Sunday Express*, *Peg's Paper* was a popular weekly magazine aimed at young working-class women – factory workers, shop-girls and domestic servants – that mainly offered fictional romances.[157] Although a true story, Beatrice's tale of suffering and suspicion fitted in rather well with the tone of such magazines, which focused on stories of love accompanied by a 'sea of jealousy, scandal, revenge, lying, guilty secrets, murder, bigamy and seduction'.[158] Even for younger women, Beatrice's dramatic experiences and post-acquittal life may have represented a fantasy of sorts. 'I have no orders to obey,' she wrote of her new situation, 'I can go where I like, and do what I like, and see what I like.'[159]

Her 'gateway' to a changed existence and 'the real beginning of my life to-day', she said, were the clothes she received in Coleford the day of her acquittal. She had wept upon seeing herself in the mirror. 'Who but a girl', she recalled thinking, 'could wear such a frock, one which ended close below the knees, and silken, flesh-colour stockings?' The exchange of garments signalled her new life. 'You've always worn long frocks nearly to your ankles, up there on Fetter Hill, and always black', commented a friend: 'it does not mean you have always got to do the same; you are starting life afresh.' Beatrice wrote that it 'didn't seem right that I should wear that frock so soon!' Nonetheless, that moment was 'the beginning point of my life to-day. A new frock and a new life – without Harry.'[160] Bobbed hair, bright fabrics and a knee-length hemline may seem insignificant, but this was an era in which women's clothing and hairstyles were relentlessly debated. Two days before Beatrice's acquittal, a commentator in the *Daily Sketch* imagined a time-travelling visitor from the past.

The 'first sight of an aeroplane' or the 'speed of traffic' might be surprising; however: 'The shortening of the skirt and the thinning of the clothes have made a more notable difference to the look of the civilised world than the war, the internal combustion engine, the kinema, and all the other changes put together.'[161] Though overstated, this suggests the cultural significance of fashion in 1920s Europe.[162]

Beatrice's new life also involved a new home. In early September, O'Donnell visited Beatrice at her 'pretty red brick villa' on the outskirts of Gloucester: 'there is considerable difference in this comfortable little place, with its six nice sized rooms, all newly decorated, and the drab little cottage ... where I first saw her'. Not only had she exchanged 'the deep black which she wore all through her long ordeal' for 'a pretty flowered frock of some light summery material', but the children 'are better dressed then ever they have been in their young lives'.

> There is an air of newness about everything in the house; new lino upon the floor, with new rugs and carpets. Then there is a huge roomy settee with two spacious armchairs. A vast improvement upon the old dilapidated sofa upon which Mrs. Pace used to lay night after night trying to snatch a few hours rest during the anxious months which followed her husband's death.[163]

Beatrice was far from the youthful 'flapper' who fascinated the 1920s press, but her post-acquittal story fitted into a related narrative of modernity centred on independent women and suburban life. Beatrice's well-established respectability and wifely suffering no doubt made her embrace of a more 'modern' womanhood unthreatening. The happy, child-centred domestic life in the Gloucester home bought with the donations of an admiring nation was certainly more than enough to allow the Pace saga, as published in *Peg's Paper*, to close on an upbeat note on the first day of January 1929. Nonetheless, its final words evoked a lingering ghost from the past: 'But there is my future – and I still wish Harry were alive and that he could share with me the good food, the warmth and comfort, our children around us, and the future ahead. It is a mad wish and illogical, but it is there.'[164] Beatrice's 'entry into modernity' in this period – perhaps like that of women more generally – would remain, in some ways, incomplete.

8

'Unimaginable agonies and degradations and cruelties': justice, politics and poverty

Alongside the personal aspects of Beatrice and Harry's life and marriage, their case raised other issues in the press and even in Parliament. Some concerned the arduous months of investigation, scrutiny, imprisonment and trial. Beatrice's idealisation as a wife and mother and the torture Harry had inflicted made her subsequent 'ordeal' at the hands of the state seem, to many, especially unjust. It was noted that the case's origin in a family quarrel complicated an already 'difficult and exciting issue' and led the justice system 'astray', and there was criticism of 'those small-town spites, those mean dislikes, those jealousies and angers that grow in the dark and by whispers, until families are filled with hatred and a rope hangs over an innocent woman'.[1] Still, the case's spectacular collapse made some ask why such an obviously innocent woman was even tried. More concretely, journalists and politicians used Beatrice's personal experiences to highlight institutional, legal and social critiques during a period already marked by discontent about the criminal justice system.

Praise and criticism

The case generated some praise of Britain's courts as well as Britons' fundamental good sense. The *Manchester Guardian* believed it affirmed the principle of placing the burden of proof on the prosecution.[2] The *Sunday Express* thought both 'our law' and 'the popular instinct' were vindicated: 'the people' had 'divined' the truth.[3] Its editor praised the 'chivalrous instincts of the good common people who rallied round Mrs. Pace'.[4] O'Donnell highlighted the nation's intuitive feelings for 'this amazing woman with the pretty bright eyes and slender figure'.[5] Noting 'general satisfaction' with the acquittal, the *Daily Mail* condemned the inquest's 'intolerable strain'.[6] The *Daily News* could not recall a case 'in which there was from the beginning a more deep and spontaneous public sympathy with a person accused of murder or a more definite public view as to the weakness of the case of the prosecution'.[7] Some were more ambivalent about the public's reactions. The *Morning Post* thought partisanship in trials should be 'wholly deprecated' even if expecting indifference to this particular case would have been 'to ask too much of human nature'.[8] The *Daily Mirror* likewise deemed the 'clamour' of the 'emotional multitude' to be 'human enough; though deplorable as a precedent'.[9] The Cheltenham *Echo* was more critical: 'There is a right way and a wrong way of expressing sympathy, and the demonstrations in Gloucester streets were the wrong way.' 'The only purpose of popular outbursts of the kind', it continued, 'is to influence the course of justice, and that is wholly reprehensible.'[10] (The *Manchester Guardian* was relieved that the directed verdict meant nobody could claim the 'popular demonstrations of sympathy with the accused' affected the jury's decision.[11])

Some institutions were applauded. Beatrice emphasised how 'wonderfully kind' her treatment in prison had been, saying she had never been made to feel like a prisoner.[12] The fairness of the prosecution was universally noted. Though the *Sunday Observer* thought the trial 'should never have taken place', it had been 'presented with a fairness which scrupulously revealed its inherent weakness'.[13] Merriman, said the *Daily Mail*, had done his job with the 'scrupulous fairness and impartiality which is expected from a Law Officer of the Crown'.[14] (Even Purcell – who critiqued nearly every other aspect of the case – praised Merriman personally.[15]) The *Daily Telegraph* speculated that 'a Law Officer of the Crown has rarely felt so little confidence in his case as the Solicitor-General' and applauded his 'scrupulously fair' prosecution. Still, 'the jury may well have wondered why, upon such guess-work and suspicion, Mrs. Pace was ever put in the dock'.[16]

That raised a key issue. Referring to the acquittal as 'the people's verdict', the *Daily Mail* urged that 'it is absolutely necessary that the whole of the circumstances attending the case should be investigated'.[17] The *Echo* thought the case 'revealed abuse of procedure from the start': the inquest was 'absurd', the magistrates' hearing was 'inefficient' and the grand jury 'failed to function'. 'There was no case to answer', and it was 'a scandal it should have got beyond the magistrates in petty sessions'.[18] *Reynolds's Illustrated News* decried Beatrice's 'prolonged torture', which 'would have been almost inhuman even if she had actually been guilty of murder'.[19] (T. A. Hannam also referred to her 'unseemly torture' as did an editorial in the communist *Sunday Worker*.[20]) The *Daily Herald* suggested that 'no murder case within the compass of living memory has caused such grave and general disquiet', the inquest showing the 'machinery of justice' to be 'creaking and groaning in every joint'. The coroner's actions had been 'extraordinary', leading to a trial in which the prosecution 'had no case'.[21] The *Daily News* expressed a widely shared view: 'It is greatly to be hoped that a direct consequence of the poignant court drama will be a rigorous tightening up of procedure at Coroner's inquests and a closer inquiry than ever into the methods of police investigation.'[22] As suggested, two institutions were particularly scrutinised: the police and the coroner.

Secrets, lies and the 'third degree': the police and Mrs Pace

On 18 March 1928, *The People* printed a short editorial titled 'Third degree', pointing out that while confessions had once been won 'by the agony of the rack' the advancement of 'the public conscience' had made torture intolerable. However, police in some countries (notably the United States) had discovered a substitute in 'the third degree': 'A merciless, ceaseless, nerve-shattering bombardment of questions and accusations' that 'induces the wretched suspect to make admission, indeed to say anything which will end his intolerable mental anguish.' It then noted that Harry Pace's widow had been 'interrogated by Scotland Yard officers for thirteen hours' and left 'in a state of collapse'.[23] Possibly inspired by this article, prominent Labour MP Will Thorne submitted a written question to the Home Secretary, Sir William Joynson-Hicks, three days later. He was promised that the matter would be looked into.[24]

The next week, *The People* promoted the issue to the front page under the headline, 'Questioned till I could have screamed'.[25] A reporter had interviewed Beatrice – 'a tragic and pathetic figure' with eyes 'sunken and red rimmed' – about her interrogation:

> 'I shan't ever forget,' she said in anguish. 'It seems that I can always hear them saying, "Did you do it? Do you know who did it? Are you shielding somebody?"
>
> *'It was terrible. The police kept on until the sweat was pouring from my body, until I could have screamed, until I could have smashed the windows of the room.'*
>
> 'They are the worst thirteen hours I have ever known in my life.'

In an accompanying article, she stated that at eight in the morning on 11 March, Inspector Bent requested that she, Doris and Leslie come to Coleford.[26] ('Inspector Bent', she emphasised, 'has all along acted very fairly towards me'.) After the children were questioned separately, Beatrice met Cornish for the first time. He warned her that her comments would be taken down and could be used as evidence, but she agreed to make a statement. Insisting that Harry had done himself in, she recalled becoming 'ratty' as they went 'backwards and forwards'. At some point – the room had no clock – she went to lunch. She was 'feeling bad' when she returned, but questioning continued. She felt faint and struggled to keep her eyes open. At 9.30 p.m., Dorothy and one of Beatrice's brothers arrived, but the detectives were not finished. She later told the reporter, 'my head was reeling as if I was drunk, and I had to hold on to the banisters' to return upstairs. She claimed she was driven home after ten o'clock and had to be carried into the house. The article concludes with a brief reference to a further statement on 14 March when, alone with the detectives, 'I told them what I had to tell them about.' Without suggesting what that meant, *The People* noted that Beatrice had afterwards fainted. The day after this article, Thorne posed a second question in Parliament. He was told Joynson-Hicks had 'ascertained the facts', but it was improper to comment until the matter had been 'disposed of'.[27]

There matters rested until 23 May, the day after the inquest verdict, when Thorne reiterated his question: was the Home Secretary aware that Mrs Pace had been 'ordered by the police to proceed to Coleford Police Station to be interrogated' for thirteen hours on 11 March although 'the children were in bed at the time, with the result that the family left the house without any breakfast'? Had this 'wicked system' of 'third-degree methods' been ordered by the police leadership? Joynson-Hicks denied there was 'anything in the nature of third degree' in Britain and noted Beatrice had thanked the police for their 'consideration'. From the Labour benches Ellen Wilkinson questioned whether that gratitude could be taken seriously: 'the poor woman would be in such a condition that she would be only too thankful to get away'.[28] The *Daily Herald* – which also raised questions about Dorothy's questioning during the inquest – was scathing about Joynson-Hicks's apparent ignorance of the case: 'Does not the Home Secretary read the newspapers? ... It is passing strange that matters within the knowledge of the most casual reader of newspapers should be unknown to the Home Secretary.'[29]

Neither *The People* nor Thorne invoked 'the third degree' arbitrarily; indeed, the (originally American) phrase had become ubiquitous in inter-war Britain when the use of police powers was questioned.[30] In the late 1920s there were many such questions. Reporting Thorne's question about whether the Pace matter would be included in an upcoming parliamentary investigation into police methods, the *Dean Forest Guardian* explained that the inquiry to which he referred involved the case of 'Miss Savidge, who was acquitted recently of misconduct in Hyde Park'.[31] In May 1928, even 'the most casual reader of newspapers' would have heard of 'Miss Savidge', and concerns about the police came to clearly link her to 'Mrs Pace' in the public mind. This issue, however, takes us briefly far away from the murder investigation in the Forest of Dean.

Irene Savidge was a 22-year-old 'wireless valve inspector' from London. On the evening of 23 April, she and Sir Leo Chiozza Money – a prominent, married economist and former MP in his late fifties – were arrested in Hyde Park for 'indecency'.[32] The arrest was one of many resulting from the police's plainclothes surveillance of sexual activity in London parks. But the case was soundly dismissed by a magistrate without Savidge – whose virginity had been medically certified – having to testify. The magistrate had even raised doubts about the constables' testimony. The Director of Public Prosecutions handed the issue of possible perjury to Scotland Yard to look into. On 15 May, two detectives appeared at Savidge's workplace, asking her to accompany them for questioning.[33] What happened during her five-hour questioning was disputed; however, she later alleged that the detectives had acted in an aggressive, suggestive and offensive manner. A Labour MP presented Savidge's claims in Parliament on 17 May, sparking a scandal that occupied the front pages, stoked debate about civil liberties and forced the Home Secretary to call two parliamentary investigations: one into the Savidge case itself and another into police powers more generally. A Home Office memo in July argued that 'there can be no doubt that it was the Pace case that heated opinion to the point where it was ready to explode when the Savidge case occurred'.[34] 'This Pace case', furthermore, 'is clearly the case on which rests the greater part of the demand for a "Second Tribunal" into police methods.'[35] Indeed, when *Reynolds's Illustrated News* gave front-page coverage to Savidge's 'startling "third degree" allegations', it also referred to the allegations about the treatment of Beatrice and Dorothy Pace as causing 'public alarm at police methods'.[36] Following Beatrice's acquittal, the *Daily Herald* thought investigations into the police procedures were necessary to ensure that nothing 'in the nature of the Third Degree' had occurred in Coleford. It was 'imperative for the Government to take steps for the re-establishment of public confidence in police methods and the administration of justice'.[37] The *Daily Chronicle* and other papers similarly connected the Pace and Savidge issues.[38] (The cases were further linked by the fact that Norman Birkett, who defended Beatrice in Gloucester, was the police's advocate in the Savidge Inquiry.[39]) Of the various complaints about the police, the *Saturday Review* commented that, 'the Pace case is undoubtedly the one out of many which has most impressed the public with the need for enquiry'.[40]

The 'third-degree' allegations in the Pace case, made most directly in *The People* in March, had also provoked activity behind the scenes. Cornish discussed the matter with his superiors: he was 'strongly of the opinion' that the accusation amounted to 'a scurrilous libel'. 'I have now completed 33 years of service', he pointed out, and 'during that time I have investigated crime of practically every description in many parts of the country, and I feel very hurt about this attack upon me as it is the first time after all these years that my conduct has ever been in question.' 'If articles of this description go unchecked or unchallenged', Cornish warned, 'I submit that the duties of Scotland Yard officers investigating serious crimes in various parts of the country will be so seriously handicapped that it will be impossible for the ends of justice to be met.'[41] He received permission to contact a legal firm that represented the Metropolitan Police, and in mid-April, a solicitor wrote to the editor and publishers of *The People*, informing them of his firm's intention 'in due course' to sue for libel.[42]

Internal police statements told a different story about what had happened on 11 March, which went as follows.[43] When Cornish and Campion arrived at the police station at about a quarter to ten, they found Beatrice, Doris and Leslie eating breakfast. Cornish questioned Doris first, having been informed she 'was the child that was most partial towards her father and used to attend to him a lot'. He started with Beatrice at about 11.20 a.m. She described Harry's cruelty and his prolonged illness for over an hour, after which Cornish asked whether she would repeat her comments so they could be written down. This was 'only fair' considering the rumours concerning Harry's death and, as he put it, 'the possibilities of her accelerating it'. She agreed and was quite talkative. 'She carried on in her own way', he said, and 'the only time I put any questions to her then was to prevent her from getting too far ahead whilst Sergeant Campion was writing down her statement in longhand'. At 1.30 p.m., Cornish sent her to a pre-arranged lunch in a private room at the nearby Angel Hotel accompanied by a policewoman, Edith Lodge. Afterwards, Beatrice continued her statement up to the point of Harry's illness. At that point, Cornish revealed to her that forensic analysis indicated the presence of arsenic: 'I asked her if she could suggest how it got there, but she was unable to account for it.'

Shortly before five o'clock, Inspector Bent's wife brought in tea. Cornish consulted with Campion and Bent for nearly an hour while Lodge attended to Beatrice. Bent went to fetch Dorothy so she could answer a few more questions, and the detectives returned upstairs. 'I asked her various questions to clear up points that had arisen in statements already taken from other people', Cornish stated, finishing just before seven. Campion then read the long statement back to her and she signed it. Beatrice insisted upon waiting while Dorothy was questioned, afterward returning home in a car Cornish had arranged. 'Mrs. Pace', Cornish insisted, 'never complained then of her stay at the Station, nor did she comment adversely on anything.' She was 'quite composed' and 'certainly not in a state of collapse': 'At no time during the day did Mrs. Pace seem cross or dissatisfied.'

Other statements agreed. Campion 'never heard Mrs. Pace make any complaint of any kind', insisted that she had not left in a state of collapse and claimed there were no 'cross words at all': 'I never noticed her getting "ratty" as she suggests in her statement to *The People*.'[44] Bent and Lodge concurred, as did James Wood, a 'garage proprietor' from Coleford who had driven people back and forth between Fetter Hill and the police station.[45] He said Beatrice, Leslie and Doris had arrived in Coleford at about 9.30 a.m., and the children returned home after being questioned. 'Directly after nine o'clock that evening' (an hour earlier than *The People* claimed), he took Beatrice home. 'She walked to the car by herself', Wood recalled, 'and got out by herself at the house and I saw no appearances of fainting or collapse.' Beatrice had been at the station for eleven to eleven-and-a-half hours. (At the assize trial, Bent agreed with Birkett's statement that she was in Coleford for about twelve hours.[46])

Cornish and Campion were advised in June that the suit could begin, but the solicitor urged caution in view of 'the present state of public feeling'.[47] Whether he meant 'public feeling' for Beatrice, against the police or some combination of the two is unclear. The detectives waited, but after Beatrice's acquittal a 'very reliable source' told Cornish the paper – 'anxious to avoid litigation' – was willing to publish a retraction and offer compensation.[48] In October *The People* paid each detective ten guineas (£10 10s) and printed a brief apology. It had been 'pointed out' that an earlier article 'casts reflections on the manner in which these officers carried out their investigations' the paper wrote: 'We wish, however, to make it quite clear – and we gladly give publicity to the fact – that we are satisfied that at no time whilst making their inquiries did these two distinguished officers exceed their lawful duty, and we desire to disclaim any intention on our part to impugn their good faith and integrity.'[49]

It would have been easy to overlook this passage – buried as it was on page five, in contrast to the front-page accusations to which it responded – but Cornish and Campion were 'quite satisfied'. Police Commissioner Horwood was disappointed the compensation was not 'more substantial' but thought 'it should teach the press that they cannot libel police officers with impunity'.[50]

Cornish's concerns may have been assuaged by Beatrice's inquest comment that he had treated her 'with great consideration and kindness'.[51] George Mountjoy had even written to him in June expressing gratitude 'on behalf of Mrs Pace and the whole of the family (excluding no one)' for 'the very kind way in which you have discharged what certainly amounts to a painful and unpleasant duty'.[52] But why, then, had she claimed otherwise in *The People*? Had her words been twisted? Or had the 11 March statement been confused with another one three days later, when Beatrice *did* leave the police station in anguish? But what had so upset her on *that* occasion, and why were that statement's contents kept secret?

Although the Pace family's claims that Beatrice was unfaithful had indeed been duly reported (and any journalist spending time in the area would have encountered rumours), the widow's adamant denials were repeated many times and never officially questioned. Her statement on 14 March was never made public and was read only by the police, the prosecutor, the coroner, the magistrates, Beatrice's defence and the members of the inquest jury.[53] It is unsurprising it had 'distressed' her, as it revealed two previous untruths.[54] Although she had spoken of two 'miscarriages' on 11 March, she now stated 'I did not tell you then that they were brought about by my husband.' In 1926, Harry, knowing she was pregnant, had given her 'something' he acquired from a workmate at the quarry: within days, she miscarried. He had done 'exactly the same thing' a few months earlier. There was a related admission: five weeks after Harry's return from the hospital in late 1927, 'I found I was again pregnant and then took medicines and injections which cleared me.'[55] Cornish recounted that Beatrice spoke 'quite voluntarily' on 14 March with the exception of 'the last paragraph which was in reply to a question from me'. This referred to Beatrice's second revelation. 'I am very sorry I told you a lie', she stated, 'when I said I had never been with any other man': she had indeed had 'connections' with a man 'a few times'.[56]

It is not known what her motivation was for making the first admission; however, that for the second is known. Cornish had come to believe she had 'occasionally' had affairs despite her emphatic denials and 'an oath on the life of her children that she had never been unfaithful to her husband at any time'.

Unconvinced, he had 'looked about with the view of testing how far her testimony could be relied upon'.[57] Leonard Pace sent him to the man in question (whose name did not come up during the inquest), claiming to have found him once with Beatrice in a 'very compromising position'. Since married, the man told Cornish he had been 'regularly seducing Mrs Pace at her house whilst her husband was away at work over a period of several years'. That statement in hand, Cornish confronted Beatrice. After 'over an hour' of denials, she finally gave in. ('She is a remarkable woman', Cornish observed, 'and adopts a very strong attitude': 'By this I mean that once she says a thing she is determined to stick to it, no matter what happens, whether it is right or wrong.') He believed she had had other affairs but apparently had no proof.

Beatrice was in a difficult position. In the midst of a murder investigation, she had admitted telling two lies to the police. One was potentially relevant to the case (in that infidelity provided a motive). The other (the 'inducing' of miscarriages) was itself illegal. Her awareness of what the police knew about her may have contributed to her conciliatory words about them at the inquest. (This continued after the trial, as Dorothy expressed understanding that the officers 'could not have ignored the accusations made against my mother'.[58]) She was, in any case, fortunate that her admissions were neither made public nor used against her by the prosecution. They might have strengthened the circumstantial case against her, and they certainly would have damaged her reputation.[59]

After the trial, not all the press was as conciliatory toward the police as Beatrice and her family. The *Daily News*, condemning Beatrice's 'sustained ordeal of mental torture', referred to her 'cross-examination' – this was Birkett's word – 'for hours on end'.[60] 'The whole way in which the case has been conducted by the police is the subject of disapproving comment', observed the Gloucester *Citizen*, 'and much will be said about it in the discussions upon police methods which are about to take place.' The paper worried that police procedure was changing 'to the prejudice of accused persons and to the prejudice, also, of the sound principles and traditions by which hitherto the rights and liberties of the individual have been scrupulously safeguarded'. A full inquiry into police methods in this case 'and other recent instances' might reveal nothing more than 'the plain obligation of the police in the detection of crime and the bringing of criminals to justice'; however, 'there ought not to be dual inquiries leading to opposed or conflicting conclusions'.[61]

This was a reference to the Savidge Inquiry, which reported the week after Beatrice's acquittal. Two of the tribunal's members exonerated Scotland Yard, but a minority report by a third questioned the police's handling of the matter, the veracity of their testimony and their methods of questioning witnesses, putting further pressure on the police. A letter in *The Times* at the end of July from trade union representatives, feminists and politicians (among them Will Thorne) pressed for a searching general inquiry: citing the Pace and Savidge cases (and the paltry number of policewomen) they argued that the 'possibility of abuse, of unfair pressure on witnesses by the police' as well as 'calumnies of the police by witnesses, are at their gravest in cases in which women are concerned'.[62] Earlier that month, Labour MP Ellen Wilkinson had again raised the matter of police actions in the Pace case, especially the lengthy questioning of the children in order to 'put a rope around their mother's neck'. Referring to the equalisation of voting rights for women that year, she observed that women had become 'responsible electors' and were 'profoundly disturbed at the attitude of the police towards children, and the rigid attitude which was maintained during that case'.[63]

The police, however, had their backers. A week after Beatrice's acquittal, the *Daily Express* admitted there were 'backsliders' and 'weaker vessels' in the force but denied that they were the 'backbone' of the rank and file: Scotland Yard remained 'the best police headquarters in the world'.[64] The *World's Pictorial News* condemned the months of 'gassy, alarming talk about the terrible methods of the English police' which had been 'nuts to the Communists, and to the criminal classes of the worst species' even though the methods of '99 per cent' of the police were 'above reproach'.[65] Public concerns faded after the largely reassuring March 1929 report of the general inquiry called in the wake of the Pace and Savidge cases – the Royal Commission on Police Powers and Procedure (during which the Pace case was discussed in testimony from Major Clarke, the Chief Constable of Gloucestershire) – as well as a much-publicised effort to purge the force of 'black sheep'.[66] However, the two cases were recalled later that year in popular novelist S. Fowler Wright's polemical critique *Police and Public*. Although based largely upon the Savidge issue, a chapter on murder trials depicted the 'scandalous farce' of the Pace case as part of a common pattern:

> The malicious slander to the police-station, too easily credited: the taking of 'statements' from all concerned without any solid basis of accusation to justify such a procedure: the collection of endless trivialities of fact or chatter, to be gone over endlessly in the hope that a few could be selected which could be woven into a theory of guilt.[67]

There were few procedural changes that resulted from the concerns raised in 1928, and not until the late 1950s would the relationship between police and public be similarly ruptured.[68] Nonetheless, the Pace case played an important – if subsequently forgotten – role in a significant police crisis in the late 1920s.

'An ordeal without precedent or parallel': the coroner's court

Even more than the police, the coroner's inquest – the specific one that sat in Coleford as well as the institution itself – was heavily criticised. The case was 'destined', as the *Daily Herald* put it, 'to go down in legal history as proving the need for revision of the existing laws governing the authority of a coroner's inquest'.[69] Dorothy complained about the proceedings being 'prolonged as they were day after day, week after week, and month after month': 'Whose responsibility it was I do not know, but it did seem to me at the time, and it does still, that all those weeks – every day of which added to the torture of my mother – were unnecessary.'[70] *The People* agreed, arguing that the 'ordeal' was 'cruelly and unnecessarily long' and asserting that 'the public conscience demands that no other innocent person shall ever be allowed to suffer in the same way'. It had been 'solely' at the coroner's suggestion that the first verdict was revised: this, the paper was sure, 'must not be allowed to stand'.[71] Purcell referred to her treatment by the coroner as 'a sort of Spanish inquisition'.[72] In an essay in *John Bull* entitled 'It could happen to you!', E. Roffe Thompson argued against maintaining the 'outworn' office of the coroner, and he thought Beatrice deserved recompense: 'It is not a comforting thought that you or I, or any of us, could be arrested and taken through the whole horrible mill of the judicial machine, and, being proved innocent, left without any title to compensation.'[73]

Other criticism had appeared almost immediately after the dramatic 'double verdict' on 22 May. A week later, a letter from H. A. Hollond, Trinity College Reader in Law, appeared in *The Times*. Those many Englishmen, he wrote, who 'complacently believe' that the superiority of British law lay in the principle of innocence until guilt is proven 'must have been rudely shocked by the dramatic circumstances of the Coroner's inquest upon the body of Harry Pace'. Although 'in substance', the verdict was simply a 'charge' and 'educated persons know it to be such', he thought 'there is much virtue in words':

> If Mrs. Pace is acquitted on trial, the fact will remain that it will stand recorded in the files of all the newspapers of the country that a Coroner's jury actually found her to have killed her husband by poison. Justice, as well as logic, surely demands that this misuse of language should be removed from our Statute-book.[74]

The *Daily Express* similarly noted that 'a man proved innocent of murder in a criminal court may always bear the stigma of having been to all intents found guilty of murder in a coroner's court'.[75]

When Beatrice was indeed acquitted less than two months later, criticism focused on precisely this point. The inquest verdict, according to the *Daily Mail*, meant that the woman remained under a 'cruel slur'.[76] The refusal of the coroner, Maurice Carter, to accept the jury's first, non-specific decision was particularly condemned, alternatively depicted as an indication of a personal failure or a systemic problem. The *Daily Telegraph* thought the verdict and the 'processes by which attempts were made to build up a case against Mrs. Pace' had caused 'surprise and anxiety'.[77] The *Daily Mail* stated unequivocally that 'solicitors and barristers' believed Carter had been 'wrong in law in not accepting the original verdict of the jury'. It quoted another coroner: 'It is wrong for a coroner's jury to name any person or persons in a finding involving a criminal case unless they are satisfied beyond all reasonable doubt that there is a prima facie case for examination.'[78] In his view, the first, 'open' verdict was the legal one. In the *World's Pictorial News*, T. A. Hannam called the verdict 'absurd'. Mrs Pace – 'a poor, bewildered little mouse in a corner fearing to stir lest one Grimalkin or another would pounce on her' – had been 'prosecuted' at the inquest. Arguing that 'it was intended to charge and commit Mrs. Pace for trial from the very first', he thought the inquest was 'a humbug'; however, he noted 'it did allow a tremendous lot of irrelevant stuff to be brought out in the police court'. The 'public sense of British justice', he claimed, demanded that the verdict be 'publicly expunged, erased, and publicly reversed and declared wrong'.[79] However, as the *Citizen* pointed out, that would be redundant: the acquittal at the assizes achieved, in law, the same result. Since the prosecution had failed, 'in no sense can it be said that the [inquest] jury's verdict stands against the widow'. Nonetheless, the paper critiqued Carter for pressing for a second verdict and sensed 'a great deal of public indignation against this action of the Coroner'.[80]

Was the 'public indignation' justified? Had the coroner unfairly – even unlawfully – bullied the jury into naming Beatrice? His summary of the evidence did seem intended to steer the jury's opinion. 'Is it conceivable', he had asked them, 'that this man is going to dose himself in July with sheep-dip lotion to see how much he could take or how long he could linger before he killed himself, and then is it conceivable he is going to take one big dose within a short space of his death?'[81] The only options he seemed to offer were a continuous series of suicide attempts between July 1927 and January 1928 – which, indeed, would seem implausible – or murder. The possibility that accidental poisoning in July and Harry's resulting illness might have led to a suicidal depression was not even mentioned. However, the personal criticism Carter received centred not on his summary but on his request to the jury to reconsider their verdict. But given the law on inquests, the complicated circumstances of the case and the character of the jury's first verdict, his actions were not that remarkable.

Coroners were regulated by the 1887 Coroner's Act, as amended by subsequent Acts (the latest revision before the Pace case had been in 1926). Carter had reportedly consulted a 'legal manual', most likely the procedural guide commonly referred to as *Jervis on Coroners*. First written in the early nineteenth century by Sir John Jervis, it had been revised as required, most recently for its seventh edition in 1927. According to *Jervis*, inquest juries were obligated to not only find the cause of death but also, when possible, name a suspect.[82] They could opt to declare that the victim had been killed by 'a person or persons unknown', and it seems that some critics believed this is what the Coleford jury at first wanted. The *Justice of the Peace* thought Carter had misinterpreted the law by asking the jurors to reconsider their verdict, since their 'plain' ('if not strictly grammatical') intention had been to return just such an 'open verdict'.[83]

However, the jury foreman had stated both that Harry had been killed by arsenic 'administered by some person or persons other than himself' and that there should be further investigation. Carter noted that a verdict against 'a person or persons unknown' was possible, but he (rightly) explained that no one could be committed for trial on a coroner's 'inquisition' (as it was known) without the jury naming them. Asked whom they suspected, the foreman said they were 'not agreed'. It was for this reason that Carter asked them to reconsider, since it was suggested that the jury may have had a name in mind. He might have interpreted their ambiguous first decision as an 'open' verdict, but in choosing not to, he acted within the letter (and, arguably, the spirit) of the law. (A unanimous decision was not required: a 'majority' of jurors – with no more than two dissenters – could name a responsible party.[84]) Had the jury returned a second time and insisted upon a verdict stating an 'unknown' perpetrator, Carter would have had to accept it: coroners could not overrule their juries' decisions. (Beatrice still could have – and probably would have – been charged by the police.) In an internal police report, Cornish stated he had been 'reliably informed' that there was 'no disagreement at all' among the jury: 'The reason for the incomplete first finding', he explained, 'was because none of the jurymen desired to mention the name of Mrs Pace if it could be avoided and they thought they could get over it by returning a verdict such as they did at first.'[85] At the end of such a lengthy, high-profile inquest, it is not surprising that Carter sought a clear verdict one way or another. After the trial, he refrained from public comment.[86]

Others argued that the problem was not the means by which a specific jury had named a particular suspect but rather their power to do so at all. Here, the Pace case became embroiled in an already simmering debate. As Hollond pointed out in his letter to *The Times*, an inquest could only 'charge'; however, he was not alone in being troubled by the implication of a 'verdict' rendered by a 'jury', especially one that could hear evidence that was prohibited in trials. The *Daily Express* thought coroners should only determine the cause of death, leaving the police to charge and the courts to determine guilt.[87] The *Sunday Express* demanded an inquiry into 'the obsolete and antiquated procedure of coroners' courts' to prevent a recurrence of 'the cumbrous and clumsy methods which inflicted on Mrs. Pace an ordeal without precedent or parallel'.[88]

Criticisms were also raised in Parliament: the press reported that questions would be asked about quashing the inquest verdict and taking steps to remove Carter from office.[89] Purcell thought Beatrice was due 'adequate compensation' for what she had gone through. 'Flogging', he said, 'would have been humane in comparison with it.'[90] Attorney-General Sir Thomas Inskip had been selected to answer Purcell's questions on the case when raised in the Commons. He flatly rejected compensation: the accused had been 'acquitted by a jury after a very careful and admittedly fair trial'. Purcell responded sharply. 'Is there really no sense of decency on the part of the Crown', he asked, provoking vocal outrage from the Conservative benches. He continued undaunted:

> I repeat, is there no sense of decency on the part of the Crown in connection with a case that has resulted in half this woman's home being destroyed by members of the public who are in a morbid sense out for sight-seeing? Is nothing to be done for a woman who in this case has been thrown into prison without an atom of evidence that she was in any sense responsible for the crime?[91]

Inskip merely agreed to look more closely at the depositions Purcell had submitted: along with compensation, they demanded a public inquiry into coroners' powers and consideration of increased legal aid for the poor. The *Manchester Guardian* found Purcell's linking of 'morbid sightseers and trophy-seekers' to a demand for compensation 'lame and halting', but he was not the only one to speak.[92] Will Thorne denounced the coroner for an unnecessary trial. He was seconded by Welsh Liberal Rhys Hopkin Morris, who had told the press that 'no prosecution would have been launched against Mrs. Pace by the Director of Public Prosecutions if his hand had not been forced by the findings at the coroner's court'.[93] (Morris had also, incidentally, helped set up the Savidge Inquiry.[94]) The Pace case thus contributed to the debate about coroner's inquests. Indeed, two biographies of Norman Birkett have claimed it drove legal reforms that ended coroners' power to name suspects.[95]

This was, however, mistaken, though not for lack of trying. Left-wing MP Cecil Malone announced his intention to seek to amend upcoming legislation to ensure coroners' juries were free to return a verdict against 'persons unknown' to prevent the recurrence of incidents 'which are greatly agitating the public mind'.[96] Within days, Morris moved legislation to limit coroners to finding the cause of death.[97] At the beginning of 1929 he introduced a similar bill, citing another problematic case.[98] But there was little headway, even though the issue transcended party lines. In October 1929, Conservative MP Sir Kingsley Wood drew attention to the 'considerable public apprehension' regarding 'the recent conduct and procedure of certain Coroners' inquests' with regard to 'the ancient and well established rights and liberties of the subject'. The Home Secretary – the 1929 election had seen Joynson-Hicks replaced by Labour's John Clynes – responded that procedure had been 'brought up to date' in 1926 and he would not consider another revision 'because of what has happened in one or two quite exceptional cases'. Coroners' courts, he said, embodied the 'ancient common law of England', and given the large number of inquests – 30,000 in 1927 – there were 'remarkably few' complaints.[99]

At least for a time, however, the events in Coleford remained a reference point in press comment and parliamentary debate. In March 1929, T. A. Hannam, in the *World's Pictorial News*, condemned the actions of the coroner looking into another case – the killing of Vivian Messiter – claiming: 'It was the Mrs. Pace position all over again, and with the same unpleasant features.'[100] In May 1930, Wood and Morris participated in another committee discussion on coroners.[101] Wood thought the issue was serious: 'There is a danger of the liberty of the subject in this country being infringed upon', since some inquests had become 'inquisitions' that were used 'not to ascertain the cause of death, but ... to secure evidence which may result in a particular individual being committed for trial'. 'Many eminent lawyers and a large section of the public' had been 'disturbed' by recent cases:

> There was the case called the Pace case, in which the coroner's inquest lasted for four months. The woman concerned in that case was subjected to a considerable ordeal, and, when she came

up for trial at the Gloucester Assizes, the judge ruled that there was no case against her. I cannot help saying that in that case the coroner's duty was perfectly clear, it was to ascertain the cause of death. It was not his duty ... to subject a person to four months of interrogation and examination with a view to placing a particular person on trial.

Morris's criticism was similar: 'some of us', he stressed, had pressed for reform without 'a very great measure of success'. He condemned the way inquests fed the press's insatiable appetite for drama. His comments have a familiar ring, condemning the way that 'every sensational case gets a wide publicity in the Press, every detail is published, particularly in the Sunday papers':

> The coroner's inquiry, with its roving examination and cross-examination inquiring into anything and everything, a good deal of which is not evidence at all, results in the whole of the inquiry being published in detail. People who have to serve on the jury at the subsequent trial at the Assizes will probably have read a good deal that would influence their minds, though it is not evidence.

The committee urged limiting inquests to determining cause of death, a recommendation echoed in 1936 by a special parliamentary committee headed by Lord Wright.[102] It, too, was not implemented, and, decades later, a 1971 inquiry was left to make the same suggestion (the 'Brodrick Report').[103] Popular outcry after an inquest named the (vanished) Lord Lucan as the murderer of his children's nanny in 1975 gave new impetus for reform. The power of coroners' juries to charge suspects – an issue so central in the legal ordeal of Beatrice Pace – was finally abolished in 1977.[104]

The price of justice and 'the sorrowful sisters of Mrs. Pace'

In addition to critiques of the police and of coroners' inquests, Beatrice's case sparked debates about poverty, marriage and equality before the law. The inquest verdict had immediately raised the problem of how this impoverished woman could afford representation. Hitherto, Beatrice's brother Fred had taken responsibility for her legal fees. By early June, all of the sheep and lambs from Harry's flock had been sold to pay for rent and food. Beatrice would have been eligible for an appointed legal counsel. However, the *World's Pictorial News* argued that experience had shown 'the best legal brains in the country' would not be available even though 'no expense is spared' for funding the prosecution.[105] The array of legal and medical experts available to the prosecution contrasted dramatically with Beatrice's grim poverty: as it was pointed out, the prosecution had the resources of the Treasury on its side. (There were reports that the prosecution cost as much as £8,000; Beatrice's legal costs were estimated to have been between £1,600 and £1,700.[106])

Alongside his demands for compensating Beatrice (which were rejected) and for quashing the inquest verdict and investigating coroners' courts (neither of which happened), Purcell raised the issue of legal aid for the poor. Although his own private efforts had raised enough money to enable Beatrice to have a barrister 'equal in skill and ability to the Crown's representative', the very necessity of such a fund proved the need for reforms to ensure 'equal opportunities on both sides'. The state's ability to use its full resources 'without the same facilities being at the disposal of the defence is not fair nor justice'.[107] Interviewed by the *Daily Herald*, Purcell stated: 'My only comment is that with a galaxy of legal luminaries ranged against this or any other poor woman, it would be unfortunate if some provision were not made for their defence.'[108] Within days of the acquittal, he wrote an article for *Reynolds's Illustrated News* that emphasised Beatrice's economic straits. Not only did they argue against her having had a motive to kill her husband (on whose income she was dependent), they also exemplified the difficulties faced by poor people in mounting a competent defence.[109] There was some support expressed for Purcell's goals. The following week, *John Bull* labelled the failure to compensate Beatrice 'a grave flaw'.[110] *Time and Tide*, while arguing against generally compensating acquitted people (which would 'impede the course of justice'), favoured a public defender. Without mentioning the Pace case by name, it observed: 'The man or woman whose "story" excites sympathy or rouses other strong emotions may be helped by a subscription list or financed by a newspaper. Others, whose careers and alleged offences are merely dull, can look for no such aid.'[111] The *Empire News* called for a public defender and highlighted the disparities in treatment of the rich and poor.[112]

On 24 July, Purcell introduced legislation to create a new office for the defence of poor persons charged with offences punishable by death: the 'Defender of the Poor'.[113] It would be empowered to give those charged with capital offences 'equal facilities with those enjoyed by the Crown in regard to the availability of legal and technical experts'. 'If there were any need to argue the matter fully,' Purcell observed, 'I think we have had sufficient experience in the recent case tried in Gloucestershire.'[114] The Bill was duly read for a second time the next day and printed. The *Manchester Guardian* thought Purcell's plan 'has much to commend it' and believed that if carried through it would 'make it impossible in the case of capital charges to complain that British justice was in any way class justice'.[115] The *Sunday News* thought a public defender was a 'logical corollary' of a public prosecutor.[116] However, many papers ignored the issue, and there was also scepticism, even among those who were otherwise critical of how the Pace case was handled.[117] In the *Dean Forest Guardian*, a reader's letter, while acknowledging Purcell's generous assistance of a poor widow, mocked the left-wing MP's criticisms of British justice: 'Possibly he imagined that innocent people are convicted here like they are in Russia, under the Bolshevist government, which Mr. Purcell so greatly admires.'[118] Purcell's bill, ultimately, got no further.

Along with poverty, marriage was relevant to the social analyses that emerged in the discussions of the Pace case. As the last chapter pointed out, though there was an individual aspect to such narratives, broader perspectives were possible. An editorial published by *The People* two days after Beatrice's acquittal did not refer specifically to the case, but considering its timing and the fact that its title – 'Martyrs by choice' – echoed the frequent evocations of Beatrice's 'martyrdom', it was most likely written with her in mind.[119] It observed: 'By nature and instinct most women welcome sacrifice for those they love. They ask little in return, except appreciation. And it is only when that is denied them that they are inclined to pose as martyrs.' Too many husbands, it concluded, failed to appreciate their wives.

Other commentary mixed class and gender concerns, and Beatrice's claim that she stayed with Harry solely out of love and a sense of duty did not prevent others from arguing otherwise. James Douglas, editor of the *Sunday Express*, saw Beatrice as a 'victim of our inhuman marriage and divorce laws' and the 'obsolete view of woman as the sole property of her husband'. 'Why did not Mrs. Pace escape? The answer is that she was too poor to escape, and that she believed it was her duty as a wife to bear unimaginable agonies and degradations and cruelties.' Unable to afford a divorce (he suggested costs were typically £100, dropping to £30 when a 'charitable solicitor conducts it for nothing') poor women such as Beatrice were trapped in 'lifelong bondage': she was an 'economic slave'. Although he could not say how many men used Britain's 'pitiless laws' to 'convert marriage into a secret devilry in which they may with impunity gratify their basest and most brutal passions', there were nonetheless 'husbands like Harry Pace on every street of every village and every town'. Douglas's solution was not only to make it 'as cheap and as easy to get out of marriage as it is to get into it' but also to increase state aid to divorced mothers. 'Let us insure motherhood as we insure unemployment', he declared: 'If the bad husband is a pauper, let the State take care of the mother and her children. If he has money, let him be forced to support them after we have rescued them from him.' Douglas thought that leadership on such reforms would have to come from women themselves, using their newly granted electoral power to fight 'intrenched [sic] interests and institutions that will resist it desperately'. In their fight, he proclaimed that his newspaper would be on the side of 'the sorrowful sisters of Mrs. Pace'.[120]

Some weeks later, Douglas returned to the topic.[121] After his first article, women had sent him letters or, as he called them, 'raw slabs and slices of married life'. Some compared their experiences with Beatrice's, recounting their husbands' brutality, neglect and substance abuse. One woman had endured a morphine-addicted husband until his death. 'I am happily married now', she wrote, 'to a man who has gradually taught me that there are men worthy of the name, and that marriage can be a fine and sacred thing.' However, the emphasis remained on the need for these 'martyrs' to escape their husbands, and Douglas printed a woman's letter explaining how to get an inexpensive divorce (it had cost her 'exactly £2 10s'). Beatrice's experience was thus built up into a broad condemnation of the state's insufficient response to domestic abuse. (Lest Douglas be thought a straightforwardly progressive thinker, however, it should be noted that in his first article on Beatrice he also labelled birth control a 'blight' that turned marriage into a 'legalised form of racial suicide'.)

Beatrice's brutal marriage, her treatment by the criminal

justice system and the constraints of her poverty certainly invited analyses and commentary linking her individual experiences to problems of institutional and legal reform and social inequality. However, when given her own opportunity to speak, as we have seen, she downplayed the role of poverty, law or social attitudes in her suffering. There was a similar tension between Beatrice's simultaneous depiction as a uniquely virtuous domestic angel and as an 'everywoman'. Different commentators emphasised – according to their own assumptions and needs – alternative elements of the story. It is possible that such complexities in Beatrice's public persona aided her popularity, but gauging what 'the public' has made of popular historical figures such as herself is a difficult task. Fortunately, as the next chapter shows, it is not impossible in this case.

9

'Those who have had trouble can sympathise with you': Mrs Pace and her public

Clearly, Beatrice had press and politics on her side, and, in the wake of the acquittal, some newspapers asked a variety of prominent people for their views. T. P. O'Connor – journalist, politician and president of the British Board of Film Censors – was 'very delighted'. 'I never thought she was guilty', he explained, 'and I deplore the long and anxious time she has been through. I hope that all the people who sympathise with her will help her to rebuild her home again.' Journalist Ada Chesterton was, likewise, 'tremendously pleased' and saw the matter as 'an extraordinary case of the triumph of personality': 'Her simple steadfastness saw her through.'[1] Her brother-in-law, G. K. Chesterton, said he was 'in sympathy with Mrs Pace' and thought that 'something should be done to compensate her'. George Bernard Shaw agreed that Beatrice should be compensated just like 'anyone who has been put to great inconvenience and, as has happened in the case of Mrs Pace, discredit, when an action has been brought and failed through lack of evidence'.[2]

What indication do we have of the views of the broader public? Gifts, donations and supportive messages 'from all over the world' reportedly flowed steadily toward her. The *News of the World* stated that she 'was overwhelmed with letters and telegrams congratulating her on her triumphant acquittal'.[3] Although only a few examples were published, over two hundred letters and postcards have been preserved in a collection of case materials kept by Beatrice's solicitor, G. Trevor Wellington.[4] Their proportion of the total correspondence is unknown, as is any selection process through which some letters might have been kept and others discarded. Nor is it clear why Wellington had so many of them. Most were written within a few days of her acquittal and many were addressed vaguely (e.g., 'Mrs Pace, Fetter Hill, Forest of Dean, Gloucestershire'[5]). Since Beatrice left the area for a holiday immediately after the trial and soon moved away, they may have been given to Wellington to pass along to her. Perhaps he forgot; maybe she did not want them. Though incomplete, the sample provides insight into the public's reactions to the case, and it offers a rare glimpse of how people interacted with the press in the early twentieth century.

'I hope you will forgive me writing to you but I felt as if I must'[6]

There are 232 letters to Beatrice in the collection. It is impossible to systematically group them according to the writer's class or income level, but other distinctions are possible. Women sent 145 (62.5 per cent) and men 29 (12.5 per cent). Forty-six (19.8 per cent) of the letters provide insufficient information for determining the sender's sex, and the remaining 12 (5.2 per cent) were signed by couples, groups, children or families. They were overwhelmingly supportive: 220 (94.8 per cent) of the 232 letters were explicitly congratulatory (one written shortly before the trial's end was hopeful). [7] Only 4 (1.7 per cent) were critical of her acquittal and 8 (3.5 per cent) expressed no explicit view one way or the other. This imbalance seems to confirm journalists' reports of a groundswell of public support – possibly 'universal compassion' – for Beatrice.[8] Caution is warranted with any sample, but some hostile letters were kept in the file. All of these were anonymous, adding speculative weight to the notion that criticism of Beatrice would have been unpopular.

The Pace children were frequently mentioned: of 220 congratulatory letters, 150 (68.2 per cent) refer to 'the children' (frequently 'your dear children') or to 'your little ones' or 'your dear ones'. Except for Selwyn, who received relatively little press attention, all the other Pace children were referred to specifically. Jean (sometimes called 'the baby') – whose illness generated sympathy – was mentioned most often (twenty-two times) followed by Doris (fourteen times), Leslie (ten times) and Dorothy (five times, once as 'the eldest daughter'). Three-quarters of female writers mentioned the children (either as a group or by name), as did half of male correspondents and about three-fifths of those whose sex could not be identified. The letters and cards Beatrice received in this sample, then, were predominantly from women, were overwhelmingly congratulatory and often highlighted her role as a mother.

Two other general features – related to time and geography – can be noted. Nearly all of the letters were written within days of Beatrice's 6 July acquittal, many that very evening, emphasising how quickly the news spread. The early-afternoon verdict meant her victory made the evening papers, as some correspondents noted.[9] A few also made reference to having heard via radio reports.[10] Some letters were sent by locals who had witnessed the trial in person. A Wesleyan minister wrote on 6 July from Cinderford, near Gloucester, noting, 'As one who was present at the Court this afternoon please receive my sincere congratulations at the result.'[11] A Mrs Edwards from Gloucester – who insisted she had always thought her innocent ('I am sure all the Gloucester people were of the same opinion') – stated that her daughter 'has been down every day to catch sight of you; she saw you twice [and] also your little family'.[12] Beatrice received post not only from throughout Britain but also from abroad: Wellington's file contains letters from Ireland, Canada, Malta and South Africa.[13] Mrs Bain wrote from Alberta: 'I am thousands of miles away, but have followed your case right through on reading old country papers, & I would just like to say: here's one who believes in you.'[14] From Johannesburg, Mrs M. Marques sent a letter saying 'Although so very far away, we have all been praying that your innocence would be proved.'[15]

Some messages were brief, consisting of no more than a sentence, such as 'congratulations from the bottom of our hearts', 'mother & I have been reading your case with keen interest & we are both delighted with the result, your acquittal' or '3 big Hurrahs & cheerio is the hearty wish of a Cornish woman in Glos'ter'.[16] Others were extensive, with writers not only congratulating Beatrice but expressing something of their own experiences. Focusing on these letters, the following two sections consider correspondence written, respectively, by women and men.

'My dear sister': identification and sympathy

As Beatrice's trial opened, the *Daily Mail* observed:

> This trial, with its intimate domestic features, the stories of callous brutality, the references to the bitterness of child-bearing, the evidence of a child against his dead father, and the spectacle of a mother fighting on the side of her dead son, made a deep and wide appeal to women.[17]

As noted, the predominance of women in the crowds gathered at the inquest and trial was often commented upon. The large number of letters from women seems to confirm that Beatrice was a figure with whom many women could identify. 'Identification', in this context, refers to placing oneself into another's position or, relatedly, seeing one's experiences reflected in another's. Among the 140 congratulatory letters from women, 51 (36.4 per cent) explicitly indicated identification as women, mothers, survivors of a hard life or victims of a cruel husband. (Other writers probably felt a similar empathy, but only direct references to such motives have been counted.)

Such identification is apparent in the emotional intensity with which some women followed the case. 'I have followed your case with great interest & sympathy for you from the beginning', one wrote from London, 'and always knew you were innocent of any harm to your late husband.'[18] Another claimed, 'I have read every word from beginning to end of your case, & I knew what the result would be.'[19] From St Leonard's-on-Sea, Annie Hudson emphasised how her circumstances ('I am an invalid girl lying upon my back with spinal trouble') had given her 'every opportunity of following your case closely from the beginning until the end yesterday'. Her interest was shared by her family ('Night & day you have been in our thoughts & I may say how we have grieved for you during your great trouble') and at least one neighbour: 'A widow lady living in the flat below us have [sic] also followed your case', she wrote, '& she like ourselves have believed in your innocence from first to last.'[20] The case was intensely followed among one woman's acquaintances: 'My friends and myself have watched your case with the greatest possible interest and deepest sympathy, and we all wish to congratulate you on the splendid bravery and fortitude with which you faced the terrible ordeal.'[21] Such greetings not only originated among informal groups, as a postcard from the (largely working-class) Mothers' Union indicates:

> We women of Berks[hire] Mothers Union feel we should like you to know how much we have felt for you in your great trial. You have often been in our thoughts & prayers. We hope the rest of your life will be peaceful & happy that your children will grow up to be a credit & comfort to you.[22]

Such emotional involvement is apparent in other letters. J. J. Brooks wrote that she and a neighbour 'have had many tears over you and we were overjoyed when we heard that you had won the day: we are so glad'.[23] E. Ransome from Weymouth wrote, 'I have read your case from the start in the *Daily Mail*, and the tears have rolled down my cheeks more than once for you I might tell you'; another woman revealed, 'we used to cry reading the touching things regarding your children while you were in prison'.[24] Dora Farrow observed, 'although we have never met, to us your face is known as well as one of our own family'.[25] 'Mrs Anonymous' had 'prayed nightly, yea almost hourly' for her, and another writer stated 'we have hardly had patience to wait for the paper every morning'.[26] Mrs C. Whitford exclaimed, 'I read your case from the first and said you never done it ... and every day I had a good cry about you, and I used to say to my sons I only wish I could see dear Mrs Pace, I would kiss her for all she is worth.'[27]

Families had taken a joint interest. Cecily Coe told her daughters about Beatrice, and 'as young as they are they have hoped you would be alright & they have not forgotten you in their prayers'.[28] From Llanelly, S. Howells explained how Leslie Pace's testimony had affected her ten-year-old son Emlyn, who 'could hardly see the words through his tears': 'Only a boy of 10, [but] you won't believe, Mrs Pace, how Emlyn has taken to Leslie.'[29] Other readers' children seem to have similarly 'taken to' Beatrice. One woman's daughter 'cried with joy' when told of the acquittal: 'She said you have a nice face', and 'she has cut your picture out of the paper and hung it up'.[30] J. W. Kelly had likewise framed a photo of Beatrice and her children; the Powell family had done the same with a picture from the *News of the World*.[31] Mrs C. Smith stated: 'I have taken every photo of you and your family, and not a day has passed without kissing your photo and blessing you.'[32] Mary

A. Chapple wrote that she had kissed Beatrice's 'Dear Face' in the newspapers.[33]

News of the acquittal seems to have set off emotional scenes throughout Britain. 'When the *Manchester Evening News* arrived at 5.30 p.m. on Friday', wrote one woman, 'we ran from the house, crying with joy.'[34] Another, from Cardiff, exclaimed, 'O what joy I had today, when one of my married daughters, Mrs Owen, came running in [the] house & said "O Mother, Mrs Pace is discharged"; we both sat down and cried with over-joyment.'[35] 'My husband hurried home tea time with the paper', a correspondent from Pontypore reported, and 'when he said Mrs Pace "not guilty" I had a good cry'.[36] A 'sincere well-wisher' had 'followed your case with keen interest as though you were my own mother', recounting that she 'jumped for joy on reading the papers today, to find you are free'.[37] A Welsh woman recalled: 'I happened to be cleaning the grate when I had the news: I jumped up and clapped my hands and laughed till they thought ... I was gone mad.'[38] A woman from Brixton Hill said not only that her own 'heart bled many times for you and your dear little children' but also that her happiness was shared by her household: 'My maid has just told me that she has offered many prayers on your behalf – & is in tears – now – of joy – at the good news.'[39]

Some women even addressed Beatrice as 'sister'. While this might be in a religious context – 'remember we are *sisters* in His sight'[40] – it was not always so. One correspondent saw herself as a 'stranger but a sister in sympathy', and another noted, 'I have thought so much about you as if you were my own sister.'[41] We also find echoes of Beatrice's press idealisation: 40 of the 140 congratulatory letters sent by women (28.6 per cent) explicitly expressed identification with her as a woman or mother. 'I am sure every woman's heart in England goes out to you', Mary Gibson assured her.[42] One woman said her letter was 'a mere simple token of sympathy in your great ordeal and injustice as one of your own sex', while another wanted 'as a woman to woman' to send 'just a little word of comfort'.[43] Explaining how she cried with happiness after the acquittal, Alice Price commented, 'We women can feel for each other, can't we?'[44] From Norfolk, Dora Farrow hoped her letter would demonstrate 'how far & wide you are thought of today not only as a mother but as a devoted wife & very brave woman'.[45]

The three identities Farrow referenced – 'mother', 'devoted wife' and 'very brave woman' – were often mixed, but maternal themes were particularly strong. Hilda M. Vickery wrote from London to say, 'I have a baby nearly two, & I realize how you must have felt leaving your dear baby behind.'[46] For some women, Beatrice's separation from her family while awaiting trial was particularly painful. 'It's only a mother who can feel for you and understand the agony of another mother torn from her children', wrote one, asserting 'many of us mothers here have shared all along with you in your grief'. 'There isn't another woman in England who has borne the terrible ordeal you have,' she continued, 'but you have had splendid courage [and] you deserve the greatest admiration.'[47] A Canadian woman wrote, 'I am a mother & have two daughters, so I understand how you must feel', and two Devonshire women, 'being mothers of families and near neighbours', sent Beatrice 'all our love as women to woman'.[48] Janet Meek, in Leeds, sympathised 'as a mother, and a grand-mother' and rejoiced 'that you are back with your children'.[49]

Such sympathies were even stronger among women who saw their own experience echoed in Beatrice's victimisation. One of the few published letters stated: 'My mother and I are so sorry for you and your little ones ... There are plenty [who] believe in your innocence. Those who have had trouble can sympathise with you.'[50] This passage combines themes central to Beatrice's public persona: the good wife and mother beset by injustice who would triumph through strong character, public support and (as a few correspondents suggested) divine assistance. It also encapsulates a recurring theme of solidarity based upon common experiences. Writing from Ontario, Canada, Maisie Cooper – who also identified with Beatrice as a 'farmer's wife' – agreed: 'It's only those who have suffered that know what sympathy really means.' She too had been 'scorned' and suffered injustice through false accusations. Describing Harry as 'that brute of a man', she wrote, 'may God above deal with him & give him eternal suffering'. Chief Inspector Cornish – 'that blessed officer who tried to make you condemn yourself' – she insisted, 'will pay the penalty too, the brute'. 'Though the sea divides [us]', she concluded, 'I am with you in tenderness for your babes.'[51]

Like many correspondents, Jessie Sturgeon, from Suffolk, expressed her thankfulness that 'you are free again to be with

your children'. 'I can feel for you in every way as I've been through
so much during my married life', she wrote, admitting she would
'wake up in the middle of the night & think & pray for you'. 'I
don't know why I should think so much of you' she commented,
but she echoed a common refrain: 'only those who have to bear
so much can really have sympathy for others'.[52] One woman had
devotedly bought the *Liverpool Echo* even though she could
ill afford it, explaining 'I could not miss one word of Norman
Birkett['s] great fight for you.' (She was also following Dorothy's
series in *Thomson's Weekly News*). 'Like you', she wrote, 'I have
had a hard life and great deal of trouble', including a sick baby.[53]
There were congratulations 'from one suffering widow to another'
who stated (without providing details), 'my husband's end was
tragic like yours'.[54] A few women praised the efforts of Beatrice's
friends – such as Alice Sayes – to assist her.[55] However, a sense
of common suffering could also lead to appeals for solidarity
of a different kind. A woman named Violet wrote to Beatrice
from Southend-on-Sea, telling a long tale of 'unhappiness &
misery' due to a profligate (and deceased) husband's gambling and
drinking debts. The letter ended in a request: for £8 to cover her
local tax bill.[56]

Some women felt linked to Beatrice by the more specific
experience of unhappy or even cruel marriages. How many
correspondents had similar, though unstated, motives is unknown,
but experience with marital violence (whether as a victim or
witness, whether within one's own family or those of neighbours)
would not have been rare. Mrs F. Steer noted that she and Pace
had 'something in common', having both been married to a 'brute
husband': 'How you could stand by such a man for 18 years', she
wrote, 'beats me beyond all knowledge.' Steer had been impressed
by the devotion in Beatrice's memoir: 'I was not so young as
you when I married, yet after reading about you, I feel such a
coward, for I lived only 2 years with my man & that two years
is a nightmare to me.'[57] Though undated, Steer's letter recalls
Beatrice's comparison, in the 29 July instalment of her memoir,
between abandoning a difficult marriage and running away 'like
a coward'.[58] A note from Florrie Goodridge captures the tone of
this sort of letter well:

> When I read our *Echo* and saw you were found not guilty, I thought
> my heart was going to beat out of me with happiness … I have read

every part of your case as it have [sic] come out and in parts it used to make me break my heart, for I understand just how you must have felt, for God knows I have had a lot of it.

Goodridge identified with Beatrice ('you have seemed one of myself all through'), having left her 'beast of a husband' six years earlier and faced malicious gossip: 'I am not a saint, I know', she admitted, but asserted she was not as 'people have painted me'.[59] Mrs M. Miller identified directly with Beatrice, being a 'poor woman' who had borne ten children ('8 alive & two dead') and endured 'a rotter of a man just the same as yours'. 'I have cried my heart sore for you', she wrote, 'for I knew what it is to have a brutal husband':

I have had many a blow from him & he has threatened my family & myself with a knife & once tried to cut my eldest daughter['s] throat; he has also asked me to drink Lysol & [said] he would buy it. He has tried to drive me & my family to the streets many times, but I have always stuck to my post for I may say I have a very respectful family … [H]e has gone off now for some time now with another woman after a young girl having a baby six years ago to him. Many a wife got clear of such a man but I had no means.

Still, she hoped for justice: 'God', she wrote, 'sits high & takes his own time to punish.'[60] Women did not need to experience poverty or abuse to be fascinated by Beatrice's story: one correspondent, for example, was 'enjoying the love of one of the best of husbands'.[61] Nonetheless, it is apparent that identification based upon perceived commonalities and suffering shaped and intensified many women's reactions to the case.

'Dear madam': respect, desire and business

Fewer men than women wrote to Beatrice, but some took an equally strong interest in her case. While not without similarities with women's correspondence, letters from men were also significantly different in terms of content and perspective. Male correspondents related differently to Beatrice, as identification based on certain common experiences, obviously, was impossible. As their number is relatively small, it is difficult to generalise about male reactions to the case. Nonetheless, three prominent themes – respect, desire and business – can be identified.

Men praised, for example, Beatrice's resilience. A Congregationalist minister from Gloucester had been a spectator in the courtroom:

> I am glad you have borne the ordeal so well, and so calmly, & would like to have seen on your table (with that bottle of smelling salts – I guessed it was this – and glass of water) a bunch of flowers. I would willingly have purchased the flowers, as I told a P.C., but was afraid I should in some way do wrong. One has to be so careful. I – and others – have prayed for you, and now, prayer has been answered.[62]

A similar tone is apparent in a letter from an enlisted soldier:

> We are all very pleased to read in the papers of your successful acquittal at the trial which ended on Friday afternoon. My Platoon Corporal came into the barrack room with an evening paper containing the glad news. It was these words that made us jump for joy: Mrs Pace acquitted. We knew that you would be acquitted because we have studied the case in each evening paper and have read through the lines. My chums and I wish you and your children the very best of luck in the future.[63]

An '80-year-old Yorkshireman' stated he had contacted a London newspaper to suggest that it should start 'a shilling subscription' for her benefit. 'There are many thousands of English women and men would subscribe to such a fund who are in sympathy with your sad circumstances', he said, indicating he had posted a cheque the same day to 'commence' the subscription.[64] A Londoner sent congratulations on having passed successfully through 'the very gates of Hell': 'Happily, you have come through it all triumphantly, and are now in green pastures beside still waters.' Saying he was 'in the legal profession', he praised her barrister and the judge (whom he claimed to know well) and urged her to 'try and keep up the brave heart': 'We all have a mission to fulfil in this vale of tears. Yours is to be the guardian and protectress of your little offsprings [sic]. In years to come, let them be able to say, "Fancy, what mother should be, and she was that."'[65] Another wrote, 'I should like to receive from you one or two flowers plucked by your dear hands, (from your native home) as a souvenir of you, "such a brave & noble woman".'[66]

As that letter hinted, some male correspondents' feelings went beyond respect, perhaps encouraged by press emphasis on

Beatrice's attractiveness and the many photographs of her in the papers. One man, married for ten years, wrote to say that Harry 'was not worthy to have such a lovely young wife like you'. 'May I say here', he continued, 'that had I been a (single) man I should have liked to have had an interview with you.' As things were, he offered his 'fullest sympathy'.[67] Beatrice, along with Dorothy, received several offers of marriage. A widower from Llanelly expressed not only his 'profoundest sympathy' but also his 'truest & sincerest joy & pleasure in your very clear & definite victory'. Urging Beatrice to look after herself for her 'dear children's sake', he wrote:

> After reading what you have [gone] through during your married life, am tempted to offer myself to you, that is to say, should you at any time think of re-marrying. Naturally, of course, you cannot think of doing so at this juncture, as I am fully conscious of the terrible strain you have gone through (physically and mentally).

He wanted to correspond with Beatrice – with a 'view to matrimony' – and expressed his eagerness to 'exchange letters (privately and confidentially of course)' through which they could 'discuss matters secretly'. Offering to send 'all particulars' if she would only write back, he signed off with the phrases 'anticipating a reply' and 'believe me'.[68] An army corporal named Wilkinson got more quickly to the point in a card with only three sentences. Congratulating her on her 'glorious acquittal' and praising her 'noble exhibition of motherhood', he had always believed her innocent: 'to show my admiration I take the liberty of offering you & yours a happy home. Kindly favour an early reply.'[69] The most elaborate proposal in the small sample available came from a gas-fitter in Desborough, a widower with three children, who wrote 'I feel as if I know you quite well': 'I shall feel satisfied that I have offered to accept you into my life and your dear ones also.' Admitting that he was 'not an angel by any means' (nor was he 'a man of means', having 'nothing but what I work for') he tried 'to live out the principles of Christianity'. Desborough, he wrote, 'is quite a pretty little manufacturing town in Northamptonshire [with] fairly good prospects for children'.

> Now my Dear Mrs Pace this may be all too much of a surprise for you. I do not want you to be too hasty in your decision, but pray about it and think it well over. All I am able to promise is

that I shall do my best for your happiness as long as we are spared together; that is if you accept, and, if not, I wish your life may [be] full of joy the rest of your days.

He added in a post-script, 'Perhaps we might arrange to meet each other somewhere.'[70]

Beatrice also received proposals that, rather than love, promised money. The day after her acquittal, Hector Dinnie wrote from London, offering to write a play based on her case. 'For your permission to do this,' he wrote, 'I am willing to pay you an agreed percentage on the royalty received by me in the event of a successful production.' Dinnie appealed to both personal and public interest: 'You would no doubt find any money received in this way very useful in providing for the future of your children. And besides, the play, if passed by the Censor, would draw public attention to the danger of convicting an innocent person.'[71] (Dinnie also wrote to Wellington, wishing to 'renew' his offer and requesting 'the complete records of the case together with any other helpful information'.[72]) Beatrice received another proposition from Charles McCoy, an 'Amusement Caterer' at an unidentified 'beautiful pleasure resort' on the north-east coast. 'I am writing to make you an offer', he wrote, 'which will combine business with pleasure.'

> I can offer you three or four weeks here just for you to exhibit your pet dog. You would not be required to exert [yourself] by making any speeches or referring to yourself in any way. The little exhibit would take place in a specially prepared drawing-room at the Amusement Park here, & you would only exhibit at intervals giving you plenty of time for recreation which would mean a very healthy holiday.

Offering £10 per week (plus expenses) for an engagement of up to a month, he suggested it would be 'a splendid holiday for you all'.[73] If this seems implausible, a theatre had also offered to pay her 'a substantial sum' to appear 'for a few minutes each evening before the audience and say half-a-dozen words'.[74] The marketability of her story, of course, is best demonstrated by its sale to the *Sunday Express*. In that context, McCoy's offer may have been less than enticing.

Vengeance, salvation, guilt and the spirit world

Some themes were shared by men and women. One involved Harry's kin. In a rare compassionate gesture toward the family, a letter from Rev. W. Brownrigg in the *Dean Forest Guardian* noted that, while sympathy and 'material help' were being 'lavished' on Harry's widow, his family were 'equally deserving of consideration', especially his mother: 'Let every mother in the country picture to herself', he urged, 'the poignant grief of that poor woman who was called upon to witness the agonising death throes of her beloved son.'[75] According to this sample, Brownrigg's call fell on deaf ears. A postcard from Crouch End, London wished Beatrice 'peace from scandal mongers', and one writer spoke of 'the people who were so bitter against you', praying that God might 'forgive them for all the wrong they tried to do to you'.[76] Most were less magnanimous, one assuring that 'in time your enemies will suffer for their wickedness to a good honourable wife like you'.[77] Another referred to the 'cruel lies & accusations made by your late husband's people', but ended hopefully: 'There is always One above to see justice [done] & no doubt they will suffer as much some day: if not in this world, in the next.'[78] Mary Gibbon was scornful of 'those that have tried to down you' but asserted 'God will certainly severely punish them in good time: so cheer up, don't think any more of the past.'[79] Mrs H. Colton wrote, 'I think your late husband's friends are wicked, but God knows best how to punish them & he will do.'[80] T. A. Carpenter stated simply: 'God moves in a mysterious way – God will avenge you of your enemies.'[81]

Some saw the prospect of divine punishment as insufficient. 'I feel', wrote Emily Dunstone, 'as doubtless many others do, that you have been a victim of the hate & jealousy of your husband's family, and I think there should be a law to punish people who would maliciously hound down an innocent woman as they have done.'[82] Eleanor Jones thought there was unfinished work for the courts: 'I would give that brother-in-law of yours 5 years hard labour', she wrote, hoping Beatrice would 'have as little as possible to do with the family in the future'.[83] H. C. Gordon went so far as to insist that the 'principals' in the case would 'suffer': 'steps', he wrote, were being taken to punish various people, such as the coroner ('for abusing his position'), Harry's brother and mother ('for conspiracy & perjury') and the foreman of the inquest jury ('for failing to do his duty as a juryman').[84] Forgiving comments such as 'I can see how it happened, the bad spirit of his brothers' (expressed in one letter's post-script) were rare.[85]

Divine vengeance was not the only religious topic in the sample. Despite the fact that Beatrice herself rarely expressed religious sentiments, nearly a quarter of the 220 letters classified as congratulatory had religious themes that went beyond colloquial expressions such as 'God bless' or passing references to having 'prayed for' her.[86] Women were somewhat more likely to have written a strongly religious letter: one-quarter did so compared to approximately one-fifth of men.[87] The cross-denominational nature of the letters testifies to her broad appeal. James Kearney described himself as a Catholic priest 'who will never meet you on earth – but hopes to join you with the good in heaven'.[88] Others saw divine intervention behind Beatrice's acquittal. Writing from Chesterfield, Charles Martin admitted the importance of public generosity, good legal counsel and a sympathetic jury; however,

> I want you to feel at the back of it all is God; there has [sic] been thousands of prayers gone up on your behalf, and God has answered them. I have watched the case and prayed for you, so God moved the public to sympathy, God moved the hearts to give, God suggested the Counsel, God gave him wisdom, God ordered the Jury.

He urged her to give her life to God, concluding, 'My dear girl we may never meet here but we may meet in Heaven.'[89] T. A. Carpenter referred to Beatrice's comment 'Thank God it is over' upon her acquittal (which was reported in various papers). The phrase was 'a common one', but:

> In your case, I feel it must have been a genuine expression of heartfelt gratitude to the omnipotent, omniscient and omnipresent God. During the month of May, whilst reading proceedings in [the] Coroner's Court on the day of your arrest, I felt such an *over-powering conviction in my mind that you were not guilty* – 'to me this was from God' – that ever since I have declared to friends that you were innocent.[90]

A somewhat more esoteric message was expressed by M. F. Bovenizer, two of whose letters are among the correspondence. The first refers to another letter sent to Beatrice 'some weeks ago' while she was in Cardiff Prison. 'In that letter', Bovenizer recalled, 'I told you that we as members of a Christian Spiritualist circle in Liverpool, had been told by the Spirits who come and speak to us, that you were innocent of the crime of poisoning your husband.'[91] 'Spiritualism', expressed through séances and other means of allegedly communicating with the dead, was strikingly popular in the inter-war period, partly influenced by the massive loss of life in the Great War.[92] In any case, the 'chief Spirit Guide' of Bovenizer's circle – who was named 'Bluebell' – had declared Beatrice innocent and said the 'spirit world' was working for her acquittal. ('Bluebell' also claimed Harry had not poisoned himself but apparently declined to name the true culprit.) The group rejoiced when their prayers for her release 'had been answered'. 'At our first meeting following your discharge, Bluebell told us that she had influenced the Judge's mind to discharge you, and explained that our prayers for you had done more to bring about the result than we could possibly understand.' Three days later Bovenizer wrote again to say a different spirit had described the 'false charges' against Beatrice, said kind things about her and assured the circle that 'the spirit world rejoices with her'. Bovenizer concluded: 'You have been very highly privileged in the way the spirit world have [sic] followed and worked for yourself and your children, when you were in the power of your enemies.'[93] The *Sunday News* also reprinted passages from a 'Christian spiritualist' periodical containing statements given to an American 'medium' by the deceased himself: in his 'spirit message', Harry Pace exonerated his wife, admitted suicide and urged people to help save Beatrice.[94]

Gertrude Smart, a 29-year-old 'invalid' and avid reader of the *Sunday Express* memoir, saw a deep religious significance in Beatrice's experiences. 'After reading this week's instalment', she wrote, 'I have tried to put myself in your place, although I am single and inexperienced to the ways of the world.' She made a striking comparison: 'You have indeed walked side by side with the "Lord Jesus Christ himself" & have experienced a share in His own sufferings, agony of the mind, body, soul & spirit. Did He not say "Whom the Lord love, He chasteneth"? You have been one of His own chosen people to suffer for Him.' God had not only chosen Beatrice to suffer, he had also given her the strength to endure, and 'in great suffering we learn it is not the things of the world which counts [sic] the highest, but the things hidden & unseen by us'. As for Harry: 'The one you loved is now in His care, though he will always be with you in Spirit, loving him as you did with such a deep, self-sacrificing devotion.'[95] A Welsh correspondent praised God for reuniting Beatrice with her children and hoped they would 'remember the Lord, for his kindness in bringing you back to them once more'.[96]

Some correspondents urged Beatrice to save her soul. Ernest Jeffrey, 'while sympathising much with you', drew her 'kind attention' to 'an error in the *Daily Express* about you. It says you were "unsaved by *religion*". Of course *everybody* is in that boat. I am. Religion never yet saved anybody. It is Christ alone that saves not religion.'[97] Mrs J. E. Bynon had followed the case intently and pressed Beatrice to accept God as her 'personal saviour'.[98] The tone of a lengthy letter from Louth, Lincolnshire, urging Beatrice to become born again becomes clear through even a brief excerpt:

> Now, dear Friend, *will you come* to God? Do. *The Precious Blood Shed on Calvary's Cross 2000 years* back has wiped away *all* sins, all mistakes, everything you [or] I *ever did amiss*, for in God's word, the Bible, it says, *All* have *Sinned* & it says '*You must be born* again.' We all must: There is *no respect* of Persons with our Creator. The *richest & the highest* in *the Land* need '*Saving*' & all (praise His name!) *can come*, or plunge them[selves] in Calvary's stream (it's free): '*Still it flows, still it flows, still it flows as fresh as ever*' (Praise Him!) from the '*Saviour's wounded Side*': Oh – Just get to *know* Jesus.[99]

There were similar letters, and Beatrice received religious objects, such as Christian booklets and a rosary.[100]

Although the overwhelming majority of the available correspondence sent to Beatrice was congratulatory, not all of it was. As noted, Beatrice referred to (but did not quote from) letters from women questioning her judgement. Jane Goldsmith made a similar point: referring to the *Sunday Express* memoir, she thought Beatrice had been 'a great fool to stick to a man who treated you worse than a dog': 'I should think a week would be long enough for that you should have run away and have taken your chance to get a living and left him.' Wishing Beatrice luck, she could not resist a postscript: 'I can't understand any woman being beaten and knocked about by any man; if it had been my case I should have him put where I could find him.'[101]

Four letters, all anonymous, were far more critical. One, signed 'Woman', cryptically states: 'You have stolen a march on your husband, but he will grab you yet. His name indicates it.'[102] The others condemned Beatrice explicitly. One accused her of having 'played the part of the hypocrite very well for your own preservation' and referred to her memoir: 'Whilst professing to have "respect and love" for your poor husband you sat down and wrote the blackest record against his character, that it was possible for anyone to write. Had it been any other country the verdict would have been different, as we are humbugged here with a few sentimental old foggy judges.' Warning Beatrice she would face 'righteous judgement', it concluded on a note reminiscent of (by then discredited) theories of the 'born criminal': 'That twist upon your face, from a point of physiognomy is a very bad indication and counts for a good deal of wickedness.'[103] Another anonymous letter simply stated: 'Don't imagine that you are a heroine to everyone. If you did not poison your husband, who did? As no one would really be such a fool as to think he killed himself. Anyway your life will be fairly a miserable one for the future, with the awful weight you must have on your evil mind.'[104] Another letter was from a woman who had been 'ill-treated' by her husband until she left him five years previously. In her case, a common experience of suffering generated neither sympathy nor identification: she thought Beatrice guilty and accused her of tarnishing Harry's name. 'You are what I should term a Brazen Hussey', she stated, agreeing with Elton Pace's suggestion that she was a 'play actress'. 'He would not tie a woman to the bed if she was not in the habit of going out while he was at work', she continued, referring to a much publicised incident early in the Paces' marriage.

> I am sure he [would have been] just the man that would suit me: a steady, ambitious husband anxious to get a farm so that he might be his own master, which he would have done had he had a suitable partner. Ill-mated marriages generally turn out bad. You are what I should term the modern woman, neither good to *God* or man.

'You will understand by this letter', she – rather unnecessarily – added, 'that I am not your admirer.'[105] How many people shared such views is unknown, but the tiny number of critical letters here lends support to press depictions of Beatrice's widespread popularity.

Conclusion

Men and women alike saw their support of Beatrice as part of a general phenomenon. A correspondent from London wrote, 'you – I am *sure* – must realise that most people were hoping you would show the world you were not guilty'.[106] As a widow from Burnley put it: 'I know that it will comfort you to know that you have had the sympathy of the public.'[107] Mrs Blanche Cluitt wrote from the Isle of Wight 'on behalf of dozens of sympathisers'.[108] Other letters were more expansive: one rejoiced 'with many hundred more', and Florence Smith urged Beatrice to 'be happy as there are hundreds even who do not know you who wish you well for the rest of your life to live happy with your children'.[109] 'You have had my prayers (poor though they be) all along', stated one letter, '& [I] am perfectly sure there must be thousands who have done that much as well.'[110] An 'unknown devoted friend' in Liverpool wrote, 'I am very much happier myself [after the acquittal] & I'm sure there are *thousands* of *others*.'[111] From Birmingham, a woman assured Beatrice 'all our thoughts at my house are with you, leave alone many thousands besides us', and a man in London asserted 'it is the duty of every lover of truth, to write to you to encourage you for the future and also to let you know, that there are thousands in this country with deep affection towards yourself and family'.[112]

Many others emphasised the extent of public support for her with reference to their locality, whether large or small. A woman from Slough, for example, wrote that 'even in this small town you had "crowds" of sympathisers', and three married couples in Devon assured her that 'if this letter could only be shown in this little town, there would be heaps of signatures'.[113] Another group of couples from the Taunton area stated 'it is only just a little country village & I think everyone has prayed for you', a suggestion reinforced by another, anonymous letter: 'We can assure you that you are loved & honoured by us people in Taunton.'[114] A writer in the Midlands claimed that 'the whole of the little parish of Cannock Wood' wished her 'every happiness' and one from a village near Exeter wrote, 'everyone from this district is overjoyed to think that once more you are back with your little children'.[115] Mrs Trobe claimed that 'everybody in Tottenham is so happy to hear you are with your dear children again', while an anonymous letter congratulated Beatrice on her victory in the name of, alternatively, 'Greater

Brighton Hove, & all the surrounding district of Sussex' and 'all of Sussex'.[116] Closer to home, Mrs S. Baker noted 'There was joy in Gloucester, there was joy all round our countryside, & towns', and Bessie Yeo stated, 'I am sure all Bristol are rejoicing in your liberty', highlighting 'the respect there is for you and your dear children in Bristol'.[117] J. Nicholson told Beatrice she was 'the most widely known lady in the land'. He lived in London ('where public opinion almost rules that prevailing in the country'): 'The feeling here was exceedingly strong in your favour, and when the result of the trial became known, there was a great relief evinced, and sympathetic hearts went out to you by thousands.'[118] Other writers described public support for Beatrice in comprehensive terms. Mrs W. Williams, in South Wales, said that she 'and all the country at large' had thought Beatrice was innocent.[119] Mrs E. Ransome, who claimed that 'the tears have rolled down my cheeks more than once for you', told Beatrice, 'you can rest assured that you had the whole country's sympathy'.[120] H. C. Gordon was exuberant: 'The whole nation was with you,' he wrote, 'even before the conclusion of the unjust inquest, because it was evident they intended to do what they did.' He continued: 'The whole proceedings have been very closely and anxiously watched, not only in your own immediate locality, but in every town throughout the country, and there would have been great demonstrations of anger from all classes of society, had there been a different verdict.'[121]

Predominant press narratives about Beatrice Pace and her experiences are clearly reflected in these letters; however, many readers readjusted the case's meanings to suit their own experiences, needs and desires. Some merely sought an autograph or some kind of brush with celebrity (through, for example, an invitation to strike up a correspondence or to come by for a visit).[122] However, many letters, particularly those from women, made clear how much significance some people invested in the Pace case. For those who avidly followed the case day by day, framed newspaper photographs, discussed the trial at family meals, remembered Beatrice in their nightly prayers or wept tears of joy upon hearing of her acquittal, the case quite clearly stirred intense emotions. However ephemeral they might seem, these letters testify to a powerful urge that some people felt to make some sort of connection with a woman whom they never knew other than through the printed word and a selection of black-and-white photos.

Conclusion

Just after the Second World War, George Orwell looked back on the murder cases that had 'given the greatest amount of pleasure' to the British public:

> Our great period in murder, our Elizabethan period, so to speak, seems to have been between roughly 1850 and 1925, and the murderers whose reputation has stood the test of time are the following: Dr Palmer of Rugeley, Jack the Ripper, Neill Cream, Mrs Maybrick, Dr Crippen, Seddon, Joseph Smith, Armstrong, and Bywaters and Thompson.[1]

The Pace case fell just outside Britain's 'great period in murder', and since it ended in an acquittal it should perhaps not even be counted a 'murder' at all. Nonetheless, it fits some of Orwell's criteria for a satisfying murder *trial*, involving an alleged poisoning in a domestic setting motivated (some claimed) by sex and money that had come to light 'as the result of careful investigations which started off with the suspicions of neighbours or relatives'. Even if not a perfect murder 'from a *News of the World* reader's point of view', it had more than 'a touch of this atmosphere' in the courtroom and in the press.[2] Harry Pace's mysterious death was linked in court testimony and press reporting to some of the cases Orwell listed, and the public was fascinated by his 'tragic' widow, even if her case has since significantly faded from British cultural memory. It seems that the most-remembered trials have tended to involve convictions rather than acquittals, even if the lives and stories behind the latter are no less interesting than those behind the former. Were one, then, to imagine a 'perfect acquittal' – from the point of view of the *News of the World* reader or otherwise – it would be difficult to top that of Beatrice Pace.

The case's sensational quality in 1928 was a product not only of its inherent drama but also of two broader factors during the 'great period in murder': an expanding sensationalist press and a declining acceptance of domestic violence. As Chapter 4 discussed, crime stories – the more lurid the better – were a staple feature of a popular journalism that turned people almost overnight into figures of national sympathy or calumny. Those whose entrée into the world of fame resulted from an alleged crime could never be certain whether they would become truly popular or merely notorious. As Martin Wiener has observed, since the Victorian era London papers had 'made use of such sensations to carve out a role as seekers of mercy for "ordinary" persons facing execution'; however, sympathies were more easily mobilised for certain kinds of people in certain kinds of circumstances.[3]

A case that occurred about a quarter-century before Beatrice's is instructive. Alfred Baker's maltreatment of Kitty Byron unquestionably contributed to the public's support for her after she stabbed him to death on a London street in 1902.[4] Although the crime was clearly premeditated, press coverage emphasised Byron's suffering (Baker had been an often cruel drunkard) and presumed naivety. As in Beatrice's case, the authorities kept silent about some of what they knew about the young woman – such as Byron's bisexual past and unstable mentality – assisting the public's idealisation. The jury recommended mercy, and Byron's sentence was reduced to life imprisonment and subsequently commuted after seven years. It later became apparent that she had quite a violent character. In her case, narratives of suffering femininity helped a dangerous woman to beat the system. Beatrice's circumstances were obviously different: Byron's guilt was not only certain but she was young, single and morally 'fallen'. But there were also some similarities: both women were idealised while their victims (actual or alleged) were reviled, and the melodramatic reporting on each case, with its black-and-white morality, concealed a more complicated reality. Such cases illustrate the complexity of both media depictions of crime and the functioning of the justice system. Commenting on the Byron case, Ginger Frost has observed: 'That an apparently bisexual woman perpetrated a premeditated murder on a public street and spent only seven years in prison complicates historians' interpretations of the "moralistic" courtroom of the early twentieth century.[5]

Along with the undermining of the circumstantial case against Harry Pace's widow, an element in her defence was the suggestion that she was too good – too moral, too devoted, too maternal – to have killed. The viability of this strategy depended upon the information made available as well as the receptivity of officials, journalists and newspaper readers to certain cues regarding individual character. It has been argued that police and prosecutors invariably use any dirt they can dig up on female suspects to undermine their public reputations and courtroom defences and, furthermore, that the plight of abused women remained invisible in the early twentieth century.[6] We have seen, however, that the authorities certainly did not use everything they had against Beatrice and that her story of suffering was extraordinarily well suited to the pages of the late 1920s popular press, where tales of wronged women were a staple fixture. (Sharing the front page with Beatrice in *Thomson's Weekly News* in late January 1928 was Mrs Cissie Nellie Reene, who, in an article titled 'My husband's "matrimonial escapades": betrays my trust a second time after I had forgiven him', told readers about her marriage to a convicted bigamist.[7]) Fully understanding the cultural attitudes toward and institutional treatment of criminal women (or of women merely accused of crime) requires taking into account both those women who have been demonised by the public and unfairly condemned and those who received public support and were – all things considered – treated fairly.[8]

Despite a tenacious belief that women have been 'doubly damned' in the criminal justice system – that they were invariably 'on trial' not only for their alleged crimes but also for violating predominant gender norms – more systematic studies of the nineteenth and early twentieth centuries have shown that women were not generally disadvantaged.[9] Certainly, some women have been unjustly condemned on the basis of a perceived (and gender-specific) 'immorality' that had little to do with the acts for which they were punished, with Edith Thompson and Ruth Ellis as only the most well-known examples.[10] But since, compared to men, women rarely kill other adults, homicide cases may be a poor basis for broader claims about gender bias and the justice system. (Though, as I hope to have demonstrated, they are very valuable in other ways.) There has so far been too little research into the depictions of male murderers in this period, which would provide a useful cross-gender comparison. Finally, given that the world of the press was already vast by the 1920s, examining this topic will require canvassing a broader range of newspaper commentary than has (sometimes) so far been the case.

Opinions about accused killers often varied across the press spectrum, and they might, over time, shift as new information came to light.[11] Although clear press preferences often emerged – whether for or against the accused – it is often possible to find quite divergent views running parallel to one another: press unanimity of the sort found in the Pace case has probably been the exception rather than the rule. Some papers specialised in the sympathetic depiction of accused and convicted criminals, particularly those condemned to death for murder. Although it has been suggested, for example, that Louie Calvert – executed for killing another woman in 1926 – was virtually ignored by the press (and, when not 'invisible' was vilified), the *World's Pictorial News* and *Thomson's Weekly News* published several sympathetic articles (in the latter case, written by her husband) highlighting her love of her children and state of mind while awaiting the results of her ultimately unsuccessful petition for mercy.[12] Even the brutal murder of an Essex constable did not stop his killers from receiving some sympathetic coverage, with one even recounting his life in a memoir cast in the style of an adventure story.[13]

Beatrice's universally positive newspaper coverage, the crowds that cheered her and the letters she received are evidence of a distinctive popularity in the face of the weighty accusations against her. It is difficult to judge what impact, if any, popular support had on the case's legal result; however, it encouraged politicians to defend and assist her and enabled the transformation of her fame into financial security.[14] Her press depiction not only provided such tangible benefits but also appears to have offered a self-image that she embraced. Ultimately, however, her case also shows how little control she had over her story, which others used for a variety of journalistic and political purposes.

The way that the Pace case has been viewed subsequently has clearly been haunted by one question: was Beatrice *really* innocent? The contemporary press and what seems the vast majority of the public enthusiastically greeted her acquittal. Even immediately after the trial, there were speculations about how Harry had died, but these all pointed either to accidental poisoning or suicide.[15] Within a few years, an account of the case mentioned a *Lancet* article about a shepherd who developed debilitating symptoms of arsenical poisoning through accidental exposure; it also referred to suggestions that it was a common belief in the Forest of Dean that small doses of arsenic could have 'beneficial' (in fact aphrodisiacal) effects; however, there was no conclusive evidence that Harry had been an 'arsenic eater'.[16] In 1962, one of Norman Birkett's biographers presented various possibilities, all of them involving accident or suicide.[17] But here, we see a subtle shift in the case's depiction. Two years later, another biography of Beatrice's barrister argued that the verdict was clearly correct but suggested, 'some observers may possibly have been tempted to adopt the opinion expressed by a distinguished surgeon with regard to a similar case of poisoning forty years previously that, "once it was all over, she should have told us, in the interests of science, how she did it"'.[18] A 1970 biography of William Willcox makes clear that the renowned pathologist thought she had gotten away with murder and that 'popular clamour in sympathy for a dejected widow with the care of children already rendered fatherless' had motivated the judge to stop the case.[19] Subsequent opinions have ranged from assertions of accidental poisoning to suggestions that Beatrice 'probably' did kill Harry.[20]

What do I think? The legal decision to acquit Beatrice was undoubtedly correct, as the inquest evidence that had at first seemed so damning was far less convincing by the trial. There was no direct proof of her guilt and the circumstantial evidence was, ultimately, thin at best. As to what 'really' happened in Rose Cottage in the weeks leading up to Harry's death in January 1928, there is no definitive proof either way. But having wrestled with this question over more than five years of researching this case, I find it entirely plausible that Harry committed suicide (ineptly, so it seems) in the midst of a depression brought on by an initial, accidental poisoning in the summer of 1927. It may seem unlikely that a sane man would repeatedly dose himself with arsenic, as the prosecution argued; however, there were indications that Harry was perhaps not entirely mentally stable. The issue of how he might have actually done it is a difficult one. However, I would point out one crucial thing. All the attempts to retroactively 'solve' the case – no matter how different their conclusions – have shared one highly questionable assumption: that we have every relevant bit of information and all that is necessary is to reassemble them in the correct way. But part of my motivation in suggesting Beatrice's innocence (besides the fact that a duly acquitted person deserves the benefit of the doubt in the absence of any new evidence) is the realisation that there might well have been vital elements or factors in the case that we simply do not know about.

By the time Scotland Yard detectives were on the scene it had been two months since Harry's death. There had been prior searches of the house by the local police, but they do not seem to have been particularly thorough. Crime scene procedure was rudimentary in 1928, particularly in a provincial police force. An undiscovered bottle, packet or tin is very possible. Leslie described his father finding something wrapped up in paper in the 'sheep box'. Could it have contained pure arsenic? Possibly. Alternatively, as was observed with regard to the 'dusty bottle' at the trial, a solution of arsenic separated from sheep dip would have had a legitimate purpose for a sheep farmer. A bottle containing something similar may have been in the 'sheep box' in Harry's room. There was plenty of time after Harry's death for a bottle or a bit of wrapping paper to be removed or destroyed – quite innocently – by any one of the people who went in and out of the house. Beatrice, as we have seen, was quite reticent about a great many things. It is not implausible that she had thrown something out (or knew that someone else had) and then, later, realising how suspicious that would look as the rumours mounted, never mentioned it again. As this makes clear, once in the realm of speculation, many things are possible; however, I suggest we should regard Beatrice's acquittal as correct – both in law and in fact – in the absence of any compelling reason to do otherwise. I have sought to point out the weaknesses in claims of Beatrice's guilt, whether those by the Crown or by Mountjoy and Sayes. Nonetheless, I have also tried to present enough information for readers to make up their own minds. All of the sources, of course, are open to the public.

A different – and in some ways equally difficult – question continues to preoccupy me: who *was* Beatrice Pace? After countless hours sifting through newspaper stories, police reports and her own statements – and even after speaking to people who knew her personally – she remains, for me, very much a mysterious figure. Here, the historian (and, perhaps, his readers) are like those many observers in 1928 who, as one journalist put it, were unable to 'solve the enigma of Mrs. Pace'.[21] The press clearly simplified her relationships with her husband, her children and her friends. No one, in fact, could have lived up to her relentlessly idealised public persona. But still, what motivated her? What, really, did she make of the events that she went through? What did she think of the hundreds of heartfelt messages she received from complete strangers? Did she really love Harry to the end, as she claimed, or was that assertion shaped more by her need to justify her choices to herself or to others (or, alternatively, by the invisible hand of a ghost-writer wishing to tell a particularly poignant tale)? In the end, these are things that we will probably never know; however, I do think that it was precisely such complexities that helped make her so intriguing to her contemporaries. Though depicted as a victim, she was not seen as powerless. Exemplifying dutiful domesticity, she built a new, independent life after her acquittal. However dramatic her situation, her experiences were common to working-class women, making her seem approachable. As we have seen, many complete strangers treated her almost as a friend or family member.

I have aimed to present the Pace case not only as a 'crime' story (though it is also that) but also as one about an inter-war 'celebrity culture' that is, perhaps, more familiar than we often realise. It was not only an era in which the gossip columns were full of news about the latest doings of the stars of stage and (increasingly) screen, but also one in which 'ordinary' people could – however fleetingly – become household names and the object of an intense degree of emotional identification. Beatrice's ambiguous position – both the 'most remarkable woman in England' and the woman next door – made her, like many other instant celebrities of the inter-war decades, a figure of fascination. For this reason, though it may forever remain unsolved, the 'Fetter Hill mystery' has much to tell us.

Postscript

Of course, the name 'Mrs Pace' eventually faded from the headlines. The sensational-sounding 'new developments' sparked by Mountjoy and Sayes trailed off in September, and soon thereafter the case was officially closed. After selling her story, Beatrice does not seem to have sought out any publicity; to the contrary, she appears to have been content to disappear from view. New events, crimes, personalities and scandals were never in short supply, and journalists' attention moved elsewhere. Before closing this history of the 'Fetter Hill mystery', however, I would like to trace what happened in the following years to some of the key players in the dramatic events of 1928.

The most renowned figure involved directly in the case was Norman Birkett, and the next few years would see his path intersect with those of other people we have encountered. For example, in the same month as Beatrice's acquittal, Radclyffe Hall's novel *The Well of Loneliness* was published. Although it dealt with the controversial topic of lesbianism, it received, at first, some rather positive commentary.[1] One important exception was a disparaging review written by one of Beatrice's ardent supporters, *Sunday Express* editor James Douglas. He wrote that he would rather give 'a healthy boy or a healthy girl a phial of prussic acid than this novel'.[2] The intimidated publishers wrote to the Home Secretary offering to withdraw the book, which he gratefully accepted. Another press printed copies of it in France and sought to import them, but they were seized by customs officials. At the book's subsequent obscenity trial, Birkett led the case for the defence.[3] William Willcox, who had provided so much forensic testimony in the Pace case, wrote a medical opinion for the court that depicted the novel as obscene and dangerous. His report described lesbianism as a

> form of unnatural vice known for thousands of years and fully described in medico-legal works. It is well known to have debasing effects on those practising it, of a mental, physical and moral character. It leads to nervous instability and in some cases to suicide. If widespread, it becomes a danger to a nation. It is antisocial.[4]

Willcox's view carried the day, and Birkett lost the case. *The Well of Loneliness* was not published in Britain until the late 1940s.

In 1930, Birkett again found himself before Mr Justice Horridge. Coincidentally, the matter related to Barbu Jonescu, the Romanian businessman and associate of Prince Carol who had donated £500 to Beatrice's defence fund. Two newspapers had published critical articles about Jonescu and even suggested he had lied about his identity. Jonescu had sued one of them, the *Evening Standard*, for libel. Birkett defended the paper and lost.[5] In 1931, Birkett successfully defended another woman against charges of arsenic murder. Sarah Ann Hearn had been charged with poisoning her sister and a neighbour. Dealing with a complex mixture of forensic and circumstantial evidence – and once again defending a woman whose local reputation appears to have been at least somewhat ambiguous – Birkett achieved a decisive acquittal on both counts.[6] In 1934, Birkett again defended a widow accused of having poisoned her husband. As in Beatrice's case, Ethel Major's late husband had been both unfaithful and abusive. However, Birkett's efforts on this occasion were fruitless: Major was convicted, sentenced to death and hanged shortly afterward.[7] Despite such defeats, his career was extraordinarily successful. He was knighted for unpaid services to the government at the beginning of the Second World War, and in November 1941 he accepted an offer to sit as a high-court judge. He would also serve as the British alternate judge at the Nuremberg trials. He continued to serve on the bench until his retirement in 1956 and two years later entered the House of Lords as Baron Birkett of Ulverston. Birkett died in London in 1962.[8]

And what of Beatrice's other erstwhile defenders? A. A. Purcell left his parliamentary seat in the Forest of Dean to contest Moss

Side in Manchester in the 1929 general election. Despite Labour's overall success that year (which saw the formation of the second Labour government), he lost. He was instead elected secretary of the Manchester and Salford Trades Council, a position he took on with great enthusiasm until he died suddenly at his home in Manchester on Christmas Eve 1935. With an echo of the appeal he had himself launched for the benefit of an impoverished constituent, an appeal from a trade union council raised over £1,200 for his widow.[9] Gilbert Trevor Wellington continued his successful legal practice in Gloucester. (The firm he helped found still exists, though under a different name.[10]) In 1937 he became sheriff of the city, and, in 1939, its mayor. Wellington died on 3 February 1963 at the Royal Hospital in Gloucester.[11] Bernard O'Donnell continued to write about crime: he claimed to have attended 321 murder trials over the course of his career. After the Second World War, he wrote several books on crime-related topics, including one entitled *Should Women Hang?* He also spent many years investigating 'Jack the Ripper', writing an unpublished manuscript on his findings that was only made available to the public in 2006.[12] O'Donnell died in 1969, aged eighty-three.[13]

Despite a conclusion to the Pace case that was, from the police perspective, distinctly unsatisfying, Chief Inspector George Cornish was officially 'highly commended' for 'ability in a difficult case of alleged murder'.[14] Shortly thereafter, in February 1929, he was promoted to superintendent, taking over command of London's East End.[15] Subsequently running 'detective work in the whole of North London', he retired at the end of October 1933.[16] On that occasion, the *Daily Mirror* referred to him as the 'murder wizard' for his skill in solving suspicious killings, and it observed that he was 'one of Britain's best-known detective chiefs'.[17] After 1928, newspaper articles might list other cases in which Cornish was involved, but they tended to avoid mentioning his dogged efforts to convict Beatrice Pace. In 1935, he published a memoir, *Cornish of the 'Yard'*, in which he described his almost thirty-nine-year career. What he made of the Pace case in retrospect is unknown, as it is a notable absence in the book. However, there is one passage with more than a hint of his experience in the Forest of Dean. In poisoning cases, he wrote, 'The murderer does not attempt to hide himself or to conceal the body, his efforts are directed in one direction only, that the death may be thought a natural one, or in some circumstances suicide. [...] Poisons too, are tricky things, and medical evidence can often vary as to facts, probabilities and possibilities.'[18] The next year, another book was published entitled *Six Against the Yard*, in which half-a-dozen popular mystery writers concocted various imaginary perfect crimes; in each case, Cornish then described whether – and how – the case might be solved. In responding to one of them, Cornish, perhaps ruefully, observed: 'In many unsolved murder mysteries, the true difficulty which has confronted the police is not that of finding the criminal, but that of proving his guilt in a way which will convince a jury.'[19] He enjoyed a lengthy retirement – one punctuated by occasional visits from Bernard O'Donnell – and died in 1959.[20]

Clarence Campion also received official praise for his 'invaluable assistance' to Cornish in the Forest of Dean case.[21] In the years that followed, he would also rise through the ranks, becoming Superintendent of the Criminal Records Department. In February 1940, Superintendent Campion led a select group of nineteen detectives to France in order to help military police prevent thefts from British Expeditionary Force (BEF) bases. Campion was given an army commission at the rank of major, and this mission is seen as a founding moment in the creation of the Special Investigations Branch (SIB) of the Royal Military Police. Soon after Campion and his men arrived, in May 1940, British forces were routed. During the Dunkirk evacuation, Campion received a fatal shrapnel wound to the head, becoming the only SIB casualty of the BEF. Today, the force Campion helped to found is headquartered in a building named for him.[22]

After the Pace trial, William Willcox remained active in the field of toxicology. He was head of the Medico-Legal Society in 1928–29, during which time he invited Professor Walker Hall to give a talk on his research into the effects of sheep dip.[23] Walker Hall and Willcox, in fact, had struck up an enduring friendship during the case, and the Bristol professor was often invited to stay with Willcox when he was in London. The Home Office sent Willcox copies of the documents gathered during the Mountjoy/ Sayes affair in August and September 1928. Curiously, while his notes record the various allegations made against Beatrice, they do not seem to point out that the methods claimed (putting powdered sheep dip in food) had been rejected by his own analysis. (This omission is also repeated by Willcox's son in the course of a rather tendentious depiction of the trial's evidence.[24]) Taking a leadership role in several medical and pharmacological organisations, he continued to work avidly in the fields that interested him until his death from a stroke in 1941.[25]

And what of Beatrice Pace? As we have seen, her efforts to build a new life were plagued by problems, such as local gossip and the new investigations beginning in August. In January 1929, even her illness made the papers: she was admitted to Gloucester Royal Infirmary for appendicitis, having what was described as a 'severe' operation.[26] Then, on 6 January, the *Sunday Express* made a brief, front-page announcement that Beatrice would be remarrying 'next Easter'. Describing the prospective bridegroom as 'a dark, handsome man about thirty years old' and a 'native of Gloucester', it reported comments she made while recovering from surgery. Reminded by the reporter that she had forsworn marriage at the end of her memoir, Beatrice replied that it was 'a woman's privilege to change her mind'. She demurred when asked to name her intended, saying only, 'That is going to remain a secret until next Easter.'[27] Bernard O'Donnell published an article the following week also speculating on Beatrice's marriage plans: before Christmas, he had visited her in Gloucester and she told him how lonely she was. Soon, he promised, 'when the time comes to reveal the identity of the mystery bridegroom, concerning whom there is considerable speculation, it will come as a surprise to many'.[28] However, on 19 January, an article in *Thomson's Weekly News* under Beatrice's own name denied the 'unkind and untruthful' things that had been said. Surmising that rumours began after people had seen her in the company of a young man who was the son of a family friend, she said the episode showed 'how careful a woman who has come prominently into the public eye must be'. As to marriage, 'there is no possibility of it for a very long time, and probably none at all'.[29] She reiterated that claim in an interview with the *Sunday News* later that month. 'All I want', she said, 'is to be left alone.'[30]

However, not six months later a case came before the Gloucester Police Court which once again brought the name 'Mrs Pace' into the headlines. As the *News of the World* reported in June, Reginald Clarke, an unemployed taxi driver, had applied to have his maintenance payments to his estranged wife halved. Clarke was also living in Beatrice's house, and the nature of their relationship was one of the crucial issues in the case. Clarke claimed he was merely a lodger and denied going away with Beatrice on holiday. The solicitor representing Mrs Clarke (also named Beatrice) suggested that the two had a more intimate relationship. Clarke had first met Beatrice during her trial, when he was the driver of the car that took her back and forth between prison and the Shire Hall. After her acquittal, he had attended a party she had hosted, and he admitted that he might have been 'dead drunk' when he returned home at four o'clock in the morning. Clarke said Beatrice had visited him at the taxi stand, but he denied that he had lost his job as a result of his association with her. His wife's solicitor, however, stated that Beatrice was 'keeping' Clarke and possibly buying him new clothes. Clarke, apparently, had also gone with Beatrice to see Harry's grave, and he had visited her at Gloucester Infirmary during her illness. The solicitor even read aloud a letter Beatrice had allegedly sent Clarke while recovering. In it, she thanked him for the 'lovely things' he had sent her, and, asking him to bring the car for her when she would be sent home again, she wrote, 'I hope you have been a good boy' since they had last seen one another: 'You know I shall be able to tell.' At this point, Mrs Clarke's solicitor paused, stating that 'he could not read the rest in court', but he read out the letter's closing statement: 'I am longing to see you and to have a nice kiss. You know it's nice, but naughty.'[31] Mrs Clarke herself entered the witness box and accused Beatrice of having 'ruined her home and forced her to go and live with her father. She led a happy life with her husband, she said, until Mrs. Pace came along with her money.' The court rejected Clarke's request to reduce the maintenance order.[32] Similar stories on the episode also appeared in the *Daily Mail*, the *Daily Telegraph* and the *Daily Express*.[33]

Perhaps due to the new notoriety that this incident brought to her, Beatrice left Gloucester altogether. Indeed, she may have already done so as the Clarke issue was brewing. At the end of July, the *Sunday News* reported that she had moved the previous month. Leaving behind 'the scene of one of the most sensational cases of recent years', she had reportedly bought a house in Pontnewynydd in south Wales. There, close to the main road and 'at the rear of the police-station', she had so successfully kept her secret 'that even neighbours did not know her identity'. Her sister

9 A family photo of Beatrice in her garden in Stroud, in the 1950s.
(Courtesy of Tony Martin)

lived in an adjoining street, 'and is assisting the tragic widow to live quietly with her five children in the house she has bought'.[34]

By the end of the 1930s, Beatrice was living in Stroud, Gloucestershire, where she bought a semi-detached house in which she would spend the remainder of her life.[35] As part of her quest to live down her past, she reverted to her maiden name. In Stroud, she suffered a further tragedy: her daughter Jean – whose fragile health as an infant had received so much attention – died in December 1941 (she was fourteen) of congenital cerebral diplegia, a form of cerebral palsy.[36] Two of Beatrice's grandsons recall her as living a quiet and even 'reclusive' life.[37] The promise that she had made at the end of her memoir held true: she never re-married. The case, it seems, was rarely discussed with the family's next generation. Beatrice, like her children, appears to have been determined to leave the events of 1928 behind her. She seems to have succeeded in living out the rest of her long life in obscurity. Beatrice Martin died at the Royal Hospital in Gloucester on 1 March 1973.[38]

Notes

Introduction

1 The crowd was estimated as 'at least 3,000' in *News of the World* (8 July 1928), p. 9 and *Daily Mirror* (7 July 1928), p. 3. The *Daily Chronicle* (7 July 1928), p. 3 reported 'a crowd of 10,000'.

2 *Daily Mirror* (7 July 1928), p. 3.

3 *The People* (8 July 1928), p. 2.

4 *Daily Mirror* (7 July 1928), p. 3.

5 *The People* (8 July 1928), p. 2.

6 *Citizen* (Gloucester) (6 July 1928), p. 6. *News of the World* (8 July 1928), p. 9: 'The crowd immediately surged across the road, broke through the police cordon, and went frantic with excitement. Many people were knocked down and some slightly injured in the press.'

7 *Daily Mirror* (7 July 1928), p. 3.

8 *Ibid.*; *The People* (8 July 1928), p. 2.

9 *The People* (8 July 1928), p. 2; *News of the World* (8 July 1928), p. 9.

10 She is described so in the *World's Pictorial News* (20 May 1928), p. 1 and *Reynolds's Illustrated News* (27 May 1928), p. 11; she was also referred to as 'the tragic widow of Gloucestershire' by the *Daily Mail*, quoted in the *Dean Forest Guardian* (20 April 1928), p. 6. References to her simply as 'the tragic widow' were ubiquitous, e.g., *Sunday News* (3 June 1928), p. 1.

11 *Daily Mirror* (7 July 1928), p. 3.

12 *News of the World* (8 July 1928), p. 9.

13 *World's Pictorial News* (15 July 1928), p. 1.

14 *Thomson's Weekly News* (4 August 1928), p. 3; *Daily Express* (7 July 1928), p. 1.

15 *News of the World* (8 July 1928), p. 9; *Daily Mail* (7 July 1928), p. 10.

16 *Sunday Express* (8 July 1928), p. 12; advertisement for *Sunday Express* series in the *Daily Mail* (13 July 1928), p. 19.

17 Among others, cover stories or images appeared in the *Daily Chronicle*, *Daily Herald*, *Sunday Express*, *Daily Express*, *Daily Mail*, *Daily Mirror* and *World's Pictorial News*.

18 *Sunday Express* (8 July 1928), p. 12.

19 A week after Pace's acquittal, a front-page headline exclaimed 'Another arsenic mystery' in reference to the sudden death of Mrs Jessie Llewellyn in Llanelly, South Wales: *News of the World* (15 July 1928), p. 1.

20 D. Bardens, *Lord Justice Birkett* (London: Robert Hale, 1962), pp. 105–18; H. M. Hyde, *Norman Birkett: The Life of Lord Birkett of Ulverston* (London: Hamish Hamilton, 1964), pp. 246–54; P. H. A. Willcox, *The Detective-Physician: The Life and Work of Sir William Willcox* (Chichester: William Heinemann Medical Books, 1970), pp. 208–17.

21 R. Church, *Accidents of Murder: Ten Cases Re-Examined* (London: Robert Hale, 1989); R. Church, 'Double jeopardy: the ordeal of Beatrice Pace', *The Criminologist* 18:2 (1994), 113–19; L. Stratmann, *Gloucestershire Murders* (Stroud: Sutton, 2005), pp. 104–19. In 1996, the case was included in an episode of the Granada television series *In suspicious circumstances* entitled *Who's sorry now?* In June 2010, a BBC radio play, *Norman Birkett and the case of the Coleford poisoner*, offered a dramatised version of the case. A description of the case is in H. Phelps, *The Forest of Dean* (Stroud: Amberley, 2008), pp. 91–7. It concludes: 'But did she or did she not? The mystery remains ... '.

22 The case was reported upon in the *New York Times* (3 July 1928), p. 4 and (7 July 1928), p. 30. It also was covered in Australia: see, e.g., *Advertiser* (Adelaide) (9 July 1928), p. 13 and the *Brisbane Courier* (4 July 1928), p. 15.

23 A recent summary of this work is provided by S. D'Cruze and L. Jackson, *Women, Crime and Justice in England since 1660* (Basingstoke: Palgrave Macmillan, 2009). More specific references to this historiography will be provided in relevant chapters.

24 *News of the World* (8 July 1928), p. 9.

1 The 'Fetter Hill mystery'

1 *World's Pictorial News* (5 February 1928), p. 1.

2 C. Hart, *The Free Miners of the Royal Forest of Dean and Hundred of St. Briavels* (Lydney, Glos.: Lightmoor Press, 2nd edn, 2002), p. xvi.

3 N. M. Herbert (ed.), *A History of Gloucestershire* (Oxford: Oxford University Press, 1996), pp. 337–8.

4 Hart, *Free Miners*, p. xiv.

5 C. Hart, *The Commoners of Dean Forest* (Lydney, Glos.: Lightmoor Press, 2nd edn, 2002), p. xv. See also Phelps, *Forest of Dean*, pp. 25–6.

6 W. Foley, *Full Hearts and Empty Bellies: A 1920s Childhood from the Forest of Dean to the Streets of London* (London: Abacus, 2009), pp. 5–6.

7 *Dean Forest Guardian* (20 January 1928), p. 5. Some newspaper stories refer to the village as 'Fetter Hill' while others use 'Fetterhill'; the former is correct: Herbert (ed.), *History of Gloucestershire*, p. 320.

8 *Daily Mail* (16 April 1928), p. 13.

9 *Daily Mail* (16 January 1928), p. 9; *World's Pictorial News* (29 April 1928), p. 20; *World's Pictorial News* (13 May 1928), p. 10.

10 *Daily News and Westminster Gazette* (9 July 1928), p. 9.

11 *Evening News* (3 March 1928) in The National Archives (hereafter TNA) HO 144/10854/1a. It was a 'bleak and lonely cottage': Hyde, *Birkett*, p. 246.

12 TNA MEPO 3/1638/5a, Report by CI George Cornish, 17 March 1928, pp. 46–7.

13 Beatrice told police: 'The rent of our house and garden is 5/- per week, in addition I rent regularly one small field at £4 per year rent. In addition to this I usually hire a field for which we pay £5.' Mrs Pace Papers, NCCL [National Centre for Citizenship and the Law] Galleries of Justice, Beatrice Pace, Statement to Police, 11 March 1928, p. 13 (hereafter: 'Pace Statement, 11 March 1928').

14 Approximate ages for the children are given in Pace Statement, 11 March 1928; those for Leslie and Selwyn have been corrected based on exact birth dates. For these, I thank Barry Martin. The baby's first name was Isobel, but she was consistently referred to by her middle name, 'Jean'.

15 Pace Statement, 11 March 1928, p. 2; *Thomson's Weekly News* (28 July 1928), p. 13.

16 *Dean Forest Guardian* (20 January 1928), p. 5. He is said to have had about a hundred sheep in *News of the World* (15 January 1928), in TNA HO 144/10854/1a. The number is given as more than a hundred in *World's Pictorial News* (22 January 1928), p. 3 and *World's Pictorial News* (5 February 1928), p. 1. Leonard Pace claimed that Harry had '84 or 86' sheep in July 1927: TNA ASSI 6/63/2, Inquest Depositions, p. 2.

17 *World's Pictorial News* (5 August 1928), p. 8; *Thomson's Weekly News* (28 July 1928), p. 13.

18 Pace Statement, 11 March 1928, p. 5.

19 His name was spelled differently in various media; I have adopted the spelling in the *Dean Forest Guardian*.

20 Some press reports put Harry's illness at the end of June, but Du Pré dated it from 'three weeks or a month' before entering the Infirmary, thus in mid-to-late July: TNA ASSI 6/63/2, Inquest Depositions, p. 125. Beatrice said the lambs had been dipped on 23 July, observing: 'I remember the dates because on the Monday 25th July 1927 I went into Coleford and registered my baby Jean.' Pace Statement, 11 March 1928, p. 5. Doris suggested it took place four days earlier: *Dean Forest Guardian* (20 April 1928), p. 6.

21 *Daily Mail* (3 July 1928), p. 7. In this book 'arsenic' refers to arsenious oxide, known as 'white arsenic', the most common form in general use and the key ingredient in sheep dip. S. Smith (ed.), *Taylor's Principles and Practice of Medical Jurisprudence*, vol. 2 (London: J & A Churchill, 9th edn, 1934), pp. 479–80.

22 *Dean Forest Guardian* (4 May 1928), p. 3.

23 *Dean Forest Guardian* (20 April 1928), p. 6.

24 *Dean Forest Guardian* (4 May 1928), p. 5.

25 *Dean Forest Guardian* (18 May 1928), p. 6. See also, Pace Statement, 11 March 1928, p. 5.

26 *Dean Forest Guardian* (1 June 1928), p. 5.

27 *Dean Forest Guardian* (11 May 1928), p. 3; TNA ASSI 6/63/2, Inquest Depositions, p. 135.

28 TNA MEPO 3/1638/5a, Report by CI George Cornish, 17 March 1928, p. 10.

29 *Dean Forest Guardian* (11 May 1928), p. 3.

30 *Dean Forest Guardian* (20 January 1928), p. 5.

31 Nanda agreed it was 'well known that peripheral neuritis can be caused by arsenic poisoning': *Dean Forest Guardian* (11 May 1928), p. 3.

32 *World's Pictorial News* (5 February 1928), p. 1. 'They thought this was from the sheep dip': *Dean Forest Guardian* (20 January 1928), p. 5.

33 TNA ASSI 6/63/2, Assize Depositions, p. 40.

34 *Ibid.*, p. 34. Beatrice reportedly stated that the Infirmary doctors had informed Du Pré that Harry 'was suffering from arsenical poisoning due to sheep dipping': *The People* (25 March 1928), p. 2; Testimony of Arthur Smith: *Dean Forest Guardian* (27 April 1928), p. 5.

35 *Dean Forest Guardian* (1 June 1928), p. 5.

36 TNA MEPO 3/1638/5a, Report by CI George Cornish, 17 March 1928, p. 7.

37 TNA ASSI 6/63/2, Inquest Depositions, p. 2.

38 Testimony of Joseph Martin: *Dean Forest Guardian* (20 April 1928), p. 5.

39 *Dean Forest Guardian* (20 April 1928), p. 5.
40 Testimony of Fletcher and Thorne: *Dean Forest Guardian* (20 April 1928), p. 5.
41 *Dean Forest Guardian* (30 March 1928), p. 5.
42 *Dean Forest Guardian* (20 April 1928), p. 5.
43 Pace Statement, 11 March 1928, p. 6.
44 Testimony of Harry John Winter: *Dean Forest Guardian* (4 May 1928), p. 3; Testimony of Arthur Smith: *Dean Forest Guardian* (27 April 1928), p. 5.
45 Charles Fletcher: 'He seemed very depressed and thought he would not recover.': *Dean Forest Guardian* (20 April 1928), p. 5. Edwin Morgan noted Harry's despondency and frequent outbursts of crying and conviction that his health would never improve. It was 'impossible to cheer him up': *Dean Forest Guardian* (27 April 1928), p. 5.
46 TNA ASSI 6/63/2, Assize Depositions, p. 40.
47 Leonard Pace and Elizabeth Porter both denied this (though Porter admitted her son was 'depressed' in hospital): *Dean Forest Guardian* (30 March 1928), pp. 5, 8. 'My husband told me if I did not take him home he would crawl out of bed and throw himself out of the verandah.': Pace Statement, 11 March 1928, p. 6. Arthur Smith claimed Harry had been despondent, convinced he would be crippled for life, and had spoken of 'doing himself in': *Dean Forest Guardian* (27 April 1928), p. 5. Rosa Kear: 'I have known him threaten to take his own life. In the week following Xmas day.' TNA ASSI 6/63/2, Inquest Depositions, p. 120.
48 Pace Statement, 11 March 1928, p. 6.
49 *World's Pictorial News* (22 January 1928), p. 3.
50 Pace Statement, 11 March 1928, pp. 6–7; *Dean Forest Guardian* (30 March 1928), p. 5.
51 *Dean Forest Guardian* (4 May 1928), p. 5.
52 *Dean Forest Guardian* (20 April 1928), p. 5.
53 *Dean Forest Guardian* (20 April 1928), p. 6 and (11 May 1928), p. 3; *Thomson's Weekly News* (21 July 1928), p. 13; Pace Statement, 11 March 1928, p. 7.
54 *Dean Forest Guardian* (11 May 1928), p. 5.
55 Dorothy's testimony: *Dean Forest Guardian* (20 April 1928), p. 6.
56 Testimony of Joseph Martin: TNA ASSI 6/63/2, Inquest Depositions, p. 25.
57 See Dorothy's testimony: *Dean Forest Guardian* (20 April 1928), p. 6. Martin's testimony: *Dean Forest Guardian* (20 April 1928), p. 5; Pace Statement, 11 March 1928, p. 7.
58 *Dean Forest Guardian* (11 May 1928), p. 3.
59 *Dean Forest Guardian* (20 April 1928), pp. 5 and 6.

60 *Ibid.*, p. 5.
61 *Dean Forest Guardian* (30 March 1928), p. 5.
62 *Dean Forest Guardian* (20 April 1928), p. 5.
63 *Dean Forest Guardian* (11 May 1928), p. 3.
64 *Dean Forest Guardian* (4 May 1928), p. 5.
65 *Dean Forest Guardian* (13 April 1928), p. 5.
66 Du Pré: *Dean Forest Guardian* (11 May 1928), p. 3.
67 *Dean Forest Guardian* (4 May 1928), p. 5. There was no running water in the house. Beatrice: 'We had drinking water from three places – Mrs Kear, Mrs Sayes and the well at Fetter Hill.' TNA ASSI 6/63/2, Inquest Depositions, p. 153.
68 *Thomson's Weekly News* (21 January 1928), p. 1. Dorothy: 'It was the knowledge that the last words my father said were "Beat, Beat". With his dying breath he spoke her name, and that she took as a token of his realisation at the last that she had played her part as a wife.' *Thomson's Weekly News* (4 August 1928), p. 3.
69 'I saw my brother Harry on the 10th Jan. 1928, I was fetched by my brother Elton between 10 a.m. and 10.35 a.m.' ASSI 6/63/2, Inquest Depositions, p. 27. At the trial she claimed to have arrived '15 minutes before he died'. *Dean Forest Guardian* (6 July 1928), p. 3. *Dean Forest Guardian* (13 April 1928), p. 5.
70 *Dean Forest Guardian* (4 May 1928), p. 5.
71 *Dean Forest Guardian* (27 April 1928), p. 5.
72 K. Watson, *Poisoned Lives: English Poisoners and Their Victims* (London: Hambledon and London, 2004), p. 1.
73 Beatrice, however, said: 'He was conscious up to the last and wished his children "good morning" and died about half past ten to eleven.' Pace Statement, 11 March 1928, p. 8.
74 *Dean Forest Guardian* (11 May 1928), p. 3.
75 *Daily Mail* (16 January 1928), p. 9.
76 *Dean Forest Guardian* (20 April 1928), p. 6.
77 *World's Pictorial News* (22 January 1928), p. 3.
78 Dorothy wrote her mother was seventeen when married and her father, 'a boy just a year older': *Thomson's Weekly News* (28 July 1928), p. 13.
79 *World's Pictorial News* (15 July 1928), p. 2. Emphasis added.
80 'And Harry, too, was only seventeen': *Sunday Express* (15 July 1928), pp. 1, 11.
81 I thank Margaret Gregory and the Gloucestershire Registry Office for the relevant certificates.
82 Even Harry's death certificate stated he was thirty-six. Going by his birth certificate, however, he was thirty-seven.
83 B. O'Donnell, *Crimes That Made News* (London: Burke, 1954), p. 93.

84 *Ibid.*, p. 1. Emphasis in original.

85 *World's Pictorial News* (12 August 1928), p. 14. An article by O'Donnell on the case also appeared in the *Empire News* (8 July 1928).

86 There may be a glancing reference to the Pace case, though not by name, in the biography of ghost-writer Maude ffoulkes: V. Powell, *A Substantial Ghost: The Literary Adventures of Maude ffoulkes* (London: Heinemann, 1967), p. 160. She did not ghost-write the Pace story, but a comment assumes that someone would have. I thank Andrew Parry for the reference.

87 *World's Pictorial News* (15 July 1928), p. 1.

88 *Thomson's Weekly News* (21 July 1928), p. 12.

89 *Sunday Express* (15 July 1928), p. 1.

90 Pace Statement, 11 March 1928, p. 1.

91 *Sunday Express* (15 July 1928), p. 1.

92 *World's Pictorial News* (15 July 1928), p. 2.

93 *Sunday Express* (15 July 1928), p. 1. O'Donnell's reference to 'several' younger children that Beatrice 'looked after' is thus exaggerated, as is Dorothy's comment that she played 'the part of a little mother to her younger brothers and sisters' since she only had one of each: *World's Pictorial News* (15 July 1928), p. 2; *Thomson's Weekly News* (21 July 1928), p. 12.

94 Pace Statement, 11 March 1928, p. 1.

95 *Thomson's Weekly News* (21 July 1928), p. 12.

96 *Sunday Express* (15 July 1928), p. 1.

97 *World's Pictorial News* (15 July 1928), p. 2.

98 *Thomson's Weekly News* (21 July 1928), p. 12.

99 Pace Statement, 11 March 1928, p. 1.

100 *Thomson's Weekly News* (21 July 1928), p. 12.

101 *World's Pictorial News* (15 July 1928), p. 1.

102 *Sunday Express* (15 July 1928), p. 1.

103 Pace Statement, 11 March 1928, p. 1. *Thomson's Weekly News* (21 July 1928), p. 12.

104 *Thomson's Weekly News* (21 July 1928), p. 12.

105 *World's Pictorial News* (15 July 1928), p. 2.

106 *Ibid.*

107 *Thomson's Weekly News* (21 July 1928), p. 12.

108 *Sunday Express* (15 July 1928), pp. 1, 11.

109 *Ibid.*, p. 11; *Thomson's Weekly News* (21 July 1928), pp. 12–13.

110 Harry, as noted, was actually almost a year younger than Beatrice.

111 *World's Pictorial News* (15 July 1928), p. 2.

112 *Sunday Express* (15 July 1928), p. 11; *World's Pictorial News* (15 July 1928), p. 2; *Thomson's Weekly News* (21 July 1928), p. 13. O'Donnell wrote that Beatrice stayed in the home of Mrs Martin,

her sister-in-law; Dorothy wrote: 'When she left London mother returned to her father's cottage at St. Briavels and she continued to live there until her wedding day.'

113 *Sunday Express* (15 July 1928), p. 11.

114 *Ibid.*

115 *World's Pictorial News* (15 July 1928), p. 2.

116 *Ibid.*

117 *Sunday Express* (15 July 1928), p. 11; *Thomson's Weekly News* (21 July 1928), p. 13.

118 *Dean Forest Guardian* (13 January 1928), p. 8. As noted, Harry was actually thirty-seven.

119 *Dean Forest Guardian* (20 January 1928), p. 5.

120 TNA MEPO 3/1638/5a, Report by CI George Cornish, 17 March 1928, pp. 7, 16.

121 TNA ASSI 6/63/2, Inquest Depositions, p. 113; *Dean Forest Guardian* (27 April 1928), p. 5.

122 TNA ASSI 6/63/2, Inquest Depositions, p. 113.

123 *Dean Forest Guardian* (27 April 1928), p. 5.

124 TNA ASSI 6/63/2, Inquest Depositions, p. 114. *Dean Forest Guardian* (27 April 1928), p. 5.

125 *Thomson's Weekly News* (4 August 1928), p. 3.

126 *Dean Forest Guardian* (13 April 1928), p. 5 and (27 April 1928), p. 5.

127 TNA ASSI 6/63/2, Inquest Depositions, p. 139.

128 *Ibid.*, p. 115. Some earlier reports gave Walker Hall's name as 'Hall Walker', e.g., *Daily Mail* (16 January 1928), p. 9 and *Dean Forest Guardian* (20 January 1928), p. 5. This misspelling was picked up in some subsequent commentary on the case, e.g., Church, *Accidents of Murder*, p. 136.

129 *Dean Forest Guardian* (20 January 1928), p. 5.

130 *World's Pictorial News* (29 April 1928), p. 20.

131 Hyde, *Birkett*, p. 246; see also Bardens, *Birkett*, p. 106; C. J. S. Thompson, *Poisons and Poisoners: With Historical Accounts of Some Famous Mysteries in Ancient and Modern Times* (London: Harold Shaylor, [1931]), p. 345.

132 All nine jurors were men: 'E. J. Smith (foreman), H. Birt, E. L. Jenkins, ... F. W. Adams, T. Higgins, H. A. Dangerfield, J. E. Bartlett, T. Bolter, and Ralph Morgan.' *Dean Forest Guardian* (20 January 1928), p. 5. They are also named in Gloucestershire Archives CO4-2-7, Coroner's Minute Book for the Forest of Dean Division, p. 13. I thank Andrew Parry for this reference.

133 O'Donnell, *Crimes That Made News*, p. 91.

134 *Dean Forest Guardian* (20 January 1928), p. 5; see also *Daily Mail* (17 January 1928), p. 7.

135 A photo of the funeral is shown in *Dean Forest Guardian* (20 January 1928), p. 5.
136 *Ibid.*

2 'Where there are so many cruel tongues'

1 *Dean Forest Guardian* (17 February 1928), p. 5; *World's Pictorial News* (5 February 1928), p. 1.
2 *Daily Express* (16 February 1928), in TNA HO 144/10854/1a.
3 *Daily Mail* (30 January 1928), in TNA HO 144/10854/1a.
4 *Dean Forest Guardian* (17 February 1928), p. 5.
5 *World's Pictorial News* (22 January 1928), p. 3 and (5 February 1928), p. 1.
6 *Dean Forest Guardian* (20 January 1928), p. 5.
7 *Daily Mail* (16 January 1928), p. 9.
8 *Dean Forest Guardian* (13 April 1928), p. 5.
9 *Dean Forest Guardian* (9 March 1928), p. 5; *Daily Mail* (16 January 1928), p. 9. Cross-examined, the Pace family admitted they were unaware Harry had left the Infirmary against the advice of his wife, the doctors and the nurses: *Dean Forest Guardian* (30 March 1928), p. 5. Wellington read out a statement from a 'Sister Arthur', a nurse, confirming Harry's discharge was against Beatrice's wishes. A fellow patient agreed: *Dean Forest Guardian* (27 April 1928), p. 5.
10 *Dean Forest Guardian* (20 January 1928), p. 5.
11 Bent's testimony: *Dean Forest Guardian* (27 April 1928), p. 6; Blanch's testimony: *Dean Forest Guardian* (4 May 1928), p. 3.
12 TNA ASSI 6/63/2, Inquest Depositions, p. 115.
13 Mrs Pace Papers, NCCL Galleries of Justice, Beatrice Pace, Statement to Police, 15 February 1928, p. 1 (hereafter: 'Pace Statement, 15 February 1928').
14 *World's Pictorial News* (5 February 1928), p. 1; *Dean Forest Guardian* (9 March 1928), p. 5.
15 Bent's testimony: *Dean Forest Guardian* (27 April 1928), p. 5.
16 TNA MEPO 3/1638/1a, Metropolitan Police telegrams, 6 and 7 March. See also TNA HO 144/10854/1, Clarke to Under Secretary of State, 7 March 1928.
17 O'Donnell later described Cornish as an 'old friend': O'Donnell, *Crimes That Made News*, pp. 6–7.
18 G. W. Cornish, *Cornish of the 'Yard': His Reminiscences and Cases* (London: John Lane, 1935), pp. 31–2. On the Crippen case, see J. E. Early, 'Keeping ourselves to ourselves: violence in the Edwardian suburb', in S. D'Cruze (ed.), *Everyday Violence in Britain, 1850–1950: Gender and Class* (Harlow: Pearson, 2000), pp. 170–84.

19 *The Times* (23 May 1922), p. 5.
20 *The Times* (20 May 1927), p. 16; (14 July 1927), p. 8; (13 August 1927), p. 7.
21 *The People* (8 July 1928), p. 7.
22 *The Times* (22 April 1927), p. 9.
23 *Dean Forest Guardian* (16 March 1928), p. 5.
24 *Daily Chronicle* (10 March 1928), in TNA HO 144/10854/1a. See also *Daily Mail* (10 March 1928), in TNA HO 144/10854/1a.
25 Cornish's testimony: *Dean Forest Guardian* (13 July 1928), p. 2.
26 *Evening News* (7 March 1928), in TNA HO 144/10854/1a.
27 TNA ASSI 6/63/2, Inquest Depositions, pp. 114–15.
28 Cornish's testimony: *Dean Forest Guardian* (11 May 1928), p. 5.
29 TNA ASSI 6/63/2, Inquest Depositions, p. 115; *Dean Forest Guardian* (11 May 1928), p. 3.
30 *Dean Forest Guardian* (16 March 1928), p. 5.
31 TNA MEPO 3/1638/5a, Report by CI George Cornish, 17 March 1928, pp. 4–5.
32 *Ibid.*, p. 27.
33 *Ibid.*, p. 39.
34 All references in this paragraph, *ibid.*, pp. 39–42.
35 All references in this paragraph, *ibid.*, pp. 42–7.
36 TNA MEPO 3/1638/11b, Rowland H. Ellis to Chief Constable of Gloucestershire (Major Stanley Clarke), 23 March 1928.
37 TNA MEPO 3/1638/21c, Alan Bent to Superintendent Shelswell, 5 April 1928.
38 TNA MEPO 3/1638/19b, Report from Karl B. Edwards, Director of the Cooper Technical Bureau, 30 March 1928.
39 TNA MEPO 3/1638/12a, Cornish to Superintendent Savage, 27 March 1928.
40 *Dean Forest Guardian* (30 March 1928), p. 5; *World's Pictorial News* (29 April 1928), p. 20.
41 *Dean Forest Guardian* (30 March 1928), p. 5.
42 F. D. Thomas, *Sir John Jervis on the Office and Duties of Coroners* (London: Sweet and Maxwell, 7th edn, 1927), p. 55, citing Coroners Act 1887, S. 4 (1).
43 *Dean Forest Guardian* (11 May 1928), p. 3. See also, TNA HO 144/10854/31a, p. 1 for comments on Paling's role.
44 Wellington had become Gloucester City Coroner in 1921: *Citizen* (Gloucester) (4 February 1963), p. 1.
45 *Dean Forest Guardian* (25 May 1928), p. 5.
46 *Dean Forest Guardian* (30 March 1928), p. 5.
47 *Dean Forest Guardian* (18 May 1928), p. 6.
48 *World's Pictorial News* (20 May 1928), p. 1.
49 *Thomson's Weekly News* (26 May 1928), p. 1. At times, she sat in

the body of the court with friends 'immediately behind the relatives of the dead man, who, dressed in sombre black, occupied nearly a complete row': *Thomson's Weekly News* (19 May 1928), p. 12.

50 *Dean Forest Guardian* (20 January 1928), p. 5 and (1 June 1928), p. 5.

51 TNA MEPO 3/1638/5a, Report by CI George Cornish, 17 March 1928, p. 17.

52 *Dean Forest Guardian* (30 March 1928), p. 5.

53 *Daily Mail* (3 July 1928), p. 11.

54 *Dean Forest Guardian* (30 March 1928), p. 5.

55 *Ibid.*, p. 8.

56 TNA ASSI 6/63/2, Inquest Depositions, pp. 1, 7.

57 *Dean Forest Guardian* (30 March 1928), p. 8.

58 *Dean Forest Guardian* (20 April 1928), p. 6.

59 *Dean Forest Guardian* (30 March 1928), p. 5.

60 Timing recounted in TNA MEPO 3/1638/5a, Report by CI George Cornish, 17 March 1928, p. 8.

61 *Dean Forest Guardian* (30 March 1928), p. 5.

62 *Ibid.*, p. 8.

63 Elton's testimony: *Dean Forest Guardian* (13 April 1928), p. 5 and TNA ASSI 6/63/2, Inquest Depositions, pp. 20–6.

64 *Dean Forest Guardian* (13 April 1928), p. 5.

65 Dr Nanda's testimony: *Dean Forest Guardian* (11 May 1928), p. 5.

66 *Dean Forest Guardian* (13 April 1928), p. 5; *Sunday News* (15 April 1928), p. 9.

67 *Dean Forest Guardian* (13 April 1928), p. 5.

68 *Daily Mail* (13 April 1928), p. 12; see also *Dean Forest Guardian* (13 April 1928), p. 5.

69 *Dean Forest Guardian* (20 April 1928), p. 6.

70 *Dean Forest Guardian* (4 May 1928), p. 3.

71 *World's Pictorial News* (29 April 1928), p. 20.

72 *Dean Forest Guardian* (4 May 1928), p. 5.

73 *Ibid.* Also: TNA ASSI 6/63/2, Inquest Depositions, p. 89.

74 *Dean Forest Guardian* (4 May 1928), p. 5.

75 My summary of the Armstrong case is based on *The Times* (3 January 1922), p. 10; (5 January 1922), p. 10; (11 January 1922), p. 5; (12 January 1922), p. 5; (18 February 1922), p. 4; (4 April 1922), p. 14; (8 April 1922), p. 7; (15 April 1922), p. 12; (17 April 1922), p. 17; (16 May 1922), p. 17; (1 June 1922), p. 7. See also J. Emsley, *The Elements of Murder: A History of Poison* (Oxford: Oxford University Press, 2006), p. 163 and R. Odell, *Exhumation of a Murder: The Life and Trial of Major Armstrong* (London: Harrap, 1975).

76 *The Times* (5 January 1922), p. 10.

77 *The Times* (15 April 1922), p. 12.
78 *The Times* (16 May 1922), p. 17.
79 Watson, *Poisoned Lives*, pp. 45–9, 208–9.
80 A. Ballinger, *Dead Woman Walking: Executed Women in England and Wales, 1900–1955* (Aldershot: Ashgate, 2000), pp. 168–9.
81 *The Times* (16 May 1922), p. 17.
82 Watson, *Poisoned Lives*, p. 149.
83 *Dean Forest Guardian* (13 April 1928), p. 5.
84 Watson, *Poisoned Lives*, p. 67.

3 'I cannot tell you sir – I cannot tell you'

1 *Reynolds's Illustrated News* (6 May 1928), p. 13.
2 *World's Pictorial News* (13 May 1928), p. 10.
3 *Dean Forest Guardian* (20 April 1928), p. 6; *Sunday News* (22 April 1928), p. 5.
4 *Dean Forest Guardian* (11 May 1928), p. 3. TNA ASSI 6/63/2, Inquest Depositions, pp. 40–50.
5 Smith (ed.), *Taylor's Principles*, p. 386.
6 *Dean Forest Guardian* (11 May 1928), p. 3.
7 *Dean Forest Guardian* (20 April 1928), p. 5.
8 *Dean Forest Guardian* (4 May 1928), p. 5.
9 As described by Doris: *Dean Forest Guardian* (20 April 1928), p. 6; Leslie's testimony: *Dean Forest Guardian* (4 May 1928), p. 5.
10 Sgt Hamblin also testified briefly; his comments were confined to Beatrice handing him the bottle labelled 'Butter of Antimony', a matter also mentioned by Bent: *Dean Forest Guardian* (13 April 1928), p. 5.
11 See, e.g., *Daily Mail* (27 April 1928), p. 13.
12 *Dean Forest Guardian* (27 April 1928), p. 5.
13 Beatrice claimed Harry was also fined 14s. Pace Statement, 11 March 1928, p. 4.
14 Hale's name was not mentioned in the local press coverage, but comparison of the comments in court with the original statement shows it was a reference to him. Pace Statement, 15 February 1928, p. 2.
15 *Dean Forest Guardian* (27 April 1928), p. 5.
16 Pace Statement, 15 February 1928, p. 1.
17 The receipt appears to be in the Mrs. Pace Papers, NCCL Galleries of Justice: item #252.
18 *Dean Forest Guardian* (27 April 1928), p. 5.
19 *Dean Forest Guardian* (11 May 1928), p. 5.
20 Incorrectly stated as 'Wednesday 18 March' in the *Dean Forest Guardian* (11 May 1928), p. 5.

21 TNA ASSI 6/63/2, Inquest Depositions, p. 164.
22 *Dean Forest Guardian* (11 May 1928), p. 5.
23 *Dean Forest Guardian* (27 April 1928), p. 5.
24 *Dean Forest Guardian* (11 May 1928), p. 5.
25 *Dean Forest Guardian* (27 April 1928), p. 5.
26 *Dean Forest Guardian* (4 May 1928), p. 3.
27 *Dean Forest Guardian* (27 April 1928), p. 5.
28 *Dean Forest Guardian* (20 April 1928), p. 5.
29 *Dean Forest Guardian* (11 May 1928), p. 5.
30 *Dean Forest Guardian* (20 April 1928), p. 5.
31 *Dean Forest Guardian* (13 April 1928), p. 5.
32 TNA MEPO 3/1638/5a, Report by CI George Cornish, 17 March 1928, p. 12.
33 TNA ASSI 6/63/2, Inquest Depositions, p. 134.
34 *Dean Forest Guardian* (4 May 1928), p. 5.
35 A copy of Harry's will is in TNA ASSI 6/63/2.
36 The sheep had been sold to Matthew Hoare (a collier who also dealt in pigs and sheep) and Caleb John Miles. Hoare bought 22 sheep and 14 lambs in late August 1927 for £40, and on 11 October 1927 Miles bought 14 ewes and 8 lambs for £34 8s. TNA ASSI 6/63/2, Inquest Depositions, pp., 107, 123.
37 *Dean Forest Guardian* (4 May 1928), p. 3.
38 TNA ASSI 6/63/2, Inquest Depositions, p. 156. In 2009, based upon an 'average earnings' comparison, the equivalent value would have been roughly £13,300: www.measuringworth.com, accessed 21 February 2011.
39 *Dean Forest Guardian* (20 April 1928), p. 5.
40 *Dean Forest Guardian* (4 May 1928), p. 5.
41 *Ibid.*
42 *Dean Forest Guardian* (20 April 1928), p. 5.
43 *Ibid.*
44 *Daily Mail* (20 April 1928), p. 14.
45 *Daily Mail* (27 April 1928), p. 11.
46 *Daily Mail* (5 May 1928), p. 10.
47 *Dean Forest Guardian* (11 May 1928), p. 5.
48 *Dean Forest Guardian* (11 May 1928), p. 3.
49 *Ibid.*
50 *Ibid.*, p. 5.
51 *Ibid.*, p. 3.
52 TNA MEPO 3/1638/5a, Report by CI George Cornish, 17 March 1928, pp. 39, 48.
53 TNA MEPO 3/1638/12a, Cornish to Superintendent Savage, 27 March 1928, p. 1.
54 *Sunday News* (20 May 1928), p. 5.

55 Willcox, *Detective-Physician*, p. xii.
56 *Ibid.*, p. 210.
57 Willcox's testimony: *Dean Forest Guardian* (18 May 1928), p. 6.
58 *Dean Forest Guardian* (11 May 1928), p. 5.
59 *Daily Mail* (11 May 1928), p. 13; *The People* (13 May 1928), p. 4.
    There were nineteenth-century cases in which 88 grains or more
    than 154 grains of arsenic were found in the deceased: Thompson,
    Poisons and Poisoners, pp. 260–1.
60 *Thomson's Weekly News* (19 May 1928), p. 12. The combination
    of chronic and acute poisoning was brought out most clearly in
    Walker Hall's trial testimony: *Dean Forest Guardian* (13 July
    1928), p. 2.
61 *Dean Forest Guardian* (18 May 1928), p. 6.
62 *Sunday News* (20 May 1928), p. 5.
63 *Dean Forest Guardian* (18 May 1928), p. 6.
64 *News of the World* (8 July 1928), p. 9.
65 *Dean Forest Guardian* (18 May 1928), p. 6.
66 *The Times* (18 February 1922) p. 4.
67 'The witness said it was difficult to diagnose cases of arsenical
    poisoning during life, and where there were no grounds for suspicion,
    as many of the symptoms of arsenical poisoning occurred in natural
    diseases or in cases of so-called ptomaine poisoning.' *Ibid.*
68 Ellis's testimony: 'The green bottle (found in the fender) was
    empty and had the smell of nitrous ether. It contained only traces
    of a mixture which gave negative results as to traces of arsenic or
    antimony. The second, a small bottle labelled "eye drops", contained
    a few drops of colourless liquid which gave negative results. The
    third bottle contained ordinary embrocation and held no arsenic or
    antimony. The fourth bottle, with a label as to taking the mixture,
    contained a brown-coloured liquid and was principally opium, and
    had no trace of arsenic or antimony. The fifth bottle, having a label
    with writing on it which he thought was "butter of antimony",
    contained an orange-coloured liquid, which he found to contain
    hydrochloric acid and antimony chloride, but no arsenic. This was
    an extremely corrosive poison. The red powder used for marking
    sheep was ordinary raddle and did not contain arsenic. The grey
    powder was a sheep medicine, containing principally Epsom salts,
    bone meal, sulphur, etc., and contained no arsenic. The white
    powder was ordinary boracic acid powder, a dark purple powder
    was potassium permanganate.' *Dean Forest Guardian* (11 May
    1928), p. 5.
69 *Dean Forest Guardian* (18 May 1928), p. 6.
70 *Ibid.*, p. 7.
71 *World's Pictorial News* (20 May 1928), p. 20.

72 *Thomson's Weekly News* (19 May 1928), p. 12.
73 *World's Pictorial News* (27 May 1928), p. 10.
74 *Ibid.*
75 *Thomson's Weekly News* (26 May 1928), p. 1.
76 *World's Pictorial News* (27 May 1928), p. 10.
77 *Daily Mail* (23 May 1928), p. 13.
78 *Thomson's Weekly News* (26 May 1928), p. 1.
79 *Daily Mail* (23 May 1928), p. 1; *Thomson's Weekly News* (26 May 1928), p. 1. He was also described as 'openly crying and struggling to master his emotion': *Reynolds's Illustrated News* (27 May 1928), p. 11.
80 *World's Pictorial News* (27 May 1928), p. 10. This moment is described somewhat differently in the *Mail*: 'The stunning effect of the verdict returned against her was so great that she crumpled up instantly. She was able only to shout out, "No, I didn't; no, I didn't" and had to be helped out of the coroner's court after sinking to floor. A policewoman and an inspector gathered her in their arms, where she lay inanimate. Medical aid was called, but even under the care of two doctors and Mrs. Bent, the wife of Mr. Alan Bent, the local police inspector, two hours elapsed before she was in a condition to hear the charge.' *Daily Mail* (23 May 1928), p. 13. See also *Thomson's Weekly News* (26 May 1928), p. 1.
81 *World's Pictorial News* (27 May 1928), p. 10.
82 *Thomson's Weekly News* (26 May 1928), p. 1.
83 *World's Pictorial News* (27 May 1928), p. 10.
84 *Daily Mail* (23 May 1928), p. 13.
85 *Dean Forest Guardian* (25 May 1928), p. 5.
86 *Ibid.*

4 'Easing the burden of the tragic widow'

1 Between 1900 and 1929, 413 men and eight women were executed in England and Wales: C. Emsley, *Hard Men: Violence in England Since 1750* (London: Hambledon and London, 2005), p. 169. The two women executed for murder in the 1920s were Edith Thompson (1923) and Louie Calvert (1926).
2 K. Williams, *Get Me a Murder a Day! A History of Mass Communication in Britain* (London: Arnold, 1998), pp. 50–7.
3 T. Jeffery and K. McClelland, 'A world fit to live in: the *Daily Mail* and the middle classes 1918–1939', in J. Curran, A. Smith and P. Wingate (eds), *Impacts and Influences: Essays on Media Power in the Twentieth Century* (London: Methuen, 1987), p. 29.
4 J. Curran, A. Douglas and G. Whannel, 'The political economy of the human-interest story', in A. Smith (ed.), *Newspapers*

and Democracy: International Essays on a Changing Medium (Cambridge, MA: The MIT Press, 1980), pp. 288–347.

5 R. Shoemaker, *The London Mob: Violence and Disorder in Eighteenth-Century England* (London: Hambledon and London, 2004), pp. 241–73; R. Altick, *Victorian Studies in Scarlet* (New York: W.W. Norton, 1970).

6 M. Pugh, *We Danced All Night: A Social History of Britain between the Wars* (London: Vintage, 2009), p. 102.

7 C. Emsley, 'Violent crime in England in 1919: post-war anxieties and press narratives', *Continuity and Change* 23 (2008), 173–95. Emsley, *Hard Men*, pp. 19–22. M. Kohn, *Dope Girls: The Birth of the British Drug Underground* (London: Granta, 2001 [1992]).

8 *Daily Herald* (12 May 1927), p. 4.

9 J. Scaggs, *Crime Fiction* (Abingdon: Routledge, 2005), pp. 33–54.

10 A. Christie, *The Mysterious Affair at Styles* (London: HarperCollins, 1994 [1920]), pp. 120–1, 135.

11 G. Frost, '"She is but a woman": Kitty Byron and the English Edwardian criminal justice system', *Gender and History* 16 (2004), 538–60; Early, 'Keeping ourselves to ourselves'.

12 L. Bland, 'The trials and tribulations of Edith Thompson: the capital crime of sexual incitement in 1920s England', *Journal of British Studies* 47 (2008), 624–48.

13 A. Ballinger, 'The guilt of the innocent and the innocence of the guilty: the cases of Marie Fahmy and Ruth Ellis', in A. Myers and S. Wight (eds), *No Angels* (London: Pandora, 1996), pp. 1–28; L. Bland, 'The trial of Madame Fahmy: orientalism, violence, sexual perversity and the fear of miscegenation', in D'Cruze (ed.), *Everyday Violence in Britain, 1850–1950*, pp. 185–97.

14 J. Knelman, *Twisting in the Wind: The Murderess and the English Press* (Toronto: Toronto University Press, 1997). B. Morrissey, *When Women Kill: Questions of Agency and Subjectivity* (London: Routledge, 2003), esp. pp. 1–30. For a late 1920s American case, see J. Ramey, 'The bloody blonde and the marble woman: gender and power in the case of Ruth Snyder', *Journal of Social History* 37 (2004), 625–50.

15 M. Eisner, 'Long-term historical trends in violent crime', *Crime and Justice: A Review of Research* 30 (2003), 109–12.

16 A. Ballinger, '"Reasonable" women who kill: re-interpreting and re-defining women's responses to domestic violence in England and Wales, 1900–1965', *Outlines* 2 (2005), 74–8.

17 A. Ballinger, 'Masculinity in the dock: legal responses to male violence and female retaliation in England and Wales, 1900–1965', *Social and Legal Studies* 16 (2007), 465–9.

18 A. Bingham, *Gender, Modernity and the Popular Press in Inter-War*

Britain (Oxford: Clarendon Press, 2004), pp. 48–9. In April 1927 *Newspaper World* quipped: 'In the old days ... a two-page account of a murder ... was the great attraction; now it seems to be what some well-known man or woman thinks of the modern girl.' Quoted *ibid.*, p. 48.

19   A. Light, *Forever England: Femininity, Literature and Conservatism between the Wars* (London: Routledge, 1991), pp. 18, 211; Bingham, *Gender, Modernity and the Popular Press*, pp. 236–43; Ballinger, 'Masculinity in the dock', 462–3, 467. M. Houlbrook, '"The man with the powder puff" in interwar London', *Historical Journal* 50 (2007), 160.

20   A. J. Hammerton, *Cruelty and Companionship: Conflict in Nineteenth-Century Married Life* (London: Routledge, 1992); M. Wiener, *Men of Blood: Violence, Manliness, and Criminal Justice in Victorian England* (Cambridge: Cambridge University Press, 2004); Emsley, *Hard Men*, pp. 60–9.

21   'To-day, although a Coroner's warrant can commit a person for trial and has the effect of an indictment and is equivalent to the finding of a Grand Jury at the Assize Court, it is the invariable practice – although it is not necessary in law for the accused person to be brought before a Magisterial Court – for the Magistrate to examine the case and come to a decision whether a prima facie case has been made out.' Comments of R. Hopkin Morris, *HC Deb* 11 July 1928 vol 219 c2245.

22   The following summary is from *Dean Forest Guardian* (1 June 1928), p. 5.

23   *Dean Forest Guardian* (8 June 1928), p. 2. The room plan is in ASSI 6/63/2.

24   *Dean Forest Guardian* (8 June 1928), p. 2.

25   *Ibid.*, p. 3.

26   *Ibid.*

27   *World's Pictorial News* (10 June 1928), p. 1.

28   *Dean Forest Guardian* (8 June 1928), p. 3.

29   *World's Pictorial News* (10 June 1928), p. 2.

30   Pace Statement, 11 March 1928, pp. 2–4. See also, e.g., the summary in *News of the World* (8 July 1928), p. 9.

31   *Daily Mail* (5 June 1928), p. 7.

32   *Sunday News* (3 June 1928), p. 1; *The People* (3 June 1928), p. 1.

33   *World's Pictorial News* (10 June 1928), p. 1; *Daily Mail* (4 June 1928), p. 7.

34   *The People* (3 June 1928), p. 1.

35   *World's Pictorial News* (10 June 1928), p. 1.

36   *Dean Forest Guardian* (8 June 1928), p. 3.

37   *Ibid.*

38 *World's Pictorial News* (10 June 1928), p. 2.

39 *Dean Forest Guardian* (8 June 1928), p. 3.

40 *World's Pictorial News* (10 June 1928), p. 2.

41 *Dean Forest Guardian* (8 June 1928), p. 3.

42 *World's Pictorial News* (10 June 1928), p. 1.

43 *Dean Forest Guardian* (8 June 1928), p. 3.

44 *Daily Mail* (5 June 1928), p. 12.

45 *Thomson's Weekly News* (9 June 1928), p. 1.

46 The 'friend' may have been journalist Bernard O'Donnell: *World's Pictorial News* (10 June 1928), p. 1.

47 *Dean Forest Guardian* (8 June 1928), p. 5.

48 *Ibid.*

49 *Ibid.*

50 *World's Pictorial News* (3 June 1928), p. 9.

51 *World's Pictorial News* (24 June 1928), p. 3.

52 *The People* (8 July 1928), p. 2.

53 *World's Pictorial News* (24 June 1928), p. 3. *Thomson's Weekly News* (14 July 1928), p. 13.

54 TNA MEPO 3/1638/75a, letter from Beatrice Pace to Alice Sayes, 23 May 1928. Parts of some letters were printed after her trial in *News of the World* (8 July 1928), p. 9.

55 *Ibid.*, Letter, 20 June.

56 *Ibid.*, Letter, 27 June.

57 *Ibid.*, Letter, 12 June; Letter 27 June.

58 *Ibid.*, Letter, 20 June.

59 *Ibid.*, Letter, 20 June. 'Are you lonesome tonight?': music by Lou Handman, lyrics by Roy Turk, published 1926.

60 *Ibid.*, Letter, 27 June 1928.

61 'I am doing my best, my very best to keep up as I don't want the good people here to think I am not well and happy but they don't know how I feel, how I am longing to see my dear children.' *Ibid.*, Letter, 20 June.

62 TNA ASSI 6/63/2, Prison Medical Officer's Report, 18 June 1928.

63 *The People* (8 April 1928), p. 3; (15 April 1928), p. 4; (22 April 1928), p. 4.

64 *Daily Mail* (13 April 1928), p. 11; (19 April 1928), p. 11; (20 April 1928), p. 14; (27 April 1928), p. 11.

65 *World's Pictorial News* (29 April 1928), p. 20; (13 May 1928), p. 10; (24 June 1928), p. 3.

66 The paper suggested that she might even face a new 'ordeal' by having to travel every day from Birmingham, since Gloucester prison lacked accommodation for women prisoners. *Sunday Express* (24 June 1928), p. 13. As Chapter 5 notes, this did not happen.

67 *World's Pictorial News* (3 June 1928), p. 9.

68 *Sunday News* (27 May 1928), p. 3.
69 Frost, 'She is but a woman'.
70 Early, 'Keeping ourselves to ourselves', pp. 170–2, 180.
71 Bland, 'Edith Thompson', 626–8. See also Ballinger, *Dead Woman Walking*, pp. 221–57.
72 Bland, 'Fahmy'; Ballinger, 'Guilt of the innocent'.
73 Most stories were not by-lined. Almost all of those that were had been written by men. A 1927 International Labour Organisation study estimated that about 400 of 7,000 journalists in Britain (less than six per cent) were women. Bingham, *Gender, Modernity, and the Popular Press*, p. 40.
74 *The People* (15 April 1928), p. 4.
75 *Daily Mail* (13 April 1928), p. 11.
76 Bland, 'Edith Thompson', 631.
77 *Thomson's Weekly News* (2 June 1928), p. 13.
78 *Daily Mail* (23 May 1928), p. 13.
79 Beatrice depended on a widow's pension of twenty-four shillings a week and the assistance of family, friends and anonymous donors. *Thomson's Weekly News* (28 July 1928), p. 13.
80 *Thomson's Weekly News* (2 June 1928), p. 13.
81 *World's Pictorial News* (27 May 1928), p. 10.
82 *The People* (3 June 1928), p. 1.
83 *Sunday Express* (3 June 1928), p. 1 and (17 June 1928), p. 1. See also *Reynolds's Illustrated News* (10 June 1928), p. 17.
84 *Daily Mail* (4 June 1928), in TNA HO 144/10854/13.
85 *The People* (17 June 1928), p. 4.
86 *Thomson's Weekly News* (9 June 1928), p. 1.
87 *Dean Forest Guardian* (1 June 1928), p. 5.
88 *World's Pictorial News* (3 June 1928), p. 9; *World's Pictorial News* (27 May 1928), p. 10. 'As usual at the week-end hundreds of cars line the road near the little cottage, and from all parts of the country people swarm round the house and garden. Many hunt for souvenirs and take away a little stone from the wall or a plant from the garden.': *Reynolds's Illustrated News* (17 June 1928), p. 7. See the Mrs Pace Papers, NCCL Galleries of Justice, letter #156, for a letter from a woman who took part in one such outing.
89 J. Dawson, *Fred and Edie* (London: Hodder and Stoughton, 2000), p. 276.
90 *Thomson's Weekly News* (2 June 1928), p. 13.
91 *World's Pictorial News* (13 May 1928), p. 10.
92 *World's Pictorial News* (29 July 1928), p. 14.
93 *The People* (8 April 1928), p. 3.
94 *Thomson's Weekly News* (2 June 1928), p. 16.
95 This description based on K. Morgan, 'Purcell, Albert Arthur

(1872–1935)', *Oxford Dictionary of National Biography*, Oxford University Press, 2004, www.oxforddnb.com/view/article/35632, accessed 30 January 2011.

96 *Dean Forest Guardian* (8 June 1928), p. 2. He was (wrongly) referred to as 'A. E. Purcell' in *World's Pictorial News* (10 June 1928), p. 1.

97 TNA HO 144/10854/21, Memo by Arthur Locke. Emphasis in original.

98 They were, however, noted in the press, e.g., *Reynolds's Illustrated News* (10 June 1928), p. 1; *Sunday News* (10 June 1928), p. 3.

99 *Dean Forest Guardian* (1 June 1928), p. 3.

100 *Sunday News* (10 June 1928), p. 3.

101 *Dean Forest Guardian* (1 June 1928), p. 3.

102 *The People* (3 June 1928), p. 2; *Dean Forest Guardian* (8 June 1928), p. 2.

103 *Sunday News* (10 June 1928), in HO 144/10854/29a.

104 *Dean Forest Guardian* (8 June 1928), p. 3.

105 *Sunday News* (10 June 1928), in HO 144/10854/29a.

106 *Reynolds's Illustrated News* (1 July 1928), p. 3.

107 Jonescu was described as the brother of a former Romanian prime minister: *World's Pictorial News* (13 May 1928), p. 11.

108 *Ibid.*

109 *Daily Express* (8 May 1928), p. 1.

110 *The Times* (9 May 1928), p. 16.

111 *The Times* (10 May 1928), p. 16.

112 *Daily Mail* (5 June 1928), pp. 11–12.

113 *World's Pictorial News* (1 July 1928), p. 1.

5 'Every wife in the country has opportunity'

1 *Daily Herald* (7 June 1928), in TNA HO 144/10854/29a.

2 *Daily Mail* (3 July 1928), p. 11; *Daily Mail* (8 June 1928), in TNA HO 144/10854/29a.

3 [Patrick Arthur] Devlin, 'Birkett (William) Norman, first Baron Birkett (1883–1962)', rev. *Oxford Dictionary of National Biography*, Oxford University Press, 2004, www.oxforddnb.com/view/article/31899, accessed 6 February 2011.

4 Hyde, *Birkett*, p. 49.

5 Bardens, *Birkett*, p. 105.

6 Hyde, *Birkett*, p. 119.

7 *Ibid.*, p. 247.

8 Devlin, 'Birkett'.

9 *World's Pictorial News* (1 July 1928), p. 1.

10 Devlin, 'Birkett'.

11 *World's Pictorial News* (1 July 1928), p. 1.

12 *Daily Mail* (3 July 1928), p. 11.

13 *Manchester Guardian* (2 July 1928), p. 10. 'There is tonight scarcely a room to be secured in Gloucester city, and every hotel is booked up for a week.': *Daily Express* (2 July 1928), p. 1.

14 *The People* (1 July 1928), p. 3. See also *Liverpool Echo* (2 July 1928), p. 12.

15 *Daily Express* (2 July 1928), p. 1.

16 *Liverpool Echo* (4 July 1928), p. 12.

17 David Davies, 'Horridge, Sir Thomas Gardner (1857–1938)', rev. Hugh Mooney, *Oxford Dictionary of National Biography*, Oxford University Press, 2004, www.oxforddnb.com/view/article/33996, accessed 6 February 2011.

18 *World's Pictorial News* (1 July 1928), p. 1.

19 Hyde, *Birkett*, pp. 86–90.

20 *Ibid.*, p. 103. Sentenced to imprisonment with hard labour, Birkett's client collapsed.

21 *World's Pictorial News* (1 July 1928), p. 1.

22 Hyde, *Birkett*, p. 104.

23 *World's Pictorial News* (1 July 1928), p. 1.

24 *Daily Express* (2 July 1928), p. 1.

25 *Ibid.*; *Sunday News* (1 July 1928), p. 3.

26 Hyde, *Birkett*, p. 203.

27 *Daily Express* (2 July 1928), p. 1.

28 Spilsbury's presence is mentioned in the *Daily Express* (2 July 1928), p. 1 and *Daily Herald* (2 July 1928), p. 1.

29 Bardens, *Birkett*, p. 109.

30 *Manchester Guardian* (3 July 1928), p. 7.

31 *Liverpool Echo* (2 July 1928), p. 12.

32 *Daily Express* (2 July 1928), p. 1.

33 *World's Pictorial News* (8 July 1928), p. 1.

34 *Manchester Guardian* (3 July 1928), p. 7.

35 *Dean Forest Guardian* (29 June 1928), p. 5. The *Manchester Guardian* reported, 'a number of well-known novelists had secured places': (3 July 1928), p. 7. 'Several well-known novelists, eager for material, have asked to be allowed to attend.': *The People* (1 July 1928), p. 3. Also: *Liverpool Echo* (2 July 1928), p. 12 and *Sunday News* (24 June 1928), p. 1.

36 *Liverpool Echo* (2 July 1928), p. 12.

37 *Daily Mail* (3 July 1928), p. 11.

38 *Liverpool Echo* (3 July 1928), p. 7.

39 *Daily Mail* (6 July 1928), p. 12.

40 *Liverpool Echo* (2 July 1928), p. 7.

41 *The People* (8 July 1928), p. 7.

42 *Manchester Guardian* (2 July 1928), p. 10.
43 *The People* (1 July 1928), p. 3. It was (wrongly) reported that Beatrice would stay in a 'room in the Shire Hall' during the trial: *Liverpool Echo* (2 July 1928), p. 12. *Daily Express* (4 July 1928), p. 1.
44 *Liverpool Echo* (3 July 1928), p. 12.
45 *Ibid.*, p. 7.
46 *Daily Mirror* (3 July 1928), p. 3.
47 *Daily Express* (3 July 1928), p. 1.
48 *Daily Mirror* (5 July 1928), p. 2.
49 *Daily Express* (3 July 1928), p. 1.
50 *Daily Express* (4 July 1928), p. 1.
51 *Manchester Guardian* (4 July 1928), p. 11.
52 *Daily Express* (4 July 1928), p. 1.
53 *Ibid.*
54 *Liverpool Echo* (4 July 1928), p. 12.
55 *The People* (8 July 1928), p. 7.
56 *Daily Express* (4 July 1928), p. 1.
57 *Daily Chronicle* (5 July 1928), p. 3; *Manchester Guardian* (5 July 1928), p. 11.
58 *Manchester Guardian* (2 July 1928), p. 10; *World's Pictorial News* (8 July 1928), p. 1; *Daily Mirror* (5 July 1928), p. 2.
59 *Daily Mirror* (5 July 1928), p. 2.
60 *Liverpool Echo* (5 July 1928), p. 12.
61 *Ibid.*
62 *Liverpool Echo* (6 July 1928), p. 9.
63 *Liverpool Echo* (2 July 1928), p. 7.
64 *Daily Express* (3 July 1928), p. 1.
65 The following summary is based upon *Daily Mail* (3 July 1928), p. 7, *Manchester Guardian* (3 July 1928), p. 7 and *News of the World* (8 July 1928), p. 9.
66 *Daily Mail* (3 July 1928), p. 7.
67 *Ibid.*
68 *Manchester Guardian* (3 July 1928), p. 7.
69 *Daily Mail* (3 July 1928), p. 7.
70 *Ibid.*
71 *Liverpool Echo* (2 July 1928), p. 12.
72 *Ibid.*
73 *Daily Express* (3 July 1928), p. 1; *World's Pictorial News* (8 July 1928), p. 2.
74 *Daily Mail* (3 July 1928), p. 7.
75 *Ibid.*
76 *Ibid.*, p. 11.
77 *Daily Mirror* (4 July 1928), p. 4.
78 *The People* (8 July 1928), p. 7.

79 *Daily Mail* (4 July 1928), p. 6.
80 *Liverpool Echo* (3 July 1928), p. 7.
81 *Thomson's Weekly News* (7 July 1928), p. 12.
82 *Liverpool Echo* (3 July 1928), p. 7.
83 *Daily Mail* (4 July 1928), p. 6.
84 *Liverpool Echo* (3 July 1928), p. 7.
85 *Ibid.*; *Daily Mail* (4 July 1928), p. 6.
86 *Thomson's Weekly News* (7 July 1928), p. 12; *Liverpool Echo* (3 July 1928), p. 7.
87 *Liverpool Echo* (3 July 1928), p. 7.
88 *Ibid.*, p. 12.
89 *Daily Mail* (5 July 1928), p. 7.
90 *Ibid.*
91 *Dean Forest Guardian* (6 July 1928), p. 5.
92 *The People* (8 July 1928), p. 7.
93 *Liverpool Echo* (5 July 1928), p. 12.
94 On the Judges' Rules, see J. C. Wood, '"The third degree": press reporting, crime fiction and police powers in 1920s Britain', *Twentieth Century British History* 21 (2010), 464–85.
95 *Dean Forest Guardian* (13 July 1928), p. 2.
96 *News of the World* (8 July 1928), p. 9.
97 *Liverpool Echo* (5 July 1928), p. 12.
98 Joseph Martin agreed that Beatrice 'seemed to be doing everything that a devoted wife could do to get him better', and he stated that Harry never complained about her: *Liverpool Echo* (4 July 1928), p. 12.
99 *Ibid.*
100 *Daily Mail* (5 July 1928), p. 7.
101 *Daily Mirror* (5 July 1928), p. 20; *News of the World* (8 July 1928), p. 9.
102 *Daily Mail* (5 July 1928), p. 7.
103 *Ibid.*
104 *News of the World* (8 July 1928), p. 9.
105 *Daily Mirror* (5 July 1928), p. 20. Harry was 'a very peculiar sides' man: *Liverpool Echo* (4 July 1928), p. 12.
106 *Daily Mail* (4 July 1928), p. 6.
107 *News of the World* (8 July 1928), p. 9.
108 *Dean Forest Guardian* (6 July 1928), p. 5.
109 *Dean Forest Guardian* (13 July 1928), p. 2.
110 *World's Pictorial News* (15 July 1928), p. 2.
111 *Dean Forest Guardian* (13 July 1928), p. 2.
112 *Ibid.*, p. 3.
113 *Ibid.*, p. 3; *Daily Mirror* (7 July 1928), p. 4.
114 *Dean Forest Guardian* (13 July 1928), p. 3.

115 *Liverpool Echo* (4 July 1928), p. 12.
116 *Dean Forest Guardian* (6 July 1928), p. 5.
117 *Liverpool Echo* (6 July 1928), p. 9.
118 *Dean Forest Guardian* (13 July 1928), p. 2.
119 *Daily Mirror* (7 July 1928), p. 4.
120 Hyde, *Birkett*, p. 253.
121 *Daily Mirror* (7 July 1928), p. 4.
122 *Daily Express* (7 July 1928), p. 1.
123 *Ibid.*
124 *Sunday Express* (8 July 1928), p. 1.
125 *Daily Express* (7 July 1928), p. 1. *The People* (8 July 1928), p. 1.
126 *The People* (8 July 1928), p. 2.
127 *Daily Express* (7 July 1928), p. 1.
128 *The People* (8 July 1928), p. 2; *Daily Express* (7 July 1928), p. 1.
129 *Daily Herald* (7 July 1928), p. 1.
130 *The People* (8 July 1928), p. 2.
131 *Daily Express* (7 July 1928), p. 1; *The People* (8 July 1928), p. 2.
132 O'Donnell: 'As I greeted her, she gave me a resounding kiss, and produced from her handbag a photograph of my two young sons, Roy and Peter, aged eleven and eight respectively. I had sent it to her saying that "the imps" would bring her luck. She waved the picture before my eyes, "I've kept the photograph of the imps," she cried, "and they brought me luck as you said they would."' O'Donnell, *Crimes That Made News*, p. 103.

6 'The matter is dead'

1 *Daily Express* (7 July 1928), p. 1.
2 *The People* (8 July 1928), p. 2.
3 *Daily Mirror* (7 July 1928), pp. 3, 30.
4 *The People* (8 July 1928), p. 2.
5 *Daily Mirror* (7 July 1928), pp. 3, 30.
6 *News of the World* (8 July 1928), p. 9.
7 *Daily News and Westminster Gazette* (9 July 1928), p. 9.
8 *The People* (8 July 1928), p. 2.
9 *Daily News and Westminster Gazette* (7 July 1928), p. 8.
10 Mrs Pace Papers, NCCL Galleries of Justice. All references to letters are from this collection and numbered according to a transcript provided to me by the Galleries of Justice. Letter #2, 6 July 1928, Forest of Dean Miners' Assoc.
11 Letter #89, 7 July 1928, Transport and General Workers' Union.
12 Letter #150, 9 July 1928, Wellington to W. Shepherd.
13 Letter #221, 12 July 1928, Wellington to A. E. Smith.
14 Letter #52, 7 July 1928, S. G. Harvey to Wellington.

15 *Reynolds's Illustrated News* (8 July 1928), p. 9.
16 Letter #213, 11 July 1928, Wellington to J. A. Johnstone.
17 Letter #152, 9 July 1928, Wellington to H. C. Philpotts.
18 *The People* (8 July 1928), p. 2.
19 *News of the World* (8 July 1928), p. 9. '[T]he windows of the house are broken, and morbid sightseers have removed bits of stone to take away as souvenirs': *Sunday Times* (8 July 1928), p. 18.
20 Elton was part owner in a silica quarry in Fetter Hill: TNA MEPO 3/1638/5a, Report by CI George Cornish, 17 March 1928, p. 22.
21 *News of the World* (8 July 1928), p. 9.
22 *The People* (8 July 1928), p. 2.
23 *Reynolds's Illustrated News* (8 July 1928), p. 1.
24 *Daily Herald* (9 July 1928), p. 1. See also, *Dean Forest Guardian* (13 July 1928), p. 3 and *Daily Mail* (9 July 1928), p. 11.
25 *Sunday Express* (15 July 1928), p. 1.
26 *Citizen* (Gloucester) (9 July 1928), p. 4.
27 TNA HO 144/10854/21.
28 TNA HO 144/10854/25. The document, unfortunately, is not in the file.
29 O'Donnell, *Crimes That Made News*, p. 105. O'Donnell's version records £3,050. A balance sheet for a trust fund supervised by Wellington's firm is among the Mrs Pace Papers, recording £3,025.
30 Values from www.measuringworth.com, accessed 21 February 2011. £3,025 in 1928 was equivalent, in 2009, to amounts between £135,000 and £918,000. Based upon changes in 'average earnings' the sum that Beatrice received would have been worth £578,000 in 2009. Prof. Samuel H. Williamson, co-creator of the website, confirmed that this is the most appropriate measurement in this context: personal correspondence, 23 March 2007.
31 Letter #151, 9 July 1928, Wellington to Harvey.
32 *Daily Herald* (9 July 1928), p. 1.
33 'I cannot draw on that money and spend it in any way I like, nor do I wish to do so. It is being kept for me so that it can produce a regular weekly income, a bigger income than I have ever had before, because it is about £3 a week instead of something between ten shillings and a pound – and sometimes nothing at all.' *Peg's Paper* 501 (25 December 1928), p. 13. A yearly income of about £150 was equivalent to the starting salary of a (female) elementary teacher in 1928 (the male rate being £168): P. Tinkler, *Constructing Girlhood: Popular Magazines for Girls Growing Up in England, 1920–1950* (London: Taylor & Francis, 1995), p. 33.
34 TNA HO 144/10854/40.
35 *Daily Telegraph* (17 August 1928) and *Daily News* (17 August, 1928), in TNA HO 144/10854/40.

36 *Daily Mail* (17 August 1928) and *Daily Chronicle* (17 August 1928), in TNA HO 144/10854/40.
37 *Daily Mail* (17 August 1928) and *Daily Chronicle* (17 August 1928), in TNA HO 144/10854/40.
38 *Evening News* (17 August 1928), in TNA HO 144/10854/40.
39 *News of the World* (19 August 1928), in TNA HO 144/10854/40.
40 *Daily Express* (1 September 1928) and *Daily Chronicle* (3 September 1928), in TNA HO 144/10854/40.
41 'I called on Sir Boyd Merriman to-day. He was playing a strenuous game of tennis in the grounds of his house. After the set I had a few minutes' conversation with him, but he declined to make any statement on the probable outcome of the new developments.' *Daily Express* (1 September 1928) and *Evening News* (1 September 1928), in TNA HO 144/10854/40.
42 *The People* (2 September 1928), p. 1.
43 *Sunday Express* (2 September 1928), pp. 1 and 13.
44 *The People* (2 September 1928), p. 1.
45 *Sunday News* (2 September 1928), in TNA HO 144/10854/40.
46 *Daily Mail* (3 September 1928), in TNA HO 144/10854/40.
47 *Daily Herald* (3 September 1928), *The Times* (4 September 1928) and *Daily Telegraph* (4 September 1928), in TNA HO 144/10854/40.
48 *News of the World* (19 August 1928), in TNA HO 144/10854/40.
49 *Reynolds's Illustrated News* (19 August 1928), p. 3.
50 *Daily Express* (3 September 1928) and *Daily Mail* (3 September 1928), in TNA HO 144/10854/40.
51 *Daily Herald* (3 September 1928), in TNA HO 144/10854/40.
52 *Daily Herald* (4 September 1928) and *Daily Mail* (3 September 1928); his wife claimed he had been 'out of work for weeks': *Daily Express* (3 September 1928). All in TNA HO 144/10854/40.
53 *Sunday Dispatch* (2 September 1928), in TNA HO 144/10854/40; corrected in *Daily Chronicle* (4 September 1928), in TNA HO 144/10854/40. See also: *World's Pictorial News* (9 September 1928), p. 1.
54 *Evening News* (3 September 1928), in TNA HO 144/10854/40.
55 *Dean Forest Guardian* (7 September 1928), p. 5.
56 *Dean Forest Guardian* (14 September 1928), p. 5.
57 *Daily Chronicle* (3 September 1928), in TNA HO 144/10854/40.
58 *World's Pictorial News* (30 September 1928), p. 10.
59 TNA MEPO 3/1638/47a, Cornish to Superintendent, 26 July 1928.
60 TNA MEPO 3/1638/52a, Mountjoy to Cornish, 10 August 1928.
61 TNA MEPO 3/1638/52b, Cornish to ACC [Assistant Chief Constable], 14 August 1928.
62 TNA MEPO 3/1638/75a, Letter from Mountjoy, 10 August 1928, among original documents received from *Evening Express* and *Daily Chronicle*; a copy is in TNA MEPO 3/1638/54e.

63 TNA MEPO 3/1638/62a, Cornish to ACC, 24 August 1928.

64 TNA MEPO 3/1638/54b, Gittoes-Davies to Cornish, 15 August 1928.

65 TNA HO 144/10854/41, Kendal to Blackwell, August 1928.

66 Gittoes-Davies had added a note: 'You will appreciate what this means to me as a journalist, and I naturally assume that you will be kind enough to give me the first hint of any action which is taken on the strength of the statement I have put before you.' TNA HO 144/10854/41, Gittoes-Davies to Cornish, 15 August 1928.

67 TNA MEPO 3/1638/57a, Cornish to ACC, 20 August 1928.

68 TNA MEPO 3/1638/75a, Mountjoy to Bliss, 16 August 1928. Emphasis in original.

69 TNA MEPO 3/1638/55c, [Kendal] to Stephenson (Assistant Director of the DPP), [16 August 1928].

70 A minute by Ernley Blackwell commented upon the 'remarkable development' on 23 August 1928: 'He seems to have been told that the law can't touch either Mrs. P or himself. There he is wrong. Assuming his story is proved to be true he c[oul]d be convicted of being accessory before the fact and principal in 2nd degree although Mrs. P has been acquitted.' TNA HO 144/10854/41.

71 TNA MEPO 3/1638/55a, [Kendal] to Stephenson, 16 August 1928.

72 TNA MEPO 3/1638/58a, Clarke to Horwood, 20 August 1928.

73 TNA MEPO 3/1638/57a, Cornish to Mountjoy, 20 August 1928.

74 TNA HO 144/10854/41. Minute sheet.

75 TNA MEPO 3/1638/58c, Mountjoy to Gittoes-Davies, n.d.

76 *Ibid.*

77 TNA MEPO 3/1638/61c, Mountjoy to Cornish, 23 August 1928.

78 TNA MEPO 3/1638/61a, Cornish to Mountjoy, 24 August 1928.

79 TNA HO 144/10854/42. Minute sheet.

80 TNA MEPO 3/1638, letter to 'Mrs. Sayes' from 'Sister Jennie', 4 September 1928.

81 *Daily Chronicle* (4 September 1928), in TNA HO 144/10854/40.

82 TNA HO 144/10854/42. Minute sheet, noted 7 September 1928.

83 *Ibid.*, noted 8 September 1928.

84 TNA MEPO 3/1638/63b, Report by CI George Cornish, 5 September 1928.

85 *Ibid.*

86 *World's Pictorial News* (9 September 1928), p. 1.

87 TNA MEPO 3/1638/5a, Report by CI George Cornish, 17 March 1928, p. 36.

88 TNA MEPO 3/1638/63a, Cornish to Superintendent, 7 September 1928.

89 TNA MEPO 3/1638. Minute sheet, noted 14 September 1928.

90 Both comments: TNA MEPO 3/1638. Minute sheet, noted 17 September 1928.

91 TNA MEPO 3/1638/71i, Mountjoy to Cornish, 12 September 1928.

92 TNA MEPO 3/1638/71h, Cornish to Mountjoy, 17 September 1928.

93 TNA MEPO 3/1638/71g, Mountjoy to Cornish, 'Tuesday' (probably 18 September 1928).

94 *Ibid.*

95 TNA MEPO 3/1638/71f, Cornish to Mountjoy, 19 September 1928.

96 TNA MEPO 3/1638/71e, Mountjoy to Cornish, 20 September 1928.

97 TNA MEPO 3/1638/71d, Cornish to Mountjoy, 28 September 1928.

98 TNA MEPO 3/1638/75a, 'Tues', Statement by Sayes. Copy in TNA MEPO 3/1638/54c.

99 TNA MEPO 3/1638/54g, Copies of statements by Sayes.

100 *Ibid.* Emphasis in original.

101 TNA MEPO 3/1638/52a, Mountjoy to Cornish, 10 August 1928.

102 TNA MEPO 3/1638/54g, Sayes statement, 15 August 1928.

103 TNA MEPO 3/1638/5a, Report by CI George Cornish, 17 March 1928, p. 31.

104 TNA ASSI 6/63/2, Inquest Depositions, p. 132.

105 TNA MEPO 3/1638/5a, Report by CI George Cornish, 17 March 1928, p. 28.

106 TNA MEPO 3/1638/54g, Sayes statement, 15 August 1928.

107 £34 16s in 1928 is equivalent to £6,650 in 2009 using the 'average earnings' calculator at www.measuringworth.com, accessed 21 February 2011.

108 TNA MEPO 3/1638/62b, Kendal to Stephenson, 25 August 1928.

109 TNA ASSI 6/63/2, Inquest Depositions, p. 72.

110 TNA MEPO 3/1638/71e, Mountjoy to Cornish, 20 September 1928.

111 *Dean Forest Guardian* (11 May 1928), p. 3.

112 TNA ASSI 6/63/2, Inquest Depositions, p. 133.

113 *The People* (3 June 1928), p. 2. 'Was Pace physically incapable of getting out of bed 48 hours before death? – I think that he was able to 48 hours before his death, but not 12 hours before. It was between those times that he became incapable of getting out of bed unaided – probably near the latter time as he became suddenly worse then.': *Daily Mail* (4 June 1928), p. 7. See also *Reynolds's Illustrated News* (10 June 1928), p. 17.

114 *Dean Forest Guardian* (6 July 1928), p. 5.

115 TNA MEPO 3/1638/5a, Report by CI George Cornish, 17 March 1928, p. 39.

116 Both notes in TNA MEPO 3/1638/75a. One reads: 'Dear Mrs. and Mr. Sayes, I am very sorry to have your letter with such sad news. I did not know until Mr. White came in after dinner. He then told

me that Fred had fetched them. Mr. Clarke will be down tomorrow and I shall be over one day and I will see that you get your fowls back as I shall not want them. I only want a few of the ones that is with you, that is if you let me have them. If not I shall not worry, but don't you worry over yours. All will be put right when I come over. I shall soon be going from Coleford so I hear. I shall be very glad to settle down if it's only in a pig cot. I ask you in my letter how things where [sic] with you. The house I mean but you never said so I take it you have finished with me – not my fault so please don't think so. I shall be over one day so I hope you will be in. I will say I still remain, your loving Friend [signed] Beattie'.

117 TNA MEPO 3/1638/62a, Cornish to ACC, 24 August 1928.
118 TNA MEPO 3/1638/57a, Cornish to ACC, 20 August 1928. TNA MEPO 3/1638/62a, Cornish to ACC, 24 August 1928.
119 TNA MEPO 3/1638/62b, Kendal to Stephenson, 25 August 1928.
120 TNA MEPO 3/1638/73b, Clarke to Commissioner, 9 October 1928.
121 *World's Pictorial News* (30 September 1928), p. 10.
122 TNA MEPO 3/1638/73a, Cornish to Superintendent, 1 November 1928.

7 '18 years of hell'

1 K. Martin, 'Public opinion: crime and the newspapers', *Political Quarterly* 2:3 (July 1931), 428. I thank Stefan Slater for this reference.
2 Bland, 'Edith Thompson'. Calvert's coverage was affected by the General Strike that year, but she did receive substantial sensationalist coverage: see, e.g., *World's Pictorial News* (27 June 1926), p. 3 and (4 July 1926), p. 1.
3 H. Smith, 'British feminism in the 1920s', in H. Smith (ed.), *British Feminism in the Twentieth Century* (Aldershot: Elgar, 1990), pp. 47–65; M. Pugh, *Women and the Women's Movement in Britain, 1914–59* (Basingstoke: Macmillan, 1992); S. Kent, *Making Peace: The Reconstruction of Gender in Inter-war Britain* (Princeton: Princeton University Press, 1993).
4 D. Beddoe, *Back to Home and Duty: Women between the Wars, 1918–1939* (London: Pandora, 1989), p. 8. Billie Melman highlights the press's 'welter of misogyny': *Women and the Popular Imagination in the Twenties: Flappers and Nymphs* (Basingstoke: Macmillan, 1988), pp. 17–18.
5 The phrase is from Light, *Forever England*, p. 9, which argues against this view.
6 S. Todd, *Young Women, Work and Family in England, 1918–1950*

(Oxford: Oxford University Press, 2005), p. 6. D. Gittins, *Fair Sex: Family Size and Structure 1900–39* (London: Hutchinson, 1982), p. 82. S. Alexander, 'Becoming a woman in London in the 1920s and 1930s', in D. Feldman and G. S. Jones (eds), *Metropolis – London: Histories and Representatives since 1800* (London: Routledge, 1989), pp. 245–71; A. Davies, *Leisure, Gender and Poverty: Manchester and Salford 1900–1939* (Buckingham: Open University Press, 1992); C. Langhamer, *Women's Leisure in England, 1920–1960* (Manchester: Manchester University Press, 2000); A. Bingham, '"An era of domesticity"? Histories of women and gender in interwar Britain', *Cultural and Social History* 1 (2004), 225–33; B. Søland, *Becoming Modern: Young Women and the Reconstruction of Womanhood in the 1920s* (Princeton: Princeton University Press, 2000).

7 J. Bourke, *Working Class Cultures in Britain, 1890–1960* (London: Routledge, 1994), pp. 131–3; J. Bourke, *Dismembering the Male: Men's Bodies, Britain and the Great War* (London: Reaktion Books, 1996); Bingham, *Gender, Modernity, and the Popular Press*, pp. 229–36.

8 M. Anderson, 'The social implications of demographic change', in F. M. L. Thompson (ed.), *The Cambridge Social History of Britain, 1750–1950*, vol. 2 (Cambridge: Cambridge University Press, 1990), pp. 38–42; K. Fisher, *Birth Control, Sex and Marriage in Britain, 1918–1960* (Oxford: Oxford University Press, 2006), pp. 1–25; C. Law, *Suffrage and Power: The Women's Movement, 1918–1928* (London: I. B. Taurus, 1997).

9 Pugh, *We Danced All Night*, pp. 126–7.

10 R. McKibbin, *Classes and Cultures: England, 1918–1951* (Oxford: Oxford University Press, 1998), p. 519.

11 Bingham, *Gender, Modernity and the Popular Press*, pp. 236–43; Light, *Forever England*, p. 18. Hammerton, *Cruelty and Companionship*, pp. 73–101.

12 Ballinger, 'Masculinity in the dock', 462–3, 467.

13 Houlbrook, 'Man with the powder puff', 160–2.

14 Light, *Forever England*, p. 5.

15 Advertisement, *Daily Mail* (13 July 1928), p. 19.

16 *Thomson's Weekly News* (14 July 1928), p. 12.

17 *Daily Mail* (7 July 1928), p. 10.

18 *World's Pictorial News* (22 January 1928), p. 3.

19 J. Tosh, *Manliness and Masculinities in Nineteenth-Century Britain* (Harlow: Pearson Education, 2005), pp. 15, 37, 92–3.

20 *Thomson's Weekly News* (21 January 1928), p. 1. Beatrice told police that Harry 'was not in any club' and did not belong to 'any society of any description': Pace Statement, 11 March 1928, p. 13.

21 *Thomson's Weekly News* (28 July 1928), p. 13.
22 *Dean Forest Guardian* (20 January 1928), p. 5. *World's Pictorial News* (22 January 1928), p. 3.
23 *Daily Mail* (30 January 1928), in TNA HO 144/10854/1a.
24 *World's Pictorial News* (5 February 1928), p. 1.
25 *The People* (25 March 1928), p. 2.
26 All from *The People* (3 June 1928), p. 1.
27 G. Behlmer, *Child Abuse and Moral Reform in England, 1870–1908* (Stanford: Stanford University Press, 1982); S. D'Cruze, *Crimes of Outrage: Sex, Violence and Victorian Working Women* (London: UCL Press, 1998); Wiener, *Men of Blood*, pp. 40–75; J. C. Wood, *Violence and Crime in Nineteenth-Century England: The Shadow of Our Refinement* (London: Routledge, 2004), pp. 36–40, 70–94; Emsley, *Hard Men*, pp. 57–75.
28 Wiener, *Men of Blood*, pp. 198–200, 234–5, 238–9.
29 Pace Statement, 15 February 1928, p. 1.
30 *Daily Mail* (27 April 1928), p. 13; *The People* (3 June 1928), p. 1.
31 *Sunday Express* (15 July 1928), p. 11.
32 *Thomson's Weekly News* (21 July 1928), p. 13.
33 *World's Pictorial News* (29 July 1928), p. 10.
34 *The People* (8 July 1928), p. 7. Also *Sunday Express* (8 July 1928), p. 11. Beatrice said one child had been born deaf and dumb 'because Harry had beaten me with an end of wire rope before the child was born': *Sunday Express* (22 July 1928), p. 11. Jean's illness was also blamed on his violence: *World's Pictorial News* (29 July 1928), p. 10.
35 *Sunday Express* (29 July 28), p. 14.
36 *Thomson's Weekly News* (21 July 1928), p. 13.
37 *Thomson's Weekly News* (28 July 1928), p. 13.
38 *Sunday Express* (29 July 1928), p. 14.
39 *World's Pictorial News* (29 July 1928), p. 10.
40 *World's Pictorial News* (5 August 1928), p. 8. Dorothy's first memory of her father was being taken to sleep 'on straw in the pigsty': 'It was in an atmosphere like that that I grew up.': *Thomson's Weekly News* (21 July 1928), p. 13. She recalled that 'twice at least' he 'turned us all out of the house in the dead of night': *Thomson's Weekly News* (28 July 1928), p. 13.
41 *Sunday Express* (12 August 1928), p. 12.
42 *Thomson's Weekly News* (28 July 1928), p. 13.
43 *World's Pictorial News* (29 July 1928), p. 10.
44 *World's Pictorial News* (5 August 1928), p. 8.
45 See, R. Dobash and R. Dobash, *Women, Violence and Social Change* (London: Routledge, 1992), pp. 6–8; D. Sonkin and D. Dutton, 'Treating assaultive men from an attachment perspective', in

R. Geffner, D. Dutton and D. Sonkin (eds), *Intimate Violence: Contemporary Treatment Innovations* (London: Routledge, 2003), p. 119; M. Wilson and M. Daly, 'The man who mistook his wife for a chattel', in J. Barkow, L. Cosmides and J. Tooby (eds), *The Adapted Mind: Evolutionary Psychology and the Generation of Culture* (Oxford: Oxford University Press, 1995), pp. 289–322.
46 *Sunday Express* (22 July 1928), p. 11.
47 Pace Statement, 11 March 1928, p. 4.
48 *World's Pictorial News* (5 August 1928), p. 8. *Sunday Express* (22 July 1928), p. 11.
49 *Sunday Express* (22 July 1928), p. 11. *World's Pictorial News* (5 August 1928), p. 8. From Beatrice's 15 February statement: 'he had connections with my sister "Florence" when she was about 12 or 13 years of age, in consequence of which my sister was sent away from home' (p. 1).
50 Pace Statement, 11 March 1928, p. 4.
51 *World's Pictorial News* (5 August 1928), p. 8.
52 *Sunday Express* (22 July 1928), p. 11.
53 *Peg's Paper* 489 (2 October 1928), p. 18.
54 U. Vogel, 'Whose property? The double standard of adultery in nineteenth-century law', in C. Smart (ed.), *Regulating Womanhood: Historical Essays on Marriage, Motherhood and Sexuality* (London: Taylor & Francis, 1992), pp. 147–65. M. Jackson, *The Real Facts of Life: Feminism and the Politics of Sexuality, c. 1850–1940* (London: Taylor & Francis, 1994), pp. 123–6.
55 *Dean Forest Guardian* (20 April 1928), p. 5.
56 Harry was 'unquestionably a remarkable man' who 'never seems to have associated with other men', and 'when passing people whom he knew quite well he would hang his head and take no notice'. TNA MEPO 3/1638/5a, Report by CI George Cornish, 17 March 1928, p. 47. Harry's cruelty was 'corroborated to some extent' by the summons taken out against him before the Coleford magistrates. Although 'a record of this cannot be found in the books', Cornish had 'no doubt that it is true'.
57 Ballinger, 'Guilt of the innocent'; Bland, 'Fahmy'.
58 Ballinger, 'Masculinity in the dock', 467, 477.
59 Emsley, *Hard Men*, p. 74. J. Gillis, *For Better, For Worse: British Marriages, 1600 to the Present* (Oxford: Oxford University Press, 1985), p. 251.
60 Light, *Forever England*, p. 218.
61 *Daily Chronicle* (4 July 1928), p. 3.
62 *News of the World* (8 July 1928), p. 9.
63 *World's Pictorial News* (5 February 1928), p. 1.
64 *Daily Mail* (16 January 1928), p. 9.

65 The *Daily Mail* quoted in *Dean Forest Guardian* (20 April 1928), p. 6.
66 *World's Pictorial News* (29 April 1928), p. 20.
67 Houlbrook, 'Man with the powder puff', 156–7. Bingham, *Gender, Modernity and the Popular Press*, p. 146. E. Miller, *Framed: The New Woman Criminal in British Culture at the Fin de Siècle* (Ann Arbor: University of Michigan Press, 2008), pp. 89–92.
68 *Thomson's Weekly News* (21 January 1928), p. 1 and (5 May 1928), p. 14.
69 *Thomson's Weekly News* (2 June 1928), p. 13. As noted, she was actually thirty-eight.
70 *Sunday News* (8 July 1928), p. 11.
71 *The People* (8 July 1928), p. 1.
72 E.g., 'She collapsed when leaving the inquest in a motor-car and was carried across the fields to the lonely farm where her husband died.' *Daily Mail* (17 January 1928), p. 7.
73 *Thomson's Weekly News* (21 January 1928), p. 1.
74 *Daily Mail* quoted in *Dean Forest Guardian* (20 April 1928), p. 6.
75 *Thomson's Weekly News* (5 May 1928), p. 14.
76 *Daily Mail* (13 April 1928), p. 11 and (11 May 1928), p. 14; *The People* (15 April 1928), p. 4 and (27 May 1928), p. 14.
77 *Thomson's Weekly News* (19 May 1928), p. 12.
78 *Thomson's Weekly News* (26 May 1928), p. 1. She had been 'sobbing hysterically': *Reynolds's Illustrated News* (27 May 1928), p. 11.
79 *The People* (3 June 1928), p. 2; *Sunday News* (10 June 1928), p. 2.
80 *Thomson's Weekly News* (14 July 1928), p. 12.
81 *Reynolds's Illustrated News* (10 June 1928), p. 1.
82 See, e.g., Frost, 'She is but a woman', 543–4; D'Cruze, *Crimes of Outrage*, pp. 184–5; Wiener, *Men of Blood*, 128–9.
83 *World's Pictorial News* (8 July 1928), p. 1.
84 *Sunday Dispatch* (8 July 1928), in TNA HO 144/10854/29b.
85 *The People* (15 July 1928), p. 7.
86 *World's Pictorial News* (12 August 1928), p. 14.
87 *Sunday Express* (8 July 1928), p. 11.
88 *The People* (8 July 1928), p. 1 and (15 July 1928), p. 7.
89 *World's Pictorial News* (29 July 1928), p. 10 and (22 July 1928), p. 2.
90 *Sunday Express* (5 August 1928), p. 15.
91 *Sunday Express* (15 July 1928), p. 11.
92 Fisher, *Birth Control, Sex and Marriage*, pp. 26–75.
93 *Thomson's Weekly News* (28 July 1928), p. 13.
94 *Sunday Express* (8 July 1928), p. 11.
95 *Sunday Express* (15 July 1928), p. 11.
96 *Thomson's Weekly News* (4 August 1928), p. 3.

97 Over nearly two decades, 'all this torture and misery was borne almost without a complaint': *World's Pictorial News* (29 July 1928), p. 14. 'And she did it all uncomplainingly. I have never heard a murmur of discontent from her lips.': *Thomson's Weekly News* (28 July 1928), p. 13.

98 *Sunday Express* (29 July 1928), p. 14.

99 P. Thane, 'Population and the family', in P. Addison and H. Jones (eds), *Companion to Contemporary Britain, 1939–2000* (Oxford: Blackwell, 2005), p. 53.

100 *World's Pictorial News* (5 August 1928), p. 8.

101 *Peg's Paper* 489 (2 October 1928), p. 15.

102 *Sunday News* (27 May 1928), p. 3. Beatrice once stated 'I never wanted to go to the pictures', highlighting her devotion to her domestic work. *Daily Mail* (16 April 1928), p. 13.

103 Dorothy was quoted discussing her deceased siblings: 'Altogether I have had nine brothers and sisters, but only five [sic] are alive. Kathleen, Daisy and Kingsley died as infants, while Cyril, who was deaf and dumb, and Hillier lived only to the age of two. Their deaths followed one another at intervals of about two years.' *Thomson's Weekly News* (2 June 1928), p. 16. Dorothy here was evidently counting herself among the survivors.

104 *Sunday Express* (8 July 1928), p. 1.

105 *Thomson's Weekly News* (28 July 1928), p. 13. E. Ross, '"Not the sort that would sit on the doorstep": respectability in pre-World War I London neighborhoods', *International Labor and Working Class History* 27 (1985), 39–59.

106 *Thomson's Weekly News* (28 July 1928), p. 13. Søland, *Becoming Modern*, p. 69.

107 *World's Pictorial News* (27 May 1928), p. 10.

108 *World's Pictorial News* (24 June 1928), p. 3.

109 *Sunday Express* (8 July 1928), p. 11. This article includes a photograph of Beatrice knitting.

110 *Thomson's Weekly News* (28 July 1928), p. 13.

111 Bingham, *Gender, Modernity and the Popular Press*, p. 10.

112 *Daily Mail* (13 July 1928), p. 19.

113 R. Phillips, *Untying the Knot: A Short History of Divorce* (Cambridge: Cambridge University Press, 1991), pp. 36–7.

114 L. Stone, *Road to Divorce: England 1530–1987* (Oxford: Oxford University Press, 1990), p. 2. S. Cretney, *Family Law in the Twentieth Century* (Oxford: Oxford University Press, 2003), pp. 161–3. Hammerton, *Cruelty and Companionship*, pp. 118–19.

115 A. Thorpe, *The Longman Companion to Britain in the Era of the Two World Wars 1914–45* (Harlow: Longman, 1994), p. 63; Pugh, *We Danced All Night*, p. 139.

116 Hammerton, *Cruelty and Companionship*, pp. 39, 48.

117 Cretney, *Family Law*, pp. 200–1.

118 Anderson, 'Demographic change', pp. 30–1; Cretney, *Family Law*, p. 201.

119 Gillis, *For Better, For Worse*, p. 236. L. Davidoff, 'The family in Britain', in Thompson (ed.), *The Cambridge Social History of Britain, 1750–1950*, pp. 112–13.

120 'I couldn't leave him, and at bottom I didn't want to.' *Sunday Express* (29 July 1928), p. 14.

121 L. Walker, *The Battered Woman* (New York: Harper & Row, 1979).

122 D. Dutton, *The Abusive Personality: Violence and Control in Intimate Relationships* (London: Guilford Press, 2006), pp. 74–5.

123 *Ibid.*, p. 78.

124 L. Walker, *The Battered Woman Syndrome* (New York: Springer, 1999), p. 126.

125 *Sunday Express* (5 August 1928), p. 15.

126 *Thomson's Weekly News* (21 January 1928), p. 1 and (21 July 1928), p. 13. E. Roberts, *A Woman's Place: An Oral History of Working-Class Women 1890–1940* (London: Blackwell, 1984), p. 193. See also McKibbin, *Classes and Cultures*, p. 199.

127 *World's Pictorial News* (5 August 1928), p. 8.

128 *Sunday Express* (22 July 1928), p. 11.

129 Pace Statement, 11 March 1928, p. 3. See also *World's Pictorial News* (22 July 1928), p. 2.

130 *Sunday Express* (22 July 1928), p. 11. 'My brother told me I was a fool, and he was angry with me, and would not speak to me again, but though that made me unhappy, I didn't care.'

131 Pace Statement, 11 March 1928, p. 3. See also *World's Pictorial News* (5 August 1928), p. 8.

132 *Thomson's Weekly News* (21 July 1928), p. 13.

133 *World's Pictorial News* (22 July 1928), p. 2.

134 Pace Statement, 11 March 1928, p. 4; *World's Pictorial News* (5 August 1928), p. 8.

135 Pace Statement, 15 February 1928, p. 1.

136 *Sunday Express* (29 July 1928), p. 14.

137 Emsley, *Hard Men*, p. 64. Walker, *Battered Woman Syndrome*, p. 192.

138 *World's Pictorial News* (5 August 1928), p. 8.

139 *Sunday Express* (22 July 1928), p. 11. The receipt seems to be in the Mrs Pace Papers, NCCL Galleries of Justice, among the letters sent to her: item #252.

140 *World's Pictorial News* (5 August 1928), p. 8.

141 *Sunday Express* (5 August 1928), p. 15.

142 *Sunday Express* (22 July 1928), p. 11.
143 *Sunday Express* (29 July 1928), p. 14: 'It is easy to talk of running away when there is nothing to run from, when you are free, and have no responsibilities and no ties. A woman thinks then that she is going to be the master – that the can do as she likes, and that if anything goes wrong she has only to walk out like a cook giving notice.'
144 *Peg's Paper* 489 (2 October 1928), pp. 17–18.
145 *Sunday Express* (5 August 1928), p. 15.
146 *Thomson's Weekly News* (21 July 1928), p. 13.
147 *World's Pictorial News* (29 July 1928), p. 10.
148 *Sunday Express* (5 August 1928), p. 15.
149 Ballinger, 'Masculinity in the dock', 468. Emphasis in original.
150 R. Connell, *Gender and Power: Society, the Person and Sexual Politics* (Cambridge: Polity, 1987), pp. 183–4; Bland, 'Edith Thompson', 647.
151 *Sunday Express* (5 August 1928), p. 15.
152 Light, *Forever England*, p. 10. Light refers to middle-class women and literature, but the point can be applied more widely.
153 It was the first time she had been 'to any place of amusement': *Sunday Express* (15 July 1928), p. 1.
154 'What "the pictures" looked like, what they could show me, I did not know at all. People who, I realise new, have been amusing you all for years – people like Charlie Chaplin and Mary Pickford and Tom Mix – were to me only far away names.' *Peg's Paper* 487 (18 September 1928), p. 18.
155 *Sunday Express* (22 July 1928), p. 11.
156 The weekly series began 18 September 1928 and concluded 1 January 1929.
157 Tinkler, *Constructing Girlhood*, p. 54.
158 McKibbin, *Classes and Cultures*, p. 493, quoting Pearl Jephcott, *Girls Growing Up* (London: Faber, 1942).
159 *Peg's Paper* 487 (18 September 1928), p. 18.
160 *Peg's Paper* 494 (6 November 1928), pp. 9–10.
161 *Daily Sketch* (4 July 1928), p. 4.
162 M. Roberts, 'Samson and Delilah revisited: the politics of fashion in 1920s France', in W. Chadwick and T. Latimer (eds), *The Modern Woman Revisited* (New Brunswick: Rutgers University Press, 2003), p. 65. C. Usborne, 'The new woman and generation conflict: perceptions of young women's sexual mores in the Weimar Republic', in M. Roseman (ed.), *Generations in Conflict: Youth Revolt and Generation Formation in Germany 1770–1968* (Cambridge: Cambridge University Press, 1995), p. 137.
163 *World's Pictorial News* (9 September 1928), p. 1.
164 *Peg's Paper*, 502 (1 January 1929), p. 15.

8 'Unimaginable agonies and degradations and cruelties'

1 *Sunday Express* (8 July 1928), p. 11.
2 *Manchester Guardian* (7 July 1928), p. 12.
3 *Sunday Express* (8 July 1928), p. 12.
4 *Sunday Express* (15 July 1928), p. 12.
5 *World's Pictorial News* (29 July 1928), p. 14.
6 *Daily Mail* quoted in *Dean Forest Guardian* (13 July 1928), p. 3.
7 *Daily News* (7 July 1928), p. 6.
8 *Morning Post* quoted in *Dean Forest Guardian* (13 July 1928), p. 3.
9 *Daily Mirror* (7 July 1928), p. 9.
10 Cheltenham *Echo* quoted in *Dean Forest Guardian* (13 July 1928), p. 3.
11 *Manchester Guardian* (7 July 1928), p. 12.
12 *Sunday Express* (8 July 1928), p. 1.
13 *Sunday Observer* quoted in *Dean Forest Guardian* (13 July 1928), p. 3.
14 *Daily Mail* quoted in *Dean Forest Guardian* (13 July 1928), p. 3.
15 HC Deb 24 July 1928 vol 220 c1095.
16 *Daily Telegraph* quoted in *Dean Forest Guardian* (13 July 1928), p. 3.
17 *Daily Mail* (7 July 1928), p. 10.
18 Cheltenham *Echo* quoted in *Dean Forest Guardian* (13 July 1928), p. 3. Grand juries were abolished in 1933.
19 *Reynolds's Illustrated News* (8 July 1928), p. 12.
20 *World's Pictorial News* (5 August 1928), p. 4; *Sunday Worker* (8 July 1928), p. 7.
21 *Daily Herald* (9 July 1928), p. 4.
22 *Daily News and Westminster Gazette* (7 July 1928), p. 6.
23 *The People* (18 March 1928), p. 10.
24 HC Deb 21 March 1928 vol 215 cc373–4.
25 *The People* (25 March 1928), p. 1.
26 *Ibid.*, p. 2. Italics in original.
27 HC Deb 26 March 1928 vol 215 cc816–17W.
28 HC Deb 23 May 1928 vol 217 cc1890–2.
29 *Daily Herald* (24 May 1928), pp. 1, 4. On accusations that, during the inquest, detectives had used excessive methods in questioning Dorothy, see also *Reynolds's Illustrated News* (6 May 1928), p. 13.
30 Wood, 'Third degree'.
31 *Dean Forest Guardian* (25 May 1928), p. 5.
32 H. Clayton, 'A bad case of police Savidgery: the interrogation of Irene Savidge at Scotland Yard', *Women's History Magazine* 61 (Autumn/Winter 2009), 30–8.

33 One of them, Chief Inspector Collins, had been mooted as a lead investigator in the Pace case before it was given to Cornish: TNA MEPO 3/1638/1a, Metropolitan Police telegram, 6 March 1928.

34 TNA HO 144/10854/31a, 'Memo in anticipation of questions being raised', Arthur Locke, 9 July 1928, p. 1. I thank Bob Morris for assistance in analysing this source.

35 TNA HO 144/10854/31, Memo (in Locke's handwriting), 9 July 1928. On the day Will Thorne raised the Pace case, the terms for the Savidge Inquiry were being debated: *Manchester Guardian* (24 May 1928), p. 11.

36 *Reynolds's Illustrated News* (20 May 1928), p. 1.

37 *Daily Herald* (9 July 1928), p. 4.

38 *Daily Chronicle* (9 July 1928), p. 3; *Daily News and Westminster Gazette* (9 July 1928), p. 10. Headlines in one issue of *Reynolds's Illustrated News* (20 May 1928) referred to 'Miss Savidge's ordeal' (p. 7) and 'Tragic widow's long ordeal' (p. 11).

39 Hyde, *Birkett*, pp. 229–45.

40 *Saturday Review* (18 August 1928), p. 22. See also *Saturday Review* (13 October 1928), p. 460.

41 TNA MEPO 3/1638, File 95/GEN/44/1a, Report by Cornish, 28 March 1928, pp. 2–3.

42 TNA HO 144/10854/5.

43 Cornish's comments are in TNA MEPO 3/1638, File 95/GEN/44/7e, Statement of George Cornish, 30 April 1928.

44 TNA MEPO 3/1638, File 95/GEN/44/7f, Statement of Clarence Campion, 30 April 1928, p. 3.

45 TNA MEPO 3/1638, File 95/GEN/44/7g, 7h and 7i, Statements of Alan Bent, Edith Mabel Lodge and James Henry Wood, all taken 17 April 1928.

46 *The People*, 8 July 1928, p. 7.

47 TNA MEPO 3/1638, File 95/GEN/44/7d, Muskett to Cornish, 8 June 1928.

48 TNA MEPO 3/1638, Report from Campion, 1 November 1928, pp. 1–2.

49 TNA MEPO 3/1638, File 95/GEN/44/7b, Muskett to Cornish, 29 October 1928; *The People* (28 October 1928), p. 5.

50 TNA MEPO 3/1638, File 95/GEN/44/. Minute sheet, noted 5 November 1928. In April, Horwood had minuted, 'I am all out for this and I hope it will be possible to obtain substantial damages for these two officers.'

51 *Dean Forest Guardian* (18 May 1928), p. 7.

52 TNA MEPO 3/1638/35c, Mountjoy to Cornish, 7 June 1928.

53 The first public disclosure of their contents appears to have been in Stratmann, *Gloucestershire Murders*.

54 *Dean Forest Guardian* (11 May 1928), p. 5.
55 Pace Statement, 14 March 1928, p. 15.
56 *Ibid.*, p. 16.
57 Cornish's comments that follow: TNA MEPO 3/1638/5a, Report by CI George Cornish, 17 March 1928, pp. 20–1, 42–3.
58 *Thomson's Weekly News* (4 August 1928), p. 3.
59 The single public reference I have found to Beatrice's admission was in the *Dean Forest Mercury*, a sister paper of the *Dean Forest Guardian*, reporting on Paling's opening speech at the magistrates' hearing: 'infidelity', he remarked, 'was not confined solely to him' (1 June 1928), p. 5. However, this appeared in neither the *Dean Forest Guardian* nor, as far as I can tell, any of the coverage in major papers.
60 *Daily News* quoted in *Dean Forest Guardian* (13 July 1928), p. 3.
61 *Citizen* (Gloucester) (9 July 1928), p. 4.
62 *The Times* (30 July 1928), p. 8. See also TNA HO 45/25860/1, Report of the Royal Commission on Police Powers and Procedures. On the issue of women and the police, see L. Jackson, *Women Police: Gender, Welfare and Surveillance in the Twentieth Century* (Manchester: Manchester University Press, 2006).
63 HC Deb 11 July 1928 vol 219 c2307.
64 *Daily Express* (14 July 1928), p. 5.
65 *World's Pictorial News* (28 October 1928), p. 11.
66 *Daily Herald* (16 January 1929), p. 2; *Manchester Guardian* (1 January 1929), p. 7; *Sunday Express* (6 January 1929), p. 13. Parliament, *Report of the Royal Commission on Police Powers and Procedure*, Cmd 3297 (London: HMSO, 1929).
67 S. Fowler Wright, *Police and Public* (London: Fowler Wright, 1928), p. 123.
68 See J. C. Wood, 'Press, politics and the "police and public" debates in late 1920s Britain', *Crime, Histoire & Sociétés / Crime, History and Societies* (forthcoming 2012).
69 *Daily Herald* (9 July 1928), p. 1.
70 *Thomson's Weekly News* (4 August 1928), p. 3.
71 *The People* (8 July 1928), p. 10.
72 *Reynolds's Illustrated News* (8 July 1928), p. 9.
73 *John Bull* (21 July 1928), p. 19.
74 *The Times* (29 May 1928), p. 13.
75 Earlier editorial quoted in *Daily Express* (7 July 1928), p. 8.
76 *Daily Mail* (9 July 1928), p. 12.
77 Quoted in *Dean Forest Guardian* (13 July 1928), p. 3.
78 *Daily Mail* (9 July 1928), p. 11.
79 *World's Pictorial News* (15 July 1928), p. 4.
80 *Citizen* (Gloucester) (9 July 1928), p. 4.
81 *Daily Mail* (23 May 1928), p. 7.

82 The jury were to state 'so far as such particularly have been proved to them, who the deceased was, and how, when, and where the deceased came by his death, and, *if he came by his death by murder or manslaughter, the person, if any, whom the jury find to have been guilty of such murder or manslaughter, or of being accessories before the fact to such murder.*' Thomas, *Jervis*, p. 59, citing Coroners Act 1887, S. 4 (3). Emphasis added.

83 *Justice of the Peace* (2 June 1928), in TNA HO 144/10854/18.

84 'Where the jury are not unanimous the coroner should collect the voices, and provided the minority consists of not more than two he takes the verdict according to the opinion of the majority ...': Thomas, *Jervis*, p. 62, citing Coroner's Act 1887, S. 4 (3). As amended in 1926, a majority of no fewer than five jurors (against two) was required: *ibid.*, p. 136.

85 TNA MEPO 3/1638/32a, Report from CI Cornish, 24 May 1928, p. 5.

86 *Sunday Times* (8 July 1928), p. 18.

87 *Daily Express* quoted in *Dean Forest Guardian* (13 July 1928), p. 3; *Daily Express* (7 July 1928), p. 8.

88 *Sunday Express* (8 July 1928), p. 12.

89 *Daily Mail* (7 July 1928), p. 11.

90 *Sunday Times* (8 July 1928), p. 18.

91 HC Deb 9 July 1928 vol 219 cc1856–61; *Daily Mail* (10 July 1928), p. 13.

92 *Manchester Guardian* (10 July 1928), p. 6.

93 *Sunday Times* (8 July 1928), p. 18.

94 *News of the World* (8 July 1928), p. 9.

95 'One immediately satisfactory result of the Pace case was the passing by Parliament of the Act which limits the duty of a coroner to finding the cause of death and debars him from specifically naming any individual as being responsible.' Hyde, *Birkett*, p. 254. Beatrice's ordeal 'aroused the sympathy of the public and, indirectly, caused a change to be made in the future conduct of coroners' inquests.' Bardens, *Birkett*, p. 106.

96 *Manchester Guardian* (9 July 1928), p. 9. As noted, juries were already free to reach such verdicts if they chose.

97 HC Deb 11 July 1928 vol 219 cc2244–7.

98 HC Deb 30 January 1929 vol 224 cc946–8.

99 HC Deb 29 October 1929 vol 231 c17.

100 *World's Pictorial News* (24 March 1929), p. 4.

101 The following quotes are taken from HC Deb 7 May 1930 vol 238 cc985–1078.

102 *The Times* (7 February 1936), p. 8.

103 *The Times* (20 June 1966), p. 9 and (11 November 1971), p. 1.

104 The law was changed by sections 56 and 65 of the Criminal Law Act of 1977. The current law is contained in section 11 (6) of the 1988 Coroners Act: 'At a coroner's inquest into the death of a person who came by his death by murder, manslaughter or infanticide, the purpose of the proceedings shall not include the finding of any person guilty of the murder, manslaughter or infanticide; and accordingly a coroner's inquisition shall in no case charge a person with any of those offences.' This law is further reinforced by Rule 42 of the Coroners Rules (1984) which states: 'No verdict shall be framed in such a way as to appear to determine any question of – (a) criminal liability on the part of a named person, or (b) civil liability.' I am grateful to Nicholas Rheinberg for helpfully explaining post-1928 inquest developments.

105 *World's Pictorial News* (3 June 1928), p. 9.

106 *News of the World* (8 July 1928), p. 9. The *Sunday Chronicle* reported that 'It cost £2,000 to prosecute Mrs. Pace and £1,700 to defend her. About £1,400 has been subscribed to the defence fund.' (8 July 1928), p. 1.

107 *Citizen* (Gloucester) (9 July 1928), p. 4.

108 *Daily Herald* (7 July 1928), p. 1.

109 *Reynolds's Illustrated News* (8 July 1928), p. 5.

110 *John Bull* (14 July 1928), p. 5.

111 *Time and Tide* (13 July 1928), p. 674.

112 *Empire News* (15 July 1928), p. 8.

113 *The People* (29 July 1928), p. 2.

114 HC Deb 24 July 1928 vol 220 cc1094–6.

115 *Manchester Guardian* (31 July 1928), p. 10.

116 *Sunday News* (29 July 1928), p. 12.

117 *World's Pictorial News* (5 August 1928), p. 4.

118 *Dean Forest Guardian* (13 July 1928), p. 5.

119 *The People* (8 July 1928), p. 10.

120 *Sunday Express* (15 July 1928), p. 12.

121 *Sunday Express* (5 August 1928), p. 10.

9 'Those who have had trouble can sympathise with you'

1 Comments from T. P. O'Connor and A. Chesterton: *Daily News and Westminster Gazette* (7 July 1928), p. 7.

2 Comments from G. K. Chesterton and G. B. Shaw: *Sunday Chronicle* (8 July 1928), p. 1.

3 *News of the World* (8 July 1928), p. 9.

4 *World's Pictorial News* (13 May 1928), p. 10. Mrs Pace Papers, NCCL Galleries of Justice. I thank the Galleries of Justice for providing a transcript of the Pace correspondence. All references

are cited by their number on the transcript. I have aimed to let the writers speak in their own voices and idioms but, in the interest of readability, have changed or added punctuation and corrected some spelling. Originally underlined text has been italicised.

5 #254, [postmarked Brixton 6 July 1928], 'R. W.'
6 #129, 7 July 1928, from H. Buckby, Burton Latimer.
7 #3, n.d., anonymous.
8 *Sunday Express* (8 July 1928), p. 12.
9 E.g., #42, 6 July 1928, Nellie Heinsen, London.
10 #8, 6 July 1928, D. Jackman, Teignmouth; #262, 6 July 1928, 'A native of Monmouth', London; #107, [6 July 1928], Mrs E. Oke, Holsworthy; #141, 8 July 1928, Olive Gundry, Bridport.
11 #251, 6 July 1928, Walter Floyd, Cinderford.
12 #10, n.d., Mrs Edwards, Gloucester.
13 #247, 28 July 1928, Maisie Cooper, Ontario, Canada; #229, 23 July 1928, N. B., Malta.
14 #250, 20 July 1928, Mrs D. Bain, Alberta, Canada.
15 #228, 10 July 1928, Mrs M. Marques, Johannesburg, South Africa.
16 #101, n.d., anonymous, Llandudno; #12, 6 July 1928, Katherine Cole, Walthamstow; #259, [6 July 1928], anonymous, [Gloucester].
17 *Daily Mail* (3 July 1928), p. 11.
18 #78, 7 July 1928, Emily Dunstone, London.
19 #115, n.d., Wisher M. Cottrell, London.
20 #77, 7 July 1928, Annie Hudson, St-Leonards-on-Sea.
21 #81, 7 July 1928, Nancy D. Griffiths, London.
22 #261, 7 July 1928, Berkshire Mothers' Union. A Norwich writer was also an 'M. U.' member: #112, 7 July 1928, anonymous.
23 #171, n.d., Mrs J. J. Brooks, Lower Cillington.
24 #48, 6 July 1928, Mrs E. Ransome, Weymouth; #109, 7 July 1928, Mrs Skinner, Epsom.
25 #181, 7 July 1928, Dora Annie Farrow, Aldeby.
26 #196, 8 July 1928, 'Mrs Anonymous'; #188, 9 July 1928, Mrs E. Gertrude Williams, Whitchurch.
27 #172, 8 July 1928, Mrs C. Whitford, St Truro.
28 #158, 10 July 1928, Cecily Coe, Foston.
29 #121, 9 July 1928, S. Howells, Llanelly.
30 #113, 7 July 1928, Edith M. Stile, Pinhoe.
31 #136, 8 July 1928, J. W. Kelly, Gt Leighs; #201, 9 July 1928, Robert P. Powell, Narbeth.
32 #194, 8 July 1928, Mrs C. Smith, Ross-on-Wye.
33 #197, 10 July 1928, Mary A. Chapple, Reading.
34 #161, 8 July 1928, Mrs S. Baker, Bowden.
35 #176, 6 July 1928, Mrs J. S. MacDonald, Cardiff.
36 #41, 6 July 1928, Alice B. Price, Pontypore.

37 #45, 6 July 1928, from Florence Wakefield, Farnham.

38 #59, n.d. [probably 9 July 1928], Mrs A. Coles, Pontypool.

39 #22, 6 July 1928, 'an Irish Catholic', London.

40 #3, n.d., anonymous, emphasis in original. See also #9, 6 July 1928, Mrs J. E. Bynon, Bristol; #95, n.d., Mrs Griggs, Woodside; #176, 6 July 1928, Mrs J. S. MacDonald, Cardiff.

41 #38, 6 July 1928, A. E. Woodcock, Rusholme; #156, n.d., Mrs Williams, Gellyyear. See also #194, 8 July 1928, Mrs C. Smith, Ross-on-Wye.

42 #116, n.d., Mrs Mary Gibbon, St Helens.

43 #46, 6 July 1928, Mrs Wootton, near Merthyr, S. Wales; #34, 7 July 1928, Mrs W. Williams, Aberdare.

44 #41, 6 July 1928, Alice B. Price, Pontypore.

45 #181, 7 July 1928, Dora Annie Farrow, Aldeby.

46 #1, 6 July 1928, Hilda M. Vickery, London.

47 #222, 5 July 1928, E. Lawrence, Bexleyheath.

48 #250, 20 July 1928, Mrs D. Bain, Alberta, Canada; #225, n.d., Mrs Olver and Mrs Tucker, Chittlehampton.

49 #210, 9 July 1928, Janet Meek, Leeds.

50 *World's Pictorial News* (29 July 1928), p. 14.

51 #247, 28 July 1928, Maisie Cooper, Southampton, Canada.

52 #246, 30 July 1928, Jessie Sturgeon, near Bury St Edmunds.

53 #248, 26 July 1928, Mrs Cannon, West Derby.

54 #209, 7 July 1928, Mrs Evie Bull, Blandford.

55 #36, 6 July 1928, Mrs S. Bassett, Littleborough; #176, 6 July 1928, Mrs J. S. MacDonald, Cardiff; #180, n.d., Emily Winch, Tredegar.

56 #224, n.d., 'Violet', Southend-on-Sea.

57 #233, n.d. (Mrs) F. Steer, Watford.

58 *Sunday Express* (29 July 1928), p. 14.

59 #203, 8 July 1928, Florrie Goodridge, Southampton.

60 #139, 8 July 1928, Mrs M. Miller, Leith.

61 #67, n.d., Mrs Allen Price, Billesdon.

62 #4, 6 July 1928, Rev. Francis George Price, Gloucester.

63 #74, 7 July 1928, Guardsman W. Short, Brookwood.

64 #207, 10 July 1928, anonymous, Bridlington.

65 #215, 8 July 1928, J. Nicholson, London.

66 #198, 11 July 1928, Charles Williams-Curgenven, Penzance.

67 #132, 8 July 1928, C. A. Needham, Manchester.

68 #159, 8 July 1928, T. Griffiths, Llanelly.

69 #175, 8 July 1928, A. Wilkinson, Bordon.

70 #241, 15 July 1928, Arthur Williams, Desborough, near Kettering.

71 #165, 7 July 1928, Hector Dinnie, London.

72 #53, 7 July 1928, Hector Dinnie, London. It is unclear whether this is the same 'well-known West-End producer' who was quoted as

saying 'if things go as planned' he 'will produce the drama [based on the life and trial of Beatrice Pace] round about Christmas': *Sunday Chronicle* (8 July 1928), p. 1. I have found no record of a contemporary play based on the case.

73 #166, 9 July 1928, Charles McCoy, Cleethorpes.
74 *News of the World* (8 July 1928), p. 9.
75 *Dean Forest Guardian* (13 July 1928), p. 5. Brownrigg wrote from Ellwood, where some of the Pace family lived.
76 #256, [postmarked 6 July 1928], E. S. Cooke, Hornsey; #208, 11 July 1928, M. Jenkins, Milford Haven.
77 #258, [postmarked 6 July 1928], Mrs R. M. Renton, London.
78 #231, [postmarked 9 July 1928], Florence Gibbons, Warwick.
79 #116, n.d., Mrs Mary Gibbon, St Helens.
80 #174, 6 July 1928, Mrs H. Colton, Blyth.
81 #111, 7 July 1928, T. A. Carpenter, Croydon. See also #204, n.d., 'A. M.'
82 #78, 7 July 1928, Emily Dunstone, London.
83 #233, 11 July 1928, Eleanor Jones, Barton-on-Irwell.
84 #205, 7 July 1928, H. C. Gordon, Twickenham.
85 #63, 7 July 1928, S. W. Darby, Old Hill.
86 A rare exception to Beatrice's general lack of religious phrasing was the claim by Nesta Ryall that Beatrice 'often' said: 'They can never find an innocent woman guilty: God would not allow it.' *Sunday News* (8 July 1928), p. 11.
87 Of 140 congratulatory letters from women, 35 had a strongly religious character as did 5 out of 24 from men; this could be said of 11 of 44 letters whose writers' sexes cannot be definitively identified and 1 of the 4 'group' letters. None of the five couples' and two children's letters could be categorised in this way, and the same could be said of the one 'family' letter.
88 #68, 7 July 1928, James Kearney, PP, Garvagh, Co. Derry, N. Ireland.
89 #240, July 1928, Charles John Martin, Chesterfield.
90 #111, 7 July 1928, T. A. Carpenter, Croydon. Emphasis in original.
91 #75, 8 July 1928, M. F. Bovenizer, Liverpool.
92 Pugh, *We Danced All Night*, pp. 9–11.
93 #220, 11 July 1928, M. F. Bovenizer, Liverpool.
94 The 'spirit message': 'I want to save my missis. Set this down for me. My name's Pace – 'Arry Pace, you know. It's my woman I want to save. They've got 'er up for murder. Don't let 'er 'ang! I done fer myself. 'Urry! 'Urry, or you'll be too late. I was crazed with pain. I didn't want to live. I thought death would end it all.' *Sunday News* (15 July 1928), p. 3. The full article, from the *Christian Spiritualist* and written by R. H. Greaves, was reprinted in *Empire News* (15 July 1928), p. 11.

95 #244, 30 July 1928, Gertrude Smart, Gillingham.

96 #208, 11 July 1928, M. Jenkins, Milford Haven.

97 #236, 14 July 1928, Ernest Jeffrey, West Wimbledon, London. I have found no such statement in the *Express*. Emphasis in original.

98 #9, 6 July 1928, Mrs J. E. Bynon, Bristol.

99 #227, n.d., Mabel Jackson, Louth. Emphasis in original.

100 #119, n.d., Maud Purslow, Manchester, and, more briefly, #23, 6 July 1928, Annie Jones, London; #118, n.d., Mrs H. Dawe, Plymouth; #187, 9 July 1928, Helena Bone, St Mawgan.

101 #243, 31 July 1928, Jane Goldsmith.

102 #226, 15 July 1928, anonymous.

103 #237, n.d., anonymous.

104 #234, n.d., anonymous.

105 #218, n.d., anonymous. Emphasis in original.

106 #19, 6 July 1928, Mrs Smythe, London. Emphasis in original.

107 #85, n.d., E. Cobbett, Burnley.

108 #65, 7 July 1928, Mrs Blanche Cuitt, Ryde.

109 #15, 6 July 1928, Mrs Lee, Bexleyheath; #178, n.d., Florence Smith, Birmingham. See also #141, 8 July 1928, Mrs Olive Gundry, Bridport.

110 #22, 6 July 1928, anonymous, London.

111 #51, n.d., 'D.S.' (an 'unknown devoted friend'), Liverpool. Emphasis in original.

112 #80, 7 July 1928, Mrs J. Burman, Birmingham; #186, 9 July 1928, 'P. A. G.', London.

113 #28, 6 July 1928, anonymous, Slough; #94, n.d., Willis, Hole and Vinnicombe, Bradninch.

114 #163, n.d., Howell, Webber and Clalwathy, Taunton; #184, n.d., anonymous, Taunton.

115 #191, 8 July 1928, Mrs Emma Derry, Cannock Wood; #113, 7 July 1928, Edith M. Stile, Pinhoe.

116 #86, 7 July 1928, Mrs Trobe, London; #127, n.d., anonymous, 'Greater Brighton Hove'.

117 #161, 8 July 1928, Mrs S. Baker, Bowden; #26, 6 July 1928, Bessie Yeo, Bristol.

118 #215, 8 July 1928, J. Nicholson, London.

119 #34, 7 July 1928, Mrs W. Williams, Aberdare.

120 #48, 6 July 1928, Mrs E. Ransome, Weymouth.

121 #205, 7 July 1928, H. C. Gordon, Twickenham.

122 'Would you be so kind as to sign your name on the little piece of Paper enclosed, for me to put into my Autograph Book': #230, n.d., from Gordon Stenning, Ditchling.

Conclusion

1 G. Orwell, 'Decline of the English murder', in S. Orwell and I. Angus (eds), *The Collected Essays, Journalism and Letters of George Orwell*, vol. 4 (Boston: Nonpareil, 2005), p. 98. Originally published in *Tribune* (15 February 1946).

2 Orwell, 'Decline of the English murder', pp. 99–100.

3 M. Wiener, 'Convicted murderers and the Victorian press: condemnation vs. sympathy', *Crimes and Misdemeanours* 1:2 (2007), 123; S. Walklate, *Imagining the Victim of Crime* (Maidenhead: Open University Press, 2007), p. 28.

4 Frost, 'She is but a woman'.

5 *Ibid.*, 558.

6 E.g.: 'Throughout this book I have argued that the Crown will employ what is "known" about female defendants as *women* for the purpose of establishing a dominant truth which is likely to secure a conviction.' Ballinger, *Dead Woman Walking*, p. 244, emphasis in original. 'Ultimately, however, the period between 1920–1970 ... lacked a strong feminist movement such as that emerging after 1970 ... to ensure cases similar to Ethel Major's were understood in the general context of male violence against women.' *Ibid.*, p. 258. Furthermore, 'discourses of the "battered wife" did not exist'. *Ibid.*, p. 270.

7 *Thomson's Weekly News* (21 January 1928), p. 1.

8 Ballinger, 'Masculinity in the dock' and 'Guilt of the innocent'; L. Seal, 'Issues of gender and class in the Mirror newspapers' campaign for the release of Edith Chubb', *Crime, Media, Culture* 5 (2009), 57–78.

9 A. Lloyd, *Doubly Deviant, Doubly Damned* (London: Penguin, 1995); L. Zedner, *Women, Crime and Custody in Victorian England* (Oxford: Clarendon, 1991); Ballinger, *Dead Woman Walking*. For evidence that questions this view, see B. Godfrey, S. Farrall and S. Karstedt, 'Explaining gendered sentencing patterns for violent men and women in the late-Victorian and Edwardian period', *British Journal of Criminology* 45 (2005), 696–720 and P. King, 'Gender, crime and justice in late eighteenth- and early nineteenth-century England', in M. Arnot and C. Usborne (eds), *Gender and Crime in Modern Europe* (London: UCL Press, 1999), pp. 44–74.

10 See Ballinger, *Dead Woman Walking*, pp. 3–6, 50–3 and *passim*. See also Bland, 'Edith Thompson'; Ramey, 'Bloody blonde'; L. Seal, 'Discourses of single women accused of murder: mid twentieth-century constructions of "lesbians" and "spinsters"', *Women's Studies International Forum* 32 (2009), 209–18; L. Seal, *Women,*

Murder and Femininity: Gender Representations of Women Who Kill (Basingstoke: Palgrave Macmillan, 2010).

11 Bland, 'Edith Thompson', deals very effectively with these complexities.

12 Ballinger, *Dead Woman Walking*, p. 131 comments on the cases of Calvert and Margaret Allen: 'As the end of their lives drew near their cases attracted barely a comment in the media or in the Home Office.' However, see, e.g., *World's Pictorial News* (6 June 1926), p. 9; (13 June 1926), p. 14; (20 June 1926), p. 3; (27 June 1926), p. 3; (4 July 1926), pp. 1–2; (14 July 1926), p. 14. *Thomson's Weekly News* (12 June 1926), p. 1; (19 June 1926), p. 11; (26 June 1926), p. 10.

13 William Kennedy and Frederick Browne: *World's Pictorial News* (27 May 1928), pp. 1–2 and 20; (3 June 1928), pp. 1–2; (10 June 1928), p. 10; (17 June 1928), p. 11. *Thomson's Weekly News* (12 May 1928), p. 12; (19 May 1928), pp. 1, 13; (26 May 1928), p. 12; (2 June 1928), pp. 1, 12. Frederick Browne's lengthy series 'My life as a bandit' began in *Reynolds's Illustrated News* (29 April 1928), p. 5.

14 A 2010 BBC radio drama based on the case, *Norman Birkett and the case of the Coleford poisoner*, suggests the Home Secretary – with an eye toward newly enfranchised women voters – put pressure on the judge to stop the case. My research suggests this is (a quite effective example of) dramatic licence.

15 *Daily Mail* (13 July 1928), p. 11; *World's Pictorial News* (15 July 1928), p. 2.

16 Thompson, *Poisons and Poisoners*, p. 350. For case-related discussion of the 'arsenic eating' topic, see *Sunday News* (20 May 1928), p. 5; *Daily Mail* (20 July 1928) p. 9; *Empire News* (29 July 1928), p. 4.

17 Bardens, *Birkett*, p. 118.

18 Hyde, *Birkett*, p. 254. The same anecdote is used in Willcox, *Detective-Physician*, p. 216. The case in question was that of Adelaide Bartlett and the speaker was Sir James Paget, Sergeant-Surgeon to Queen Victoria. The cases were 'similar' only in that Bartlett was acquitted of the poisoning (with chloroform) after a coroner's jury had recorded a verdict of murder against her.

19 Willcox, *Detective-Physician*, p. 216.

20 Church, *Accidents of Murder*, p. 139; Stratmann, *Gloucestershire Murders*, p. 119.

21 *The People* (15 July 1928), p. 7.

Postscript

1 L. Doan and J. Prosser (eds), *Palatable Poison: Critical Perspectives on the Well of Loneliness* (New York: Columbia University Press, 2001).
2 Doan and Prosser (eds), *Palatable Poison*, p. 38.
3 Hyde, *Birkett*, pp. 254–60.
4 Willcox, *Detective-Physician*, p. 204.
5 Hyde, *Birkett*, pp. 287–9.
6 *Ibid.*, pp. 310–22.
7 *Ibid.*, pp. 380–3.
8 [Patrick Arthur] Devlin, 'Birkett (William) Norman, first Baron Birkett (1883–1962)', rev. *Oxford Dictionary of National Biography*, Oxford University Press, 2004, www.oxforddnb.com/view/article/31899, accessed 6 February 2011.
9 K. Morgan, 'Purcell, Albert Arthur (1872–1935)', *Oxford Dictionary of National Biography*, Oxford University Press, 2004, www.oxforddnb.com/view/article/35632, accessed 30 January 2011.
10 I thank John Loosley of the Gloucestershire Local History Committee for this information.
11 I thank the firm of Langley Wellington Solicitors for this information.
12 See the Jack the Ripper Forum: www.jtrforums.com/forumdisplay.php?f=328, accessed 2 February 2011.
13 I thank Stewart Evans and Richard Whittington-Egan for their helpful information about O'Donnell's life and Howard Brown at the Jack the Ripper Forum for putting me in touch with them.
14 MEPO 3/1638. Minute sheet, noted 10 August 1928. It is interesting to note that on the police minute sheet – which recorded all the official actions taken in the case – the word 'alleged' was added to the typed note by hand.
15 *The Times* (2 February 1929), p. 14.
16 *The Times* (1 September 1933), p. 14.
17 *Daily Mirror* (1 September 1933), p. 5.
18 Cornish, *Cornish of the 'Yard'*, pp. 171–2.
19 *Six Against the Yard* (London: Selwyn & Blount, [1936]), p. 277. The six authors were Margery Allingham, Anthony Berkeley, Freeman Wills Crofts, Father Ronald Knox, Dorothy L. Sayers and Russell Thorndike.
20 *The Times* (7 February 1959), p. 8. O'Donnell, *Crimes That Made News*, p. 6.
21 MEPO 3/1638. Minute sheet, noted 10 August 1928.
22 *The Times* (6 February 1940), p. 10; *Daily Mirror* (23 May 1940), p. 3; 'Royal Military Police Special Investigations Branch (United

Kingdom)', www.army.mod.uk/documents/general/proRmpUnit_sib (uk).pdf, accessed 7 August 2011.

23 I. Walker Hall, 'Action of sheep dip on tissues', *Transactions of the Medico-Legal Society* 23 (1928–29), 163–9.

24 Willcox, *Detective-Physician*, pp. 208–17.

25 W. J. Bishop, 'Willcox, Sir William Henry (1870–1941)', rev. K. D. Watson, *Oxford Dictionary of National Biography*, Oxford University Press, 2004, www.oxforddnb.com/view/article/36910, accessed 24 February 2011.

26 *Daily Mail* (7 January 1929) and *Evening News* (7 January 1929), in HO 144/10854/40.

27 *Sunday Express* (6 January 1929), p. 1.

28 *World's Pictorial News* (13 January 1928), p. 3.

29 *Thomson's Weekly News* (19 January 1929), p. 17.

30 *Sunday News* (27 January 1929), in HO 144/10854/40.

31 *News of the World* (30 June 1929), in HO 144/10854/44.

32 *Ibid.*

33 *Daily Mail* (29 June 1929); *Daily Telegraph* (29 June 1929); *Daily Express* (29 June 1929), all in HO 144/10854/44.

34 *Sunday News* (28 July 1929), in HO 144/10854/44.

35 Personal communications from Keith Smart and Barry Martin.

36 Death certificate, Isobel Jean Martin. I thank Keith Smart and the Martin family for this information.

37 Personal communication from Barry Martin and Tony Martin.

38 Death certificate, Beatrice Annie Martin.

Bibliography

Newspapers and periodicals

Citizen (Gloucester)
Daily Chronicle
Daily Express
Daily Herald
Daily Mail
Daily Mirror
Daily News and Westminster Gazette
Daily Sketch
Dean Forest Guardian
Dean Forest Mercury
Economist
Empire News
John Bull
Liverpool Echo
Manchester Guardian
News of the World
Peg's Paper
The People
Reynolds's Illustrated News
Saturday Review
Sunday Express
Sunday News
Sunday Worker
Time and Tide
The Times
Thomson's Weekly News
World's Pictorial News

Archival sources

Mrs Pace Papers, NCCL Galleries of Justice, Nottingham, UK.
The National Archives, Kew, London:
ASSI 6/63/2
HO 144/10854
MEPO 3/1638

Other primary sources

Allingham, Margery, Anthony Berkeley, Freeman Wills Crofts et al., *Six Against the Yard*. London: Selwyn & Blount, [1936].

Christie, A. *The Mysterious Affair at Styles*. London: HarperCollins, 1994.

Cornish, G. W. *Cornish of the 'Yard': His Reminiscences and Cases*. London: John Lane, 1935.

Martin, K. 'Public opinion: crime and the newspapers.' *Political Quarterly* 2:3 (July 1931): 428–32.

O'Donnell, B. *Crimes That Made News*. London: Burke, 1954.

Orwell, G. 'Decline of the English murder.' In *The Collected Essays, Journalism and Letters of George Orwell*, vol. 4, ed. S. Orwell and I. Angus, pp. 98–101. Boston: Nonpareil, 2005.

Parliament. *Report of the Royal Commission on Police Powers and Procedure*. Cmd 3297. London: HMSO, 1929.

Thomas, F. D. *Sir John Jervis on the Office and Duties of Coroners*, 7th edn. London: Sweet and Maxwell, 1927.

Walker Hall, I. 'Action of sheep dip on tissues.' *Transactions of the Medico-Legal Society* 23 (1928–29): 163–9.

Wright, S. Fowler. *Police and Public*. London: Fowler Wright, 1928.

Secondary sources

Alexander, S. 'Becoming a woman in London in the 1920s and 1930s.' In *Metropolis – London: Histories and Representatives since 1800*, ed. D. Feldman and G. S. Jones, pp. 245–71. London: Routledge, 1989.

Altick, R. *Victorian Studies in Scarlet*. New York: W.W. Norton, 1970.

Anderson, M. 'The social implications of demographic change.' In *The Cambridge Social History of Britain, 1750–1950*, vol. 2, ed. F. M. L. Thompson, pp. 1–70. Cambridge: Cambridge University Press, 1990.

Ballinger, A. 'The guilt of the innocent and the innocence of the guilty: the cases of Marie Fahmy and Ruth Ellis.' In *No Angels*, ed. A. Myers and S. Wight, pp. 1–28. London: Pandora, 1996.

Ballinger, A. *Dead Woman Walking: Executed Women in England and Wales, 1900–1955*. Aldershot: Ashgate, 2000.

Ballinger, A. '"Reasonable" women who kill: re-interpreting and re-defining women's responses to domestic violence in England and Wales, 1900–1965.' *Outlines* 2 (2005): 65–82.

Ballinger, A. 'Masculinity in the dock: legal responses to male violence and female retaliation in England and Wales, 1900–1965.' *Social and Legal Studies* 16 (2007): 459–81.

Bardens, D. *Lord Justice Birkett*. London: Robert Hale, 1962.

Beddoe, D. *Back to Home and Duty: Women between the Wars, 1918–1939*. London: Pandora, 1989.

Behlmer, G. *Child Abuse and Moral Reform in England, 1870–1908*. Stanford: Stanford University Press, 1982.

Bingham, A. *Gender, Modernity and the Popular Press in Inter-War Britain*. Oxford: Clarendon Press, 2004.

Bingham, A. '"An era of domesticity"? Histories of women and gender in interwar Britain.' *Cultural and Social History* 1 (2004): 225–33.

Bland, L. 'The trial of Madame Fahmy: orientalism, violence, sexual perversity and the fear of miscegenation.' In *Everyday Violence in Britain, 1850–1950: Gender and Class*, ed. S. D'Cruze, pp. 185–97. Harlow: Pearson, 2000.

Bland, L. 'The trials and tribulations of Edith Thompson: the capital crime of sexual incitement in 1920s England.' *Journal of British Studies* 47 (2008): 624–48.

Bourke, J. *Working Class Cultures in Britain, 1890–1960*. London: Routledge, 1994.

Bourke, J. *Dismembering the Male: Men's Bodies, Britain and the Great War*. London: Reaktion Books, 1996.

Church, R. *Accidents of Murder: Ten Cases Re-Examined*. London: Robert Hale, 1989.

Church, R. 'Double jeopardy: the ordeal of Beatrice Pace.' *The Criminologist* 18:2 (1994): 113–19.

Clayton, H. 'A bad case of police Savidgery: the interrogation of Irene Savidge at Scotland Yard.' *Women's History Magazine* 61 (Autumn/Winter 2009): 30–8.

Connell, R. *Gender and Power: Society, the Person and Sexual Politics*. Cambridge: Polity, 1987.

Cretney, S. *Family Law in the Twentieth Century*. Oxford: Oxford University Press, 2003.

Curran, J., A. Douglas and G. Whannel. 'The political economy of the human-interest story.' In *Newspapers and Democracy: International Essays on a Changing Medium*, ed. A. Smith, pp. 288–347. Cambridge, MA: The MIT Press, 1980.

Davidoff, L. 'The family in Britain.' In *The Cambridge Social History of Britain, 1750–1950*, vol. 2, ed. F. M. L. Thompson, pp. 71–129. Cambridge: Cambridge University Press, 1990.

Davies, A. *Leisure, Gender and Poverty: Manchester and Salford 1900–1939*. Buckingham: Open University Press, 1992.

Dawson, J. *Fred and Edie*. London: Hodder and Stoughton, 2000.

D'Cruze, S. *Crimes of Outrage: Sex, Violence and Victorian Working Women*. London: UCL Press, 1998.

D'Cruze, S. and L. Jackson. *Women, Crime and Justice in England since 1660*. Basingstoke: Palgrave Macmillan, 2009.

Doan, L. and J. Prosser, eds. *Palatable Poison: Critical Perspectives on the Well of Loneliness*. New York: Columbia University Press, 2001.

Dobash R. and R. Dobash. *Women, Violence and Social Change*. London: Routledge, 1992.

Dutton, D. *The Abusive Personality: Violence and Control in Intimate Relationships*. London: Guilford Press, 2006.

Early, J. E. 'Keeping ourselves to ourselves: violence in the Edwardian suburb.' In *Everyday Violence in Britain, 1850–1950: Gender and Class*, ed. S. D'Cruze, pp. 170–84. Harlow: Pearson, 2000.

Eisner, M. 'Long-term historical trends in violent crime.' *Crime and Justice: A Review of Research* 30 (2003): 83–142.

Emsley, C. *Hard Men: Violence in England Since 1750*. London: Hambledon and London, 2005.

Emsley, C. 'Violent crime in England in 1919: post-war anxieties and press narratives.' *Continuity and Change* 23 (2008): 173–95.

Emsley, J. *The Elements of Murder: A History of Poison*. Oxford: Oxford University Press, 2006.

Fisher, K. *Birth Control, Sex and Marriage in Britain, 1918–1960*. Oxford: Oxford University Press, 2006.

Foley, W. *Full Hearts and Empty Bellies: A 1920s Childhood from the Forest of Dean to the Streets of London*. London: Abacus, 2009.

Frost, G. '"She is but a woman": Kitty Byron and the English Edwardian criminal justice system.' *Gender and History* 16 (2004): 538–60.

Gillis, J. *For Better, For Worse: British Marriages, 1600 to the Present*. Oxford: Oxford University Press, 1985.

Gittins, D. *Fair Sex: Family Size and Structure 1900–39*. London: Hutchinson, 1982.

Godfrey, B., S. Farrall and S. Karstedt. 'Explaining gendered sentencing patterns for violent men and women in the late-Victorian and Edwardian period.' *British Journal of Criminology* 45 (2005): 696–720.

Hammerton, A. J. *Cruelty and Companionship: Conflict in Nineteenth-Century Married Life*. London: Routledge, 1992.

Hart, C. *The Commoners of Dean Forest*, 2nd edn. Lydney, Glos.: Lightmoor Press, 2002.

Hart, C. *The Free Miners of the Royal Forest of Dean and Hundred of St. Briavels*, 2nd edn. Lydney, Glos.: Lightmoor Press, 2002.

Herbert, N. M., ed. *A History of Gloucestershire*. Oxford: Oxford University Press, 1996.

Houlbrook, M. '"The man with the powder puff" in interwar London.' *Historical Journal* 50 (2007): 145–71.

Hyde, H. M. *Norman Birkett: The Life of Lord Birkett of Ulverston*. London: Hamish Hamilton, 1964.

Jackson, L. *Women Police: Gender, Welfare and Surveillance in the Twentieth Century*. Manchester: Manchester University Press, 2006.

Jackson, M. *The Real Facts of Life: Feminism and the Politics of Sexuality, c. 1850–1940*. London: Taylor & Francis, 1994.

Jeffery, T. and K. McClelland. 'A world fit to live in: the *Daily Mail* and the middle classes 1918–1939.' In *Impacts and Influences: Essays on Media Power in the Twentieth Century*, ed. J. Curran, A. Smith and P. Wingate, pp. 27–52. London: Methuen, 1987.

Kent, S. *Making Peace: The Reconstruction of Gender in Inter-war Britain*. Princeton: Princeton University Press, 1993.

King, P. 'Gender, crime and justice in late eighteenth- and early nineteenth-century England.' In *Gender and Crime in Modern Europe*, ed. M. Arnot and C. Usborne, pp. 44–74. London: UCL Press, 1999.

Knelman, J. *Twisting in the Wind: The Murderess and the English Press*. Toronto: Toronto University Press, 1997.

Kohn, M. *Dope Girls: The Birth of the British Drug Underground*. London: Granta, 2001 [1992].

Langhamer, C. *Women's Leisure in England, 1920–1960*. Manchester: Manchester University Press, 2000.

Law, C. *Suffrage and Power: The Women's Movement, 1918–1928*. London: I. B. Taurus, 1997.

Light, A. *Forever England: Femininity, Literature and Conservatism between the Wars*. London: Routledge, 1991.

Lloyd, A. *Doubly Deviant, Doubly Damned*. London: Penguin, 1995.

McKibbin, R. *Classes and Cultures: England, 1918–1951*. Oxford: Oxford University Press, 1998.

Melman, B. *Women and the Popular Imagination in the Twenties: Flappers and Nymphs*. Basingstoke: Macmillan, 1988.

Miller, E. *Framed: The New Woman Criminal in British Culture at the Fin de Siècle*. Ann Arbor: University of Michigan Press, 2008.

Morrissey, B. *When Women Kill: Questions of Agency and Subjectivity*. London: Routledge, 2003.

Odell, R. *Exhumation of a Murder: The Life and Trial of Major Armstrong*. London: Harrap, 1975.

Phelps, H. *The Forest of Dean*. Stroud: Amberley, 2008.

Phillips, R. *Untying the Knot: A Short History of Divorce.* Cambridge: Cambridge University Press, 1991.

Powell, V. *A Substantial Ghost: The Literary Adventures of Maude ffoulkes.* London: Heinemann, 1967.

Pugh, M. *Women and the Women's Movement in Britain, 1914–59.* Basingstoke: Macmillan, 1992.

Pugh, M. *We Danced All Night: A Social History of Britain between the Wars.* London: Vintage, 2009.

Ramey, J. 'The bloody blonde and the marble woman: Gender and power in the case of Ruth Snyder.' *Journal of Social History* 37 (2004): 625–50.

Roberts, E. *A Woman's Place: An Oral History of Working-Class Women 1890–1940.* London: Blackwell, 1984.

Roberts, M. 'Samson and Delilah revisited: the politics of fashion in 1920s France.' In *The Modern Woman Revisited*, ed. W. Chadwick and T. Latimer, pp. 65–94. New Brunswick: Rutgers University Press, 2003.

Ross, E. '"Not the sort that would sit on the doorstep": respectability in pre-World War I London neighborhoods.' *International Labor and Working Class History* 27 (1985): 39–59.

Scaggs, J. *Crime Fiction.* Abingdon: Routledge, 2005.

Seal, L. 'Discourses of single women accused of murder: mid twentieth-century constructions of "lesbians" and "spinsters".' *Women's Studies International Forum* 32 (2009): 209–18.

Seal, L. 'Issues of gender and class in the Mirror newspapers' campaign for the release of Edith Chubb.' *Crime, Media, Culture* 5 (2009): 57–78.

Seal, L. *Women, Murder and Femininity: Gender Representations of Women Who Kill.* Basingstoke: Palgrave Macmillan, 2010.

Shoemaker, R. *The London Mob: Violence and Disorder in Eighteenth-Century England.* London: Hambledon and London, 2004.

Smith, H. 'British feminism in the 1920s.' In *British Feminism in the Twentieth Century*, ed. H. Smith, pp. 47–65. Aldershot: Elgar, 1990.

Smith, S., ed. *Taylor's Principles and Practice of Medical Jurisprudence*, vol. 2, 9th edn. London: J & A Churchill, 1934.

Søland, B. *Becoming Modern: Young Women and the Reconstruction of Womanhood in the 1920s.* Princeton: Princeton University Press, 2000.

Sonkin, D. and D. Dutton. 'Treating assaultive men from an attachment perspective.' In *Intimate Violence: Contemporary Treatment Innovations*, ed. R. Geffner, D. Dutton and D. Sonkin, pp. 105–33. London: Routledge, 2003.

Stone, L. *Road to Divorce: England 1530–1987.* Oxford: Oxford University Press, 1990.

Stratmann, L. *Gloucestershire Murders.* Stroud: Sutton, 2005.

Thane, P. 'Population and the family.' In *Companion to Contemporary Britain, 1939–2000*, ed. P. Addison and H. Jones, pp. 42–58. Oxford: Blackwell, 2005.

Thompson, C. J. S. *Poisons and Poisoners: With Historical Accounts of Some Famous Mysteries in Ancient and Modern Times*. London: Harold Shaylor, [1931].

Thorpe, A. *The Longman Companion to Britain in the Era of the Two World Wars 1914–45*. Harlow: Longman, 1994.

Tinkler, P. *Constructing Girlhood: Popular Magazines for Girls Growing Up in England 1920–1950*. London: Taylor & Francis, 1995.

Todd, S. *Young Women, Work and Family in England, 1918–1950*. Oxford: Oxford University Press, 2005.

Tosh, J. *Manliness and Masculinities in Nineteenth-Century Britain*. Harlow: Pearson Education, 2005.

Usborne, C. 'The new woman and generation conflict: perceptions of young women's sexual mores in the Weimar Republic.' In *Generations in Conflict: Youth Revolt and Generation Formation in Germany 1770–1968*, ed. M. Roseman, pp. 137–63. Cambridge: Cambridge University Press, 1995.

Vogel, U. 'Whose property? The double standard of adultery in nineteenth-century law.' In *Regulating Womanhood: Historical Essays on Marriage, Motherhood and Sexuality*, ed. C. Smart, pp. 147–65. London: Taylor & Francis, 1992.

Walker, L. *The Battered Woman*. New York: Harper & Row, 1979.

Walker, L. *The Battered Woman Syndrome*. New York: Springer, 1999.

Walklate, S. *Imagining the Victim of Crime*. Maidenhead: Open University Press, 2007.

Watson, K. *Poisoned Lives: English Poisoners and Their Victims*. London: Hambledon and London, 2004.

Wiener, M. *Men of Blood: Violence, Manliness, and Criminal Justice in Victorian England*. Cambridge: Cambridge University Press, 2004.

Wiener, M. 'Convicted murderers and the Victorian press: condemnation vs. sympathy.' *Crimes and Misdemeanours* 1:2 (2007): 110–25.

Willcox, P. H. A. *The Detective-Physician: The Life and Work of Sir William Willcox*. Chichester: William Heinemann Medical Books, 1970.

Williams, K. *Get Me a Murder a Day! A History of Mass Communication in Britain*. London: Arnold, 1998.

Wilson M. and M. Daly. 'The man who mistook his wife for a chattel.' In *The Adapted Mind: Evolutionary Psychology and the Generation of Culture*, ed. J. Barkow, L. Cosmides and J. Tooby, pp. 289–322. Oxford: Oxford University Press, 1995.

Wood, J. C. *Violence and Crime in Nineteenth-Century England: The Shadow of Our Refinement*. London: Routledge, 2004.

264   *Bibliography*

Wood, J. C. '"Mrs Pace" and the ambiguous language of victimisation.' In *(Re)Interpretations: The Shapes of Justice in Women's Experience*, ed. Lisa Dresdner and Laurel Peterson, pp. 79–93. Newcastle: Cambridge Scholars Publishing, 2009.

Wood, J. C. '"Those who have had trouble can sympathise with you": press writing, reader responses and a murder trial in interwar Britain.' *Journal of Social History* 43 (2009): 439–62.

Wood, J. C. '"The third degree": press reporting, crime fiction and police powers in 1920s Britain.' *Twentieth Century British History* 21 (2010): 464–85.

Zedner, L. *Women, Crime and Custody in Victorian England*. Oxford: Clarendon, 1991.

Index

Note: 'n' after a page reference indicates the number of a note on that page. Page numbers in *italic* refer to illustrations